LAW AND ECONOMICS IN CIVIL LAW COUNTRIES

THE ECONOMICS OF LEGAL RELATIONSHIPS

Series Editor: Nicholas Mercuro
Michigan State University

THE ECONOMICS OF LEGAL RELATIONSHIPS VOLUME 6

LAW AND ECONOMICS IN CIVIL LAW COUNTRIES

EDITED BY

BRUNO DEFFAINS

Université de Nancy, France

THIERRY KIRAT

IDHE – Ecole Normale Supérieure de Cachan, France

2001

JAI

An Imprint of Elsevier Science

Amsterdam – London – New York – Oxford – Paris – Shannon – Tokyo

First Published by Elsevier Science B. V. 2001
2 Park Square, Milton Park, Abingdon, Oxfordshire OX14 4RN
711 Third Avenue, New York, NY 10017

First issued in paperback 2014

Routledge is an imprint of the Taylor and Francis Group, an informa business

Transferred to Digital Printing 2005

First edition 2001

Library of Congress Cataloging in Publication Data
A catalog record from the Library of Congress has been applied for.

ISBN 978-0-7623-0712-8 (hbk)
ISBN 978-0-415-76159-8 (pbk)

CONTENTS

LIST OF CONTRIBUTORS

Benito Arruñada	University of Barcelona (Spain)
Eric Brousseau	Université de Paris X-Nanterre (France)
Gerrit De Geest	Gent University (Belgium)
Bruno Deffains	Faculté de droit-économie-gestion, Université de Nancy 2 (France)
Myriam Doriat-Duban	Faculté de droit-économie-gestion, Université de Nancy 2 (France)
Michael Faure	Maastricht University (Netherlands)
Nuno Garoupa	University of Barcelona (Spain)
Sophie Harnay	Université de Reims-Champagne Ardennes (France)
Thierry Kirat	IDHE – Ecole Normale Supérieure de Cachan (France)
Roland Kirstein	Center for the Study of Law and Economics, Universität des Saarlandes (Germany)
Ejan Mackaay	Centre de recherche en droit public, Faculté de droit, Université de Montréal (Québec)
Alain Marciano	Université de Corte (France)
Anthony Ogus	University of Manchester (U.K.)

Arianna Pretto Oxford University (U.K.) and University of Trento (Italy)

Dieter Schmidtchen Center for the Study of Law and Economics, Universität des Saarlandes (Germany)

Evelyne Serverin IDHE – Ecole Normale Supérieure de Cachan (France)

STATEMENT OF SCOPE

The Economics of Legal Relationships monograph series is dedicated to publishing original scholarly contributions that systematically analyze legal-economic issues. As with other monograph series, each monograph can take a variety of forms.

(1) Each monograph may be comprised of a collection of original articles devoted to a single theme, edited by a guest volume editor.
(2) A monograph may be a collection of refereed articles derived from the Series Editor's "call for papers" on a particular legal-economic topic.
(3) An individual may wish to author an entire monograph.

Each monograph is published in hardback, approximately 250 pages in length and is dedicated to:

- Formulate and/or critique alternative theories of law and economics – including – the new law and economics, the economics of property rights, institutionalist and neoinstitutionalist law and economics, and public choice theory.
- Analyze a variety of public policy issues related to the interface between judicial decisions and/or statutory law and the economy.
- Explore the economic impact of political and legal changes brought on by new technologies and/or environmental concerns.
- Examine the broad array of legal/economic issues surrounding the deregulation-reregulation phenomena.
- Analyze the systematic effects of legal change on incentives and economic performance.

CALL FOR AUTHORS/VOLUME EDITORS/TOPICS

An individual who is interested in either authoring an entire volume, or editing a future volume of The Economics of Legal Relationships should submit a 3–5 page prospectus to the series editor. Each prospectus must include: (1) the prospective title of the volume; (2) a brief description of the organizing theme of the volume whether single authored or edited; (3) an identification of the line of literature from which the proposed topic emanates, and (4) either a table of contents or, if edited, a list of potential contributors along with tentative titles of their contributions. Send prospectus to the series editor. Please note that the series editor only accepts individual manuscripts for publication consideration in response to a specific "Call for Papers."

Send prospectus directly to the series editor:

Professor Nicholas Mercuro
Institute of Environmental Toxicology
Michigan State University
East Lansing, MI 48824
PHONE: (517) 353-6469
FAX: (517) 355-4603
e-mail mercuro@msu.edu

INTRODUCTION

Bruno Deffains and Thierry Kirat

This book is devoted to *The Law and Economics in Civil Law Countries*. Up until now, Law and Economics was essentially developed in countries in which common law is prevalent, with the aim of re-thinking judicial functions from an economic standpoint. The method consists in giving a dynamic view of the rule of law and enabling the finalities and changes in the judicial system to be understood. The purpose of the book is indeed to encourage thought concerning the manner in which this method may be widened within those civil law countries where law displays the particularity of being codified.

For many years, the two fields have advanced quite independently from one another. Today Law and Economics is an important vector for convergence between these two subject areas. The Nobel prize awarded to Ronald Coase in 1991 attests to the increasing importance of this field of research, with numerous writers ranging from Richard Posner to Gary Becker as well as Guido Calabresi, Douglas North, James Buchanan, William Vickrey venturing into it. All of them demonstrate that Law and Economics can provide tools for scholars interested in understanding the law regulating human behavior. Richard Posner's achievement was to use economic axioms and instruments to illuminate the forces at work in the Anglo-American legal system. He laid bare the architecture of the common law by showing how much of it could be derived from the axioms of economics. The claim was never that only these mattered, but rather that even by themselves they showed that the law could have a logic and coherence that before we had only known intuitively. Of course, the posnerian approach is not exclusive and as, some papers will demonstrate, relations between law and economics can be tackled from different points of view. Here, we want to

Law and Economics in Civil Law Countries, Volume 6, pages 1–5.

ISBN: 0-7623-0712-9

understand to what extent we are founded to have an economic lecture of law in the civil law countries tradition as well as in common law tradition.

The aim of this book is twofold: first of all to highlight the interest of confronting law and economics in civil law countries and secondly to establish an initial review of research done into this area to date.

We particularly wish to emphasise the following questions: to what extent have the existing codes in civil law countries been designed to incorporate economic considerations? Can the modifications made to codified rules over time be explained by a will to react to new economic constraints? Which economic problems are at the root of the revision of codes? Of course, the Code is not the only source of law in civil law countries. This aspect will also be a subject of reflection regarding the relationship between law and economics in both legislative and courts contexts.

Contributors from a wide range of countries are being invited to compare points of view in two directions: one being the theoretical possibility of transposing the approach and categories of Anglo-Saxon Law and Economics to civil law countries whilst the other is the development of empirical analyses concerning the content and the economic effects of rules of law in civil law countries. The book is meant to be open to theoretical, empirical, normative and positive thought in the different branches of law.

Generally speaking, Law and Economics views the legal system as a means of defining rights *ex ante*, and creating incentives to govern behaviour *ex post*. In most civil law countries, law is mainly formulated by Parliament, complemented secondly through the refinement of law in the course of judicial decisions. These decisions are essentially concerned with the interpretation of legislation contrary to common law countries where judicial decisions are concerned in priority by the development of legal rules through the production of precedents. Of course, the differences in legal systems are largely based on both political and historical considerations. For example, the legal systems can be viewed as indicators of the relative power of the State vis-à-vis property owners. In particular, common law has developed in England to some extent as a defense of Parliament and property owners against the attempts by the sovereign to regulate and expropriate them. Civil law, in contrast, has developed more as an instrument used by the sovereign for State building and controlling economic life.

Moreover, this book wants to explore some of the ways in which economic analysis can contribute to an understanding of some key aspects of the relationships between legal systems and thus provide a useful methodology for comparative law and economics. This objective seems to be crucial for economic analysis of law in civil law countries. This remark specially holds in the

European context characterized by the coexistence of different national orders influenced sometimes by common law tradition and sometimes by civil romano-Germanic tradition. So, in the context of European harmonization, we have to understand if the competition between legal systems will generate a tendency for national legal principles to converge in the different domains of the law (environmental law, contract law, liability law, criminal law, procedural rules, . . .). The answer to this question will contribute to answer to the fundamental question concerning the method of law and economics in civil law countries.

The different chapters pose important legal questions and have been studied using economic analysis. Together, they opened up the civil law to economic inquiry. These researches show that we can learn from applying economic analysis to the problems in different domains of codified civil law. To us, it symbolizes the coming of age of the field of Law and Economics in civil law countries and comparative law. The Law and Economics of the civil law has now progressed to the point at which some law faculties have courses in the area and many universities offer courses for graduate students in economics. For anyone wanting to learn where we stand concerning economic analysis of european civil law, we hope that this book provides a fairly comprehensive summary of the state of the art. If we draw a conclusion from the state of the art in Europe, it could be said that it does not give the picture of a unified framework. Taken together, the fifteen chapters joined together in this book illustrate the richness and diversity of viewpoints on Law and Economics. They also confirm, in a certain sense, that Law and Economics has not yet reached in Europe the same degree of development it has in North America. It can even be considered that the interpenetration of legal and economic processes does not follow a smooth and linear path of development in European countries; the understanding of the rationale of such a diversity and openness of legal-economic studies deserve interest by itself.

The chapters of the book, written by a majority of economists and a significant number of jurists, share a common project: showing the interest of scientific exchanges between practicers of the two academic fields concerned. They advocate the necessity of a radical evolution in the relations between economists and jurists. Concerning that issue, we would like to stress four questions that, among others, deserve a particular interest.

- First, one can try to explain the traditional poor development of interdisciplinarity between economists and jurists in legal studies in Europe. Actually, a current opinion within the legal community is that Law and Economics is a discourse on law that does not allow to understand what is really going on with legal regulation in societies. Apart from epistemological and theoretical issues, the reluctance of jurists towards economic analysis is also based on unfortunate ideological considerations: economists and jurists practising economic rhetorics have been largely suspected in the past to systematically argument in favor of market-based mechanisms and against the "irrationality" of regulatory schemes or even legislation as a tool for public policy.

- The second remark we would like to make is that the traditional gross substitute to the analysis of the economic content of legal rules and institutions has been economic law (or *droit économique*), that is to say a branch of private and public law applied to economic issues (e.g. securities, competition, taxation, etc.). Such a perspective is currently used by continental jurists who for the most part raised the issue of the necessary adaptation of law to the needs of a changing capitalism, but it should however be worth rediscovering a way of practicing economic law that a jurist, G. Schrans and an economist, A. Jacquemin stated almost twenty years ago in the following terms: "Economic law is not a new field within legal analysis; it is instead new on traditional matters. . . . It is a way to address law from the viewpoint of its consequences; in others words a new way to take law into consideration".[1]
- The third point we would like to make is that a fruitful exchange between economists and jurists can be built in the field of positive and empirical approaches aimed at providing a scientifically grounded understanding of law in action. That leads to open two broad lines of enquiry: the first is theoretical, since economics should then be assessed as a provider of tools for empirical research on law. In a sense, it is unavoidable to question what is behind the curtain of economic analysis, namely the implicit institutional and legal background of American Law and Economics. If one admits that American Law and Economics has been tailored to provide insights into American common law, it becomes useful to study in what way it may become appropriate to civil law contexts. The second line of enquiry we would like to stress is methodological. Actually, quantitative studies of law in action in Europe are rather rare; one reason of that fact probably lies in the complexity of legal and judicial statistics available. If we take the example of France, the legal data published by the Ministry of Justice provide information on the activity of courts (such as: duration of litigation, legal claims) that are built on legal terms; that means that the statistical apparatus is directly connected with the institutional features of the French judicial system, and has nothing to do with behavioral features of agents when acting regarding law. May we conclude that the future development of pluridisciplinary studies in law will require economists to go further with the institutional detail of legal systems?

[1] G. Schrans and A. Jacquemin. 1982. Le droit économique. Paris: Presses Universitaires de France.

- As a fourth and last remark, we would like to stress that the future development of Law and Economics will very probably crucially depend on the legal skills of economists. What is at stake as long as European economists are concerned is to determine if it is necessary or not for them to be trained in regulation when practising regulatory economics, or in private law when practising economic analysis of contracts, torts and property. The poor development of pluridisciplinary academic programs in Economics and Law in Europe in general, in France in particular, is a challenge for the future. One dimension is particularily crucial: economists tend to implicitly consider that the implementation of legal rules consists in a smooth process of application of statutory or regulatory rules. They are led to underestimate two important issues: first, the weight of judicial interpretation and, second, the interconnection and systemic aspects of legal rules and procedures. If one admits that statutory and regulatory rules are not performative statements (i.e. they do not make it appear in a mechanical way the world they describe), it becomes then unavoidable to question the process by which they are mobilized by economic actors and, finally, are implemented and enforced.

The structure of the book is aimed at covering the range of issues raised by the current and future expansion of economic approaches to law in Europe. The first part regroups chapters that share a common line of enquiry into the relevance of Law and Economics in civil law contexts, but exhibit different viewpoints and arguments. The second part joins together chapters devoted to the implementation of tools provided by Law and Economics for the enlightenment of legal issues in the fields of private, criminal, and administrative law.

PART I

THE RELEVANCE OF LAW AND ECONOMICS FOR RESEARCH INTO CODIFIED LAW SYSTEMS

COMPETITION BETWEEN LEGAL SYSTEMS: A COMPARATIVE LAW AND ECONOMICS PERSPECTIVE

Bruno Deffains

INTRODUCTION

Relations between law and competition are complex. In European countries, the principal problem concerns the free movement of products, instituted in 1958 by the Traité de Rome, which could be limited given the differences between national legal systems. The main question is then to appreciate the need of a central authority which could impose on states a legal harmonisation. This interrogation concerns public law and, more recently, it appears in the field of private law with the project of a "European Code of Private Law".

However, this way to start on relations between law and competition is partial because it neglects the fact that law can be presented itself as a product (Romano, 1985; Ogus, 1998). For instance, in contracts law, contracting parties can often choose the applicable rules as they choose the subject of the contract or the other party. As noted by Mattei and Cafaggi (1997), the probability that the law will spread outside of its place of origin can be determined frequently by choice of law mechanisms. In this case, the creators and the users of law have a major concern in the free movement of legal rules. So, the problem becomes to analyse the nature (static or dynamic) and the result of legal competition: can the free movement of legal rules lead to a *Ius Commune* (i.e. a form of decentralised harmonisation)? Some authors already ask for a "new"

Law and Economics in Civil Law Countries, Volume 6, pages 9–21.

ISBN: 0-7623-0712-9

European freedom which should guarantee free movement of legal rules (Van den Bergh, 1998).

Theoretically, the idea of competition between legal systems is in opposition to the idea of a unitary and hierarchical law. For example in the theory of law, the positivism inherited from Kelsen, even if he accepts the idea of conflict between legal norms, appears to be incompatible with an approach of legal norms or legal systems in terms of competition. Indeed, this type of approach implies "horizontal" relationships between the different sources and legal norms whereas the hierarchical approach (Kelsen's pyramid) gives pride of place to "vertical" relationships.

My aim here is not to criticise the internal coherence of legal positivism but rather to show to what extent the competitive view seems better able to capture the present reality of implementing legal rules both on a domestic[1] and an international level. For example, how can we deny that there is a certain competition between the legal systems originating in Common Law and in the *Romano-Germanic* tradition at a time when we worry about the Americanisation of European laws especially in the areas of finance law and business law? Accepting that this competition exists does not, however, say anything about the outcome of the competitive process.

The existence of legal competition is all the easier to detect when it appears within one and the same geographical or economic area. Any "legal tourist" observing the legal dispositions of European countries will soon notice that plurality of legal orders is more often the rule rather than the exception. Of course, this pluralism does not necessarily imply competition but can be said to encourage it as States come to realise that certain mechanisms are more effective than others when attracting "forum shoppers" in the shape of companies or owners of capital.

Mireille Delmas Marty in her book entitled *Trois défis pour un droit mondial* (1998) takes up the argument that "there is a market for law which comes in answer to the law of the market". This shows itself especially in the way that the legal systems of dominant countries is exported toward those countries under domination (this strategy could enable the form of cultures and economies to be determined without the need to invest in those countries concerned). Moreover, one of the aims of this exporting of law would be to facilitate adapting rules of law to the requirements of international business at the risk of seeing law become a "market service". This interpretation suggests that actors on the market are becoming "law merchants". This could particularly be the case in the financial sector. The author fiercely criticises this privatisation of the legal norm which may lead to sovereignty in legal matters being abandoned and private interests taking on more importance than the general interest.

Greater freedom of exchange could thus be said to be responsible for a certain legal havoc. But freedom is not the only culprit. "Codes of conduct" which are developed into an "auto-referential" order contributes to this situation. In the same way, the avoiding action of judges via Alternative Disputes Resolution attempts to lighten the load of the already overworked court system. Arbitration is first in the line of fire as it has a tendency to increasingly take the place of legal proceedings in international business.

This argument has met with considerable success but has also given rise to important problems about legal competition as outcome of the free movement of legal rules. I want to look at two of them which deal with the nature of legal competition and its consequences. We will reveal how economic analysis can help to make the debate clearer with respect to these two questions.

WHAT IS THE NATURE OF LEGAL COMPETITION?

When speaking of competition between legal orders, we need first to stipulate the type of competition in question. Quite apart from knowing with which fields this competition deals (rules, sources of law, procedures, jurisdictions . . .), economists usually draw a distinction between two types of competition (see for example McNulty, 1968). The first is static competition seen as a state at a given moment and secondly dynamic competition seen as a process. In the first case, only the result matters, the reference being perfect competition. The second case is more a question of analysing the conditions of competition between actors (in this case the "creators of law").

When applied to the field of law this distinction will lead to "legal competition" being approached from the static side (indeed this is the more frequent approach in the literature). In this case, we study the way in which economic agents are influenced and guided by the performances of rules of law (in terms of expected gain). To be precise, whether it be a question of civil law, commercial law or penal law, the effects of the differences between legal systems upon the behaviour of economic agents is the first element to come under scrutiny. We are particularly interested in the efficiency of the rules of Common Law compared to those emanating from the *Romano-Germanic* tradition.

In this light, writers have taken an interest in the comparison of the liability rules in risk prevention, of the regimes of patent law regarding the incentives to innovate. The effects of the differences between inquisitorial and accusatory procedures in civil proceedings have also been analysed by seeking to single out the most efficient from the point of view of the information acquired by the judges responsible for settling disputes. Other authors have studied the impact of damages on the incentives to risk prevention in the field of civil liability. In the same way, the effects of the *quota litis* pact on the behaviour of lawyers have been analysed. More recently the question of predictability has been approached in order to discover whether *stare decisis* which states that a rule of precedent in Common Law must be respected, does indeed lead to improved legal forecasting compared to a legal order based upon a codified law. Our present article does not aim to give detailed results of this research work with which the specialists of Law and Economics are well familiar.

In my view, this static approach highlights the "demand" side: the comparative advantages of rules or legal systems are examined according to the interest of those concerned. One risk must be brought to light here. Better performances may well be attributed to given rules whereas in fact these performances are the result of different procedures (one example is the type of dispute settlement or procedures).

Tenants of legal realism gave pride of place to this approach a good while ago, as the following statement by the famous judge Holmes illustrates: "if we look at things from the point of view of the litigant, we observe that he could not care less about great theories. What he wants to know is what the courts of Massachussets or of England will decide regarding his case".[2]

It thus seems logical that this current way of thinking was to give rise to the movement of Law and Economics in the sixties, directed at the economic evaluation of rules of law. The general idea is to provide the jurist with a method enabling him to supply a description of reality (via the evaluation of the consequences of the application of the rules) and to suggest changes in the legislation in cases where the rules do not meet its intended objectives. Conceived of in this way, the movement of Law and Economics is the ultimate development of legal realism.

LEGAL COMPETITION AS A DYNAMIC PROCESS

The static approach does however have its limits in the sense that it does not account for the "strategic" behaviour of the creators of law (judges or legislators . . .). Only dynamic competition allows us to approach this question as it deals above all with the changes in the rules. To this end, it would be appropriate to examine the way in which these "creators" react to the decisions of their "competitors". Hence, at an international level, if one State implements a rule which appears more favourable to the economic actors (as regards labour law, tax law or the fight against economic crime), it is interesting to bring out the "function of legal reaction" of neighbouring countries. Indeed, as opposed to the widely studied subject of fiscal competition, legal competition brings to light the phenomenon of "voting with one's feet", i.e. companies choose to set up where the rules are the most suitable to their activities.

This analysis, it is true, complements the previous one which was based on the recognition of performance differences of legal systems but includes an extra dimension as it leads us to look at the outcome of this dynamic: will the creators of law in a situation of competition decide to cooperate (a tendency toward harmonisation) or will they be decidedly uncooperative (legal competition)?

This is a difficult question as we have seen that the same point of departure (accepting the heterogeneity of rules of law) may lead to quite opposite conclusions. Regarding the unitary and hierarchical approach, heterogeneity leads to cooperation. The non-unitary approach leads to competition. We must immediately clarify that, for the tenants of the non-unitary approach, legal order can be just as coherent as for those preferring the unitary approach. For example, Hayek attempts to show that the rules emerging from legal order after the evolutionary process are precisely those which will win the competition.

This remark is also valid both for a given legal system and between different systems. In a given legal system, a rule of law may be conceived as being the product of the action of several producers in competition (doctrine, jurisprudence, law). Ugo Mattei then demonstrates how this competition helps to spread the knowledge regarding the legal solutions to a particular problem. It is precisely this which ensures legal order. Competition, then, is not responsible for disorder but for order quite independently of the positivist paradigm: "consequently, outside of a state centered paradigm of the law, competition between components of the legal rule, rather than cooperation among sources of the law, is the appropriate tool to use".

This is the first important result to come out of an economic analysis of legal competition: the proposition "cooperation implies order whereas competition implies disorder" is largely unfounded.

The same observation is valid at an international level at which competition becomes apparent via the transposition of concepts or legal rules from one system to another. Ugo Mattei has given a very good description of the massive importing of the German doctrine to interpret the Italian Civil Code of 1865, largely based on the French model.

The major observation we can make today is that over the last twenty years a certain number of legal instruments, norms and contractual techniques often invented within the context of Anglo-Saxon law have been imposed in countries of civil law and these appear to be spreading to all industrialised countries in the wake of globalisation. The introduction and the competition of these new laws then alter the national legal environment. But by receiving these new rules the States have become "law takers" (even though the rules are not usually accepted as they stand). It would appear that by receiving these new laws, the national institutions and laws are adapting to the demands of the global economy. The argument depicting states as "law givers" or even "law merchants" is obviously in contrast to this observation.

And, as Ugo Mattei notes, barriers between legal systems are today challenged more then ever by the extent of human market transactions. Legal rules from different legal systems are often in conflict with one another when ruling on the same course of action. It is unrealistic to imagine a set of coherent and ranked legal orders issued to the people by one all powerful "law giver".

In fact, the idea of competition between legal systems is widely accepted but this competition is rarely due to "law merchants" in the sense that the creative power of the States would be highly limited. Widely speaking, competition could theoretically lead to a coherent legal order (here economists would speak of equilibrium *à la* Stigler).

Be that as it may, competition is, in practice, imperfect and the contradictions in the legal mechanisms (or in their interpretation both domestically and internationally) may encourage the actors to give precedence to a strategic use of the rules for want of a decisive creative power.

We will put the question of competition between the sources of law to one side in order to examine competition between legal systems.

CONSTRUCTIVE OR DESTRUCTIVE COMPETITION?

Beginning with the idea that there is competition between legal mechanisms, we must examine the result of this in economic terms. First of all, we can note that the fact of approaching legal competition from a dynamic side means raising two important questions:

(1) can the result of the competitive process be forecast?
(2) does competition give an efficient result?

In the present state of knowledge we can not answer in the affirmative to either of these questions. The first raises the problem of the emergence of rules. The preceding arguments have established that the interest of the "dynamic" competitive approach does not lie in its varying capacity to forecast the emergence of rules of law which will be applied tomorrow (compared to the unitary approach), but mainly in its greater realism.

The second question raises the problem of the efficiency of legal systems. The answer is delicate indeed due to the complexity of the mechanisms, the institutional and cultural constraints (transaction costs, path dependency) and the possible definitions of efficiency. For example, in the American context, Kitch (1991) considers that decentralised jurisdictions can provide efficient regulatory patterns: the scope of jurisdiction should be as small as possible in order to maximize diversity of choice as well as to promote the maximum competition among jurisdictions for laws, practices, and procedures that people prefer. In fact, Kitch rejects the traditional argument against diversity of legal systems that it leads to restrictions of interstate trade and hence hinders integration. Such impediments will be solved by competition between regulatory entities themselves: in the long run, this system will prevail because it places stronger incentives on each jurisdiction to promulgate efficient rules for both its internal and external commerce. The argument is that legal competition can lead to efficiency because there is more choice for people and, as noted by Reich (1992), there is a competitive advantage inherent in different levels of regulation.

Such a competitive advantage has been studied by Porter (1991) with a comparative cross-country empirical analysis. The author considers that legal environment can be an important factor of competitive advantage. But he notes that though standards by one jurisdiction do not necessarily lead to an opting-out of firms from the jurisdiction, therefore provoking a "negative competition between legal orders", they may encourage start-up of specialized manufacturers and service firms to help address them, which can develop strong international positions. For instance, product liability laws can benefit competitive advantage by acting like a sophisticated buyer to encourage the development of better products. But they can also stifle innovation if the legal system becomes unpredictable and provokes lengthy product liability suits: "in the United States, product liability is so extreme and uncertain as to retard innovation, . . . it places firms in constant jeopardy of costly and, as importantly, lengthy product liability suits, . . . this risk is so great, and the consequences potentially disastrous, that the inevitable result is more caution in product innovation than there is in other advanced nations". The results of Porter are important because they show in a dynamic perspective that there are situations where legal competition can lead to efficiency and others where it cannot.

Henceforth in the field of Law and Economics, some authors start on the question of efficiency (Posner, Priest . . .) with an analysis of the real effects of legal rules. These analyses have provided the jurist with a global method destined to provoke thought on the functions of the various legal institutions. However, the problem posed by Posner goes beyond this as he defends the thesis of the economic efficiency of Common Law. This thesis seeks to have Common Law explained (but not perfectly) as a system enabling the maximization of the wealth of society, i.e. the judges from Anglo-Saxon courts would make their rulings as if their implicit aim was economic efficiency. Hence, the rules regarding civil liability drawn up within the framework of Common Law (especially the evolution toward strict liability) could be thought of as efficient if they enabled the social cost of accidents to be reduced. The strength of this approach lies in the fact one does not need to presume that the aim of the judges is to attain economic efficiency for this result to be reached.

The work undertaken over the last thirty years within the framework of Law and Economics has attempted to clarify the respective efficiency of rules of law in both a normative and a positive sense. To postulate that legal systems will gradually become more efficient is quite a different problem because despite a certain uniformity between systems, competition does not appear to have given rise to a single and coherent legal order even when economic conditions are identical, as is the case in Europe.

To illustrate this we will refer to the outcome of competition linked to the freedom of exchange. We have seen, in the view of several authors that because of this freedom, legal systems are exposed to competition which is a "race-to-the-bottom" i.e. that States are becoming obliged to fall into line with that State offering the most flexible rules (in a universe where production factors are sufficiently mobile). Frydman (2000) is one writer expressing this opinion when he states that the tenants of law and economics have been led to conceal any form of legal autonomy. He considers that the purely normative dimension of the rule of law has been replaced by a purely factual approach in terms of incidence. The legal norm would be now only seen in an instrumental way, as a tool which needs to be tailored to aims and objectives that have been defined in economic terms: maximizing wealth or optimal allocation of resources. Legal order overall would become dependent on the economic system because the economic context plays a decisive role in the presentation of the functions of law.

We can remark here that in the traditional liberal model, the economy is one of free exchange in which the State does not intervene beyond its prerogative of a policeman of human activity. The main function of the courts is one of arbiter of economic and social exchange in the context of a spontaneous and evolving order. But this model cannot describe the current system in most countries. The States goes well beyond this model as they have become involved in interventionism, especially in the realm of redistribution (Welfare State). This transformation has obviously affected the functions of law as it has become an active instrument for economic and social change. Henceforth it has become a management technique aimed at the promotion of the optimum social and economic development of society. The consequence of these new conditions for the promotion of welfare through law is a considerable increase in the norms of objective law aimed at fixing the restrictive framework for economic and social activities.

One consequently understands that the major source of law has been modified. In the liberal model, the law, being abstract and general, dominates the legal sphere. The exception lies in the contract whose extreme flexibility is particularly well suited to the development of exchanges. In the current context, the law is always omnipresent but it is increasingly negotiable so as to be applied as a contract whereas the contract itself can fulfil a regulatory function (e.g. in the area of the control of natural monopolies). Such an observation leads us to insist upon the changes affecting the status and the role of the legal system. More precisely, legal regulations seem to be a sub-set included in a wider set of regulatory mechanisms within the economic system.[3]

IS THERE A "RACE-TO-THE-BOTTOM" IN LEGAL COMPETITION?

The question of "race-to-the-bottom" evokes the idea of destructive competition, a source of disorder, quite the opposite to the way in which we normally view competition. In other words, the problem is the following: although competition is good from the point of view of social welfare when it operates in the field of consumer goods, why should it be negative when operating in the field of law?

Theoretically, the most obvious answer is the following: if we consider that the rules which are put into effect are the result of the activity of national jurisdictions, the virtues of competition should answer the basic principles of the economy of well-being (although the law is generally seen as a public good in the sense that its production requires State intervention). In Europe, this question has a somewhat particular side to it as the supporters of harmonisation and those in favour of pluralism are fiercely opposed as to social or fiscal "dumping" (special ways of "race-to-the-bottom").

My intention here is to highlight the difficulty of choosing between the two approaches. Quite apart from the fact both are conceptually coherent, it is hard to decide which of the two paints the better picture of reality. However, it seems impossible to give pride of place to the hypothesis of "race-to-the-bottom".

The problem of competition between jurisdictions has attracted the attention of many economists. Mintz and Tulkens (1986) and Wildasin (1988) examined tax competition when jurisdictions behave strategically. Assuming that the jurisdictions are the players of a Nash game, they showed that the resulting Nash equilibrium is generally non-optimal. But the jurisdictions can also compete in other dimensions. In Marceau (1997), they compete in crime deterrence. The author established that this competition leads to over deterrence because, when choosing their effort in deterrence, jurisdictions neglect the harm they impose on other jurisdictions (via the displacement of criminals or the relocation of capital). This external cost implies that too much deterrence takes place relative to social optimum. In fact, I attempt to justify that the answer about efficiency is not always so clear. For demonstrating this intuition, I am referring to a paper by Revesz (1992) analysing the competition between mechanisms set up by the States of a federal system regarding protection of the environment. The main question is to decide whether federal legislation (harmonisation) is required in order to control the impact of this competition on the behaviour of investors attracted by the least restricting mechanisms.[4]

The analysis begins with the interpretation of the hypothesis of "race-to-the-bottom" as a situation of a prisoner's dilemma. In other words, the result of strategic interaction between rational players (here the State jurisdictions) may lead to a non-optimal result that cooperation may well avoid.

The idea of Revesz consists in applying this analytical framework to the problem of two States determining the "correct" level of environmental regulations. To do this, he studies in a first stage the situation of a State that is not subject to an interaction with the other (island jurisdiction). In this case, optimal regulation is a situation allowing the external effect created by pollution to be corrected (i.e. the difference between companies' social cost and private cost). These regulations may pass via civil liability (knowing that the exact form of this liability is of no importance if transaction costs are negligible, as in the theory of Coase).

In a second stage, Revesz introduces the other jurisdiction in order to obtain a situation of competition. The two jurisdictions interact in the sense that the decisions of one will influence those of the other. In a federal-type system where capital is mobile, companies will obviously choose to set up where the rules are the least restricting. States, for their part, wish to reduce pollution in such a way as to internalise the social costs of pollution. Henceforth, however, the location of companies has an effect on employment, investment and thus on salaries and taxes received. States will thus include these potential benefits into their legislation by fixing less restricting rules than other States.

In fact, Revesz has shown that "race-to-the-bottom" will show its face when one State opts for the optimal mechanism (described in stage 1) whilst the other discovers that it is able to divert the capital flow by voting a more flexible and less confining legislation for companies. This in turn will lead the first State to alter its own legislation.

Supposing that the total amount of investment is constant, the situation where States will engage in "race-to-the-bottom" is evidently the worst in terms of social welfare, as the level of pollution is higher. The problem here does not lie in the rationality of the actors but in the negative consequences their behaviour is likely to generate regarding the implementing of rules of law.

It must be pointed out, however, that this description of "destructive" competition is based upon the existence, at the stage 2, of incentives to engage in "driving the level down". It is here that the major difficulty arises in the sense that this incentive is not necessarily present. Some research (Oates & Schwab, 1988) indeed show that race-to-the-bottom (negative competition) is only possible if the value of an extra investment is overcompensated for by more lax regulations. In fact, it is perfectly possible to imagine situations in which this condition is not fulfilled.

Particularly, Oates and Schwab study jurisdictions which compete with each other for a sum of mobile capital by lowering their taxes and voting legislation regarding the environment. In return for an increase in capital, residents receive higher wages. The local community will compare the benefits of higher wages with the cost of reduced taxes on capital and more amenable environmental legislation. The authors conclude their analysis with the fact that taxation on capital at equilibrium will be nil and environmental regulations will be optimal. In other words, no "destructive legal competition" comes into play. Should we, however, conclude that this competition is efficient? The answer is most certainly "no" for one main reason which concerns the situation of the labour market. In the analysis of Oates and Schwab, it is implicitly accepted that the labour market is in a situation of full employment. It is far from certain that their conclusion would be maintained in conditions of under-employment.

The interest of linking law and economics here is to search for clues to help in deciding between the two situations. At an international (or regional) level, economists will retain two characteristics in deciding the type of competition to which creators of law can devote themselves. The first is the degree of capital mobility and the situation on the labour market to the extent that the effects of legal competition should give rise to company set-ups in those places where the rules are the most amenable. From this point of view, no study (comparable to those undertaken in the field of fiscal competition) has to date brought such a phenomenon to light. The second characteristic lies in determining the function of reaction of the producers of law enabling changes in regulations of one State following a change in regulations in another State to be brought to light. Work in this field is still insufficient.

To put things another way, we seem to be witnessing a spontaneous convergence of legal systems without seeing in this movement any proof of a deliberate will on the part of a State to export its rules to other States and even less so that of destructive competition. Moreover, its would appear that, in general, international or supranational organisations are following this movement of convergence of legal systems rather than imposing it.

NOTES

1. Following the work of Ugo Mattei on competition in domestic law, we can argue that it first of all takes on the form of a competition betweeen the various sources of law (the law, jurisprudence and doctrines).

2. In the "path of law", Harvard Law Review, 1897.

3. This presentation of the law-economics relationships based on the 'principal' and 'accessory' approach does not have the favour of jurists in countries with a civil tradition and continental countries in particular, who never miss the chance to criticise it. On a practical level this approach has nevertheless had considerable success, especially within international and supra-national organisations. At the time of the deregulation movement accompanying the phenomenon and presentation of globalisation, the legitimacy of State or infra-State rules of law is increasingly measured by the yardstick of economic performance. In other words, domestic legal rules have been challenged, invalidated or dismantled because they are said to have a negative effect upon the development of international trade. As an example we can quote the deregulation of European financial markets in 1990 in the wake of financial globalisation, or the deregulation of telecommunications imposed by the European community in 1998, the reflection of a world-wide movement. There is also the complex procedure set in place by the WTO to remove obstacles to international trade. The programmes of the IMF make financial aid conditional on abandoning certain laws limiting free trade. Finally we will mention the multilateral investment agreement plan which aims at protecting foreign investors from the consequences of modifications in domestic legislation by taking any disputes relating to State contracts away from State tribunals and jurisdictions, entrusting them to international arbitrators.

4. The article "Regulatory Competition in the Single Market" by Sun and Pelkmans (1995) should also be mentioned. It tackles the same subject in the field of European regulatory competition.

REFERENCES

Delmas-Marty, M. (1998). *Trois défis pour un droit mondial.* Paris: Editions du Seuil.

Frydman, B. (1997). Les nouveaux rapports entre droit et économie: trois hypothèses concurrentes. In: T. Kirat & E. Serverin (Eds), *Le droit dans l'action économique* (pp. 25–41). Paris: CNRS Editions.

Holmes, O. W. (1897). The Path of Law. *Harvard Law Review.*

Kitch, E. (1991). Business Organisation Law: State or Federal. In: R. Buxbaum, G. Hertig, A. Hirsch & K. Hopt (Eds), *European Business Law – Legal and Economic Analysis on Integration and Harmonization.* Berlin: De Gruyter.

Marceau, N. (1997). Competition in Crime Deterrence. *Canadian Journal of Economics, 97,* 844.

Mattei, U. (1997). *Comparative Law and Economics.* Ann Harbor: The University of Michigan Press.

Mattei, U., & Cafaggi, F. (1998). Comparative Law and Economics. In: P. Newman (Ed.), *The New Palgrave Dictionnary of Law and Economics*. London: Macmillan.

McNulty, P. (1968). Economic Theory and the Meaning of Competition. *Quarterly Journal of Economics*, 641.

Oates, W. E., & Schwab, R. M. (1988). Economics Competition Among Jurisdictions: Efficiency Enhancing or Distortion Inducing. *Journal of Public Economics*, *35*, 333.

Ogus, A. (1999). Competition between National Legal Systems: a Contribution of Economic Analysis to Comparative Law. *International and Comparative Law Quarterly*, *48*, 405.

Porter, M. (1991). *The Competitive Advantage of Nations*. New York: Free Press.

Posner, R. A. (1998). *Economic Analysis of Law* (5th ed.). New York: Aspen Law & Business.

Priest, G. (1977). The Common Law Process and the Selection of Efficient Rules. *Journal of Legal Studies*, *6*, 65.

Reich, N. (1992). Competition between Legal orders: a New Paradigm for EC Law? *Common Market Law Review*, *29*, 861.

Revesz, R. (1992). Rehabilitating Interstate Competition: Rethinking the 'Race-to-the-bottom' Rationale for Federal Environmental Regulation. *New York University Law Review*, *67*, 1210.

Romano, R. (1985). Law as a Product: Some Pieces of the Incorporation Puzzle. *Journal of Law, Economics and Organization*, 225.

Sun, J-M., & Pelkmans, J. (1995). Regulatory Competition in the Single Market? *Common Market Law Review*, 66.

Van den Bergh, R. (1998). Subsidiarity as an Economic Demarcation Principle and the Emergence of European Private Law. *Maastricht Journal of European and Comparative Law*, *5*, 152.

LAW AND ECONOMICS: WHAT'S IN IT FOR US CIVILIAN LAWYERS

Ejan Mackaay

INTRODUCTION

Law and Economics, in its current incarnation, has been with us for some forty years. From Far West for economists, it has become part of the urban sprawl of legal scholarship, at least in the United States, where it started. It has been received in many other countries: in the English-speaking first, then in continental Europe, at differing rates and with variable popular appeal. It has even, to my delight, reached the People's Republic of China, where a translation of Posner's *Economic Analysis of Law* is reported to circulate freely. On the whole, the reception outside of the United States has been relatively modest.

The proposition I wish to put to you is that law and economics is of interest not merely to economists and to lawyers in common law countries, but that it has something of consequence to tell us lawyers in the civil law tradition. And furthermore I will argue that what it has to tell us is relevant not merely to policy makers and to academics, but to practitioners in all walks of practice.

How to get the message across? In surroundings where technology has yet to penetrate, allow me a traditional mode of transmission: the rhetoric of a presentation in two parts, as the French like to structure them. The first part deals with what law and economics can do for lawyers and legal scholars, the second with how it does it.

Law and Economics in Civil Law Countries, Volume 6, pages 23–41.

ISBN: 0-7623-0712-9

I shall leave for the conclusion a question which may already be on your minds: Is law and economics a mere branch plant of the economics empire – a multinational knowing no disciplinary boundaries? Can law, or even its basic structure, be deduced from economic concepts? (Brennen, 1980).

WHAT LAW AND ECONOMICS DOES

Law and economics, broadly speaking, can do three types of things for lawyers. It allows us to foresee the main consequences of a change in the law, for instance that a raise of the minimum wage will tend to increase unemployment, particularly amongst the young.[1] Secondly, it can show a unified rationale for legal institutions, in particular for the institutions which form the backbone of private law. Law and economics detects in these institutions incentives for carefully husbanding scarce resources and for inventing ways to alleviate scarcity. This rationale allows us by extension to shake hands with historians in accounting for why legal institutions were invented or modified at earlier times in reaction to changes in society, in technology or in marketing techniques. Thirdly, in a normative sense, law and economics can help us make better informed judgements about the desirability of proposed legal changes. We may wish to help poor tenants by rent control legislation, but surely our judgement would have to be qualified if empirical studies told us that such rules largely benefit middle class tenants and tend to reduce the stock of housing offered to let.[2]

To focus ideas, I propose to run you through three examples. For us lawyers, *ius in causa positum*. Should you doubt whether these are representative, you are ready to delve into the handbooks for yourself.[3]

Spoilt Film

You organise a trip to the Canadian North to take pictures of the polar bears which a popular weekly has agreed to buy from you. Upon your return you have the pictures developed at the local camera store. They mess up and spoil your pictures. Should you be able to claim the full cost of your trip to Canada – Cdn $25 000 or so – from them?

Lawyers would reason here in terms of foreseeability and fairness. Since the camera store could not *foresee* damages of such magnitude, it would be *unfair* to hold them liable for them. Civil Codes reflect this principle by limiting damages in contractual matters to those which were foreseen or foreseeable at the time of contracting, save cases of intention to cause harm or of gross negligence.[4]

Economists tackle the problem by examining the incentives flowing from holding one party or the other party liable. Let us look at this, leaving aside for the moment the possibility of shifting burdens between the parties through contract. If the camera store is liable, they may consider adopting elaborate precautions to avoid future mishaps of this sort and the ensuing liability. The cost of these precautions would have to be borne by clients through the price of the development of films. Since this liability is part of the law, one must presume that competing snapshot development agencies would adopt similar policies and hence that this would not change the nature of the competition. Alternatively the camera store may consider insuring itself for losses such as this, if this were the cheaper option. Again the customers would pay the cost in the form of higher prices.

Let us now see how the incentives run if the customer is responsible, that is, cannot claim damages from the camera store. The customer now has an interest in exploring the ways in which he or she can reduce the risk. If he or she knows the legal rule before the trip, options such as taking multiple shots with different cameras and having films developed at different agencies may be considered.

Common sense suggests that over the broad run of conceivable circumstances the customer, having more intimate knowledge of the value of the film, is in a better position to take the appropriate precautions. He or she is, in Calabresi's terms, the cheapest cost avoider. As a simplifying rule which promises to be advantageous in most instances, it makes sense to place the burden of precautions on that person, as the Civil Code rule in fact does. In economic terms, that solution is efficient, in the sense that no further rearrangement would promise to bring gains to both parties involved. Economic reasoning coincides here with the lawyer's intuition of fairness.

Conceivably there are circumstances in which this division of responsibilities between the parties is not the best they can think of. The service agency may be able to assume certain risks at a cost below the burden they represent to the client. The parties may differ in their ability to insure the risk which cannot usefully be prevented. This points to yet another way for parties to cope with the risk, which is for the store to ask customers if their film requires special care and if the answer is affirmative, to charge a higher price, or alternatively for the customer to take the initiative and reveal the high value of the film and ask for special care, or at what price the store is willing to guarantee flawless development. The parties may even agree on an amount of liquidated damages in advance. The point is that where parties are free to negotiate, they will tailor the contract to provide the division of precautions and risks which best corresponds to their willingness and ability to assume them.

Economically, the legal rule sets the initial burdens and gives parties an incentive to reveal private information in the course of their negotiation. This information allows parties to fine-tune the agreement, that is, to determine who between them should assume which precaution and which risk. The final division depends not on the legal rule, but on the relative costs between parties.[5]

In practice the development of films is governed by a form of contract which limits the liability of the developer to the cost of a replacement film and leaves the bulk of the risk with the customer. Options are usually provided for high risk/special care developments, at a higher price. For most customers this looks like the most advantageous arrangement: low cost, most of the risk for the customer. The undertaking by the agency to replace the film in the ordinary case gives it a modest incentive to be careful. The major incentive stems from the firm's reputation and from repeat dealings with the particular customer. The business is sufficiently competitive to ensure that if this arrangement was not suitable to most customers, firms proposing a different formula would find a niche and the formula would quickly spread to the rest of the market. Hence, even though the form arrangements are not individually negotiated, there is good reason to assume that they are tailored to be prospectively advantageous to both parties. Once more justice and economics considerations coincide.

Punitive Damages

Let us now move to an example which is not common ground. The new Quebec Civil Code, in force since 1994, contains a provision dealing with punitive damages or, better, exemplary damages, the term I shall use hereafter. It reads:

> 1621. Where the awarding of punitive damages is provided for by law, the amount of such damages may not exceed what is sufficient to fulfil their preventive purpose.
>
> Punitive damages are assessed in the light of all the appropriate circumstances, in particular the gravity of the debtor's fault, his patrimonial situation, the extent of the reparation for which he is already liable to the creditor and, where such is the case, the fact that the payment of the damages is wholly or partly assumed by a third person.

The law provides for exemplary damages in several places, in particular in the rent provisions of the Civil Code,[6] in the Consumer Protection Act[7] and in the Quebec Charter of Human Rights and Freedoms.[8] This latter provision is important because the freedoms guaranteed by the Charter apply to all relationships between private individuals as well as between the latter and the State and its agencies. Article 49 of the Charter provides for exemplary damages but restricts their application to 'unlawful and intentional interference' with any right or freedom recognised in the Charter.

Exemplary damages are generally unknown in civil law. So we have a doctrinal problem here of determining their scope. A first question concerns the 'preventive purpose' in the first paragraph of article 1621; a second one relates to the role which the various factors mentioned in the second paragraph are to play in the assessment.

One strategy to address these questions is to turn to the cases. But this merely displaces the problem. How are judges to deal with this novel institution? I believe economic analysis can help here. This casts it in the role of an instrument of doctrinal analysis.

The Logic of Ordinary Damages (Civil Responsibility)

Our starting point should be that exemplary damages are meant to correct some failure in ordinary damages. Ordinary damages, you might think, merely restore the equilibrium which has been disturbed by one party's inexcusable failure to perform a contractual duty or by his negligently causing harm to a third person. Our earlier discussion of who pays what damages for the spoilt film has made it clear that whatever compensation purpose damage awards serve for the injured party, they obviously have incentive effects on both parties. An obligation to pay damages conditional upon certain behaviour will induce the person subject to that obligation to look for ways – adjustments in his or her behaviour – to reduce it. Symmetrically, uncompensated damage gives the victim an interest to see in what ways he or she can reduce that burden.

In our earlier example we detected a logic of tailoring the liability for damages so as optimally to apportion the burden of precautionary measures between the parties to a mishap. In contractual situations, parties may be assumed to grope their way towards this solution – at least prospectively – by adjustments in the terms of the contract. Outside contract, a similar logic is at work in the hands of the courts. There is no point holding a person liable for an accident over which he or she has no control, but there is good reason to do so where he or she can take precautions which would reduce the damage potentially resulting from the accident.

The question then arises as to the circumstances over which one has such control and the extent to which one should be made liable. The answer, in an economic analysis of law, is given by the famous Learned Hand formula.[9] You are negligent and should be held liable if the cost of precautions at your disposal is lower than the cost of the potential damage you cause to third persons, discounted by the probability of such a mishap occurring. Strictly speaking, economists would like to see this test applied to each additional step of precaution, such as whether in order to reduce the risk of exploding bottles a brewery should increase the inspection of its bottles from one in every hundred cases to one in every ten, or some such number. But let us leave this quibble to one side and the incentive effects of the test are obvious even in this crude form. The test solves two questions at once: when should we hold a person liable and for how much.

To lawyers, this perspective provides what I believe to be some remarkable insights in the concepts underlying the law of civil responsibility. *Faute* (*culpa*, schuld) is the decision not to engage in precautions when by the above test, they were justified considering the potential accident costs. Paying for the full cost of the damage as it actually occurred will give you the incentive to apply this test prospectively to your own behaviour. Economic considerations coincide here again with our sense of justice.

The damages which can be proven (and hence will in principle fully compensate the victim) set at the same time the cap for your precautionary efforts. There is no point spending one thousand dollars to prevent a potential mishap of fifty dollars. This explains why the damages to be paid must in principle be set exactly at the level of those actually caused. Automatic adjustment of care comes at that price. Put the damages too high, as has happened in some American professional negligence cases for failed surgical operations, and the group targeted by such liability will substantially increase precautions, hence cost and insurance, and ultimately refuse to undertake such operations. We may judge this to be excessive precaution.

Our economic analysis also gives us a handle on the two other basic concepts of civil responsibility law, to wit causality and capacity for discernment. The causality requirement can be explained as limiting one's liability to acts over which one has some control. Intervening factors should exclude it. The capacity for discernment explains why we generally do not hold young children or animals liable for accidents. In each case, however, we put the burden of liability on near-by persons who can control their accident causing behaviour: parents, educators, owners, as the case may be, rather than on the victim, some agency of the state, an insurer or the public at large.

In many cases, the victim too can affect the chances of an accident or the magnitude of the damages. The law provides incentives for the victim to engage in such precautionary behaviour by allowing for split liability and by refusing the victim recovery for aggravation of damage which he or she could have prevented.[10]

It can be shown that this machinery works to minimise the overall costs of accidents and accident prevention.[11] As a result it connects to the economist's notion of efficiency. It exhibits a remarkable parsimony in that by a single judgement it gives the correct signals to both potential injurers and potential victims.

Complications

The model we have been building leaves out many costs which are part of the real world. All models do this to an extent. It helps us to focus on the core ideas. One we have grasped these, it is time to introduce further realism by dropping some of the simplifications. An important fiction built into our initial model is that all cases of 'uneconomical' accidents lead to convictions so that the cost of imprudent behaviour is correctly driven home (*internalised*) to the persons who engage in it.

In the real world, many things may stand in the way of this fortunate outcome. Someone may sustain injury or damage without being able to trace the injurer. Others may find it too costly to sue the injurer or to wait for the judgement. If the case goes to trial, the victim may be unable to prove his or her case, the court may misunderstand it or it may incorrectly assess the damage. And even where judgement correctly goes against the injurer, he or she may be insolvent, hence insensitive to monetary signals, or unable to adjust his or her behaviour to the norms the judgement is meant to set (for instance in driving behaviour). Or the injurer may not respond to the judgement because he acted intentionally to cause harm. All of these factors are forms of what are called transaction costs. Law and economics holds that the law can be shown to exhibit a tendency to reduce transaction costs, and that this is a desirable policy.

Many institutions exemplify this tendency. Class actions and small claims courts deal with the matter of trial costs in proportion to the stakes for the plaintiffs. Evidentiary problems are addressed by factual or legal presumptions; they are also addressed by strict liability, such as products liability. For economically preventable accidents, products liability does theoretically no better than negligence-based liability; for economically inevitable accidents, it merely leads to an implicit insurance which consumers will pay for in the price of the product and which excludes the poorest amongst them. But it looks plausible as an institution to simplify the evidentiary problems in a world of increasingly technical objects for which negligence in design or production may be difficult to prove. Products liability may also improve the incentive on manufacturers to look for technical improvements which, over large numbers, reduce the burden of accidents by more than their cost.

Exemplary Damages as a Response to one Type of Complication

Exemplary damages fit into this pattern as an institution designed to correct ordinary damage rules in three sets of cases: where damaging acts can be concealed or go unprosecuted because the stakes for the victims do not justify the expense of a lawsuit; where damages are of a moral nature and impossible to assess; and where acts are intended to cause harm.

For the first set of cases, the analysis is relatively straightforward. If only one damaging act, let us say a consumer fraud, in one hundred leads to a conviction, the proper disincentive effect is created by making the wrongdoer pay for the other ninety-nine cases in which he got away with it. This requires the judge to estimate the probability of a lawsuit and a conviction. To get the proper amount of damages to be awarded, the actual damage or loss proven in court should be multiplied by the inverse of that probability – the exemplary damage multiplier.[12]

The fact that similar cases were pending elsewhere would tend to reduce the probability from which the multiplier is calculated. The exemplary damages provide what looks like a questionable windfall to the successful plaintiff. But it is not. In part it compensates him or her for the costs of taking the initiative to sue, including *horror fori*. The judge might order that part of the exemplary damage award be paid into a compensation fund for victims of the practice at issue in the trial, or some such worthwhile cause.

The point I wish to make is that exemplary damages assessed as just indicated are part of the logic underlying the ordinary law of civil responsibility. Interpreted this way, they conform to the legal requirement, couched in article 1621 of the Quebec Civil Code, that exemplary damages should not exceed what is required for their preventive function.

The test also indicates which of the factors enumerated in the second paragraph of article 1621 of the Quebec Civil Code should enter into the assessment of exemplary damages in this function. The 'gravity of the debtor's fault' and 'the extent of the reparation for which he is already liable to the creditor' could be taken as proxy for the probability of being not caught and convicted (ability to conceal). Similarly, 'the extent of the reparation for which he is already liable to the creditor' corresponds to the actual losses proven, which by our reasoning above are to be multiplied by the damage multiplier. The 'patrimonial situation' of the debtor should *not* enter into consideration. The factor in the enumeration in article 1621 of the Quebec Civil Code deals with whether the debtor is insured. If he is, premium adjustment should normally provide the correct incentives. But the adjustment may be slow and imperfect, because the insurer is unable to assess in advance the risk of this sort posed by each insured person. This would tend to undermine the disincentive effect of the exemplary damages and be a supplementary complication, which would justify further adjustment.

In the other two sets of cases the proper scope of exemplary damages is more difficult to determine. I gather this would correspond to a lawyer's intuition. The second group of cases call simply for discretionary assessment of damages without actual need to prove their extent. The difficulty is to ensure that such awards do not exceed their preventive function. I see no firm test on which a court could base itself. We enter into considerations which are normally part of criminal law and criminology.

The most difficult problem is no doubt the third group. Where one person intentionally causes harm to another, an economist would presume that such a person derives utility directly from that harm, as opposed to treating it as a cost incidental to a different and otherwise lawful activity which is the source of his utility. In the latter case, it is sufficient simply to internalise the cost to that activity, which is what ordinary liability rules are meant to do; in the former, however, the damages must offset the personal, and in principle inscrutable in the absence of an observable transaction, utility. Once more we find ourselves in the domain of criminal law and criminology, without the safeguards built into criminal law to limit arbitrariness in the exercise of the considerable discretionary power it grants to the court. My point is that the courts are unlikely to find this any easier than does the economist. In this third role, exemplary damages could properly be set taking into account the *patrimonial situation* situation of the debtor, as an indicator of the subjective utility he or she draws from the deliberately harmful activity.

Good Faith

Good faith is one of the key civil law concepts. It played a major role in late Roman law and in the pre-codification French law.[13] It plays a central role in modern German civil law and in Dutch law, where it has been codified in numerous provisions of the New Netherlands Civil Law Code.[14] The New Quebec Civil Code has given it a substantially larger place than it had under the old Code and still has in modern French law. Unidroit principles also give it a large place.[15]

Good faith is a fuzzy concept. It is used in two distinct meanings. One deals with persons such as purchasers and possessors in good faith, in multi-party relationships, where it is designed to protect those who are justifiably ignorant of a defect in their own title or that of the person they are dealing with.[16] The second meaning applies to bilateral relationships, where it qualifies actions by one party which stay clear of taking undue advantage of the other party in circumstances where the latter is vulnerable.[17] I believe that economic analysis can be used to further our understanding of these meanings.

Good Faith as Rational Ignorance

As regards persons in good faith who are excusably ignorant of defects in their own or another person's title, it may be helpful to look at the problem through the prism of economically justifiable precautions developed in the context of accident law. Consider the title defect as an accident. The precautions against it take the form of further informing oneself. A normally prudent person – by the standard of the Hand test – would inform himself up to the point where the cost of doing so exceeded the cost of the accident discounted by the likelihood of its occurrence. Beyond this point, one engages in excessive precaution, or to put it differently, one is then justified to remain *rationally ignorant*. Below it, however, one should be held liable by a standard comparable to the Learned Hand test.

How to assess the accident cost? If the good faith purchaser of a stolen object is protected, the owner loses its value. If a third party dealing with an agent on the appearance of a mandate is protected, the principal to whom the appearance is imputed incurs the cost of a contract he would not have entered into. It is these losses which should be considered the accident cost. The level of precaution should go up in proportion to the importance of such losses. The concept of good faith should be interpreted to mean that the person has informed himself up to the level justified by the discounted foreseeable cost of such losses.

Good Faith as Loyalty

Good faith in the second sense deals with bilateral relationships, such as contracts. The role of the law here is to ensure that only agreements which promise gains to both parties pass muster. The law will not correct expectations which turn out to be mistaken after the deal has been consumed. But it does and should withhold its sanction from agreements reached in circumstances leading one to apprehend that they will not work out to the advantage of both parties. 'Thus the fundamental function of contract law (and recognized as such at least since Hobbes's day) is to deter people from behaving opportunistically toward their contracting parties, in order to encourage the optimal timing of economic activity and (the same point) obviate costly self-protective measures. (. . .) Good-faith performance – which means in this context not trying to take advantage of the vulnerabilities created by the sequential character of contractual performance – is an implied term of every contract. No one would voluntarily place himself at the mercy of the other party, so it is reasonable to assume that if the parties had thought about the possibility of bad faith they would have forbidden it expressly.'[18]

Many particular institutions, dispersed throughout the Civil Code, can be read as tending to discourage bad faith dealings of particular kinds or in specific settings. Examples such as fraud, duress and mistake, arbitrary withdrawal of offer, creditors making performance impossible, exoneration clauses fully exempting the stipulating party, culpable withholding of information in insurance contracts, abuse of confidential information, disloyalty of agents against their principals come to mind.

The principle of codification requires the Civil Code to be a closed system. For any problem arising within private relationships, it should offer a solution or the principles from which to construct a solution. It therefore needs an open-ended concept to deal with all situations not directly governed by particular rules such as those mentioned. These particular rules represent known forms of exploitation of asymmetries, which have occurred in sufficient numbers or with sufficient severity for earlier generations of lawyers to have progressively discovered and articulated a rule to stop them. This knowledge has found its way into the codification. But it would be hubris to assume that we have discovered all conceivable forms of exploitation of asymmetries.

Game theory, through an analysis of the prisoner's dilemma, allows us to see reciprocity as the basis for contracts promising gains to both parties.[19] Good faith appears to be the concept allowing us to sanction the absence of reciprocity. To avoid too broad a mandate, the concept should be used sparingly and only in the absence of more particular institutions representing 'canned' solutions to lack of reciprocity. It should sanction one party's attempt to exploit a substantial asymmetry in the relationship.[20] The asymmetry may pertain to physical force or monopoly power, to access to information or to proper assessment of small probabilities or complex arrangements (bounded rationality) or again to the ability to bear risks.

Our economic analysis allows us here to provide broad outlines of how the concept should be interpreted. It explains why the concept is indispensable in a Civil Code, while a common law system might have a lesser need for it. It points to broad classes of circumstances in which it would be appropriately applied. It explains why the principles underlying good faith can be found in a host of more detailed rules designed for particular circumstances. Broad as the categories may be, they do not include a general difference in wealth between the parties to the contract, which would direct the judge to engage in general redistribution. All in all, economic analysis, I submit, here again comforts lawyers' intuitions and shows itself a valuable tool of doctrinal analysis.

HOW LAW AND ECONOMICS OPERATES

The Paths

Let us retrace our steps and look for the method in what we have been doing. Economic analysis looks at legal institutions through the effects they are expected to have, in particular as regards incentives on people's behaviour. In our first example, we looked what the incentives would be if we imposed liability on one party, then on the other. This allowed us to see that the Code rule seemed to correspond to what according to common sense would lead to the least costly way of coping with mishaps in the broad run of circumstances. To summarise, we fleshed out the incentive structure under alternative arrangements and were thereby led to discover a plausible rationale for the rule found in the Code.

We then allowed parties to negotiate. This would allow them to fine-tune their arrangement where the standard rule can be improved upon in the specific circumstances, with gains for both parties. In practice, the fine-tuning is done through standard form contracts. These have bad press amongst lawyers because they are not individually negotiated. Economic analysis, focusing again on incentives and constraints, leads us to wonder about the relevance of the latter consideration. We drew here on economic analysis of how competitive markets function. Legal terms are part of the features of a product or service. If the terms are not to the liking of a group of consumers and a different arrangement is possible for which consumers are willing to pay, competition leads us to expect that the new package will appear in the market. Conversely, this consideration allows us to conclude that in a competitive market legal arrangements, even in standard form, will generally reflect what consumers prefer at a price they are willing to pay.

In our second example, the exemplary damages, we started with an institution new to civilian systems and for which it is not immediately obvious how we should interpret it. Our initial steps focused again on the incentive effect. They led us to conclude that this institution was designed to provide higher than normal disincentives for wrongdoing. This in turn points to the idea that they are a corrective on ordinary damage rules. We briefly fleshed out the economic analysis of ordinary civil responsibility rules. The analysis presents these rules as a parsimonious and remarkably subtle incentive system to make people take proper care in situations where they may cause harm to others. The incentive structure brought to the surface for the corresponding common law institutions appears to fit the civil law institution.

We then proceeded to explore how the noble logic of this institution may come to naught because of interfering factors, which are referred to by the general term of transaction costs. We pointed to various forms of such costs and the legal institutions – class actions, small claims courts, presumptions of fact or of law and reversal of burdens of proof, product liability – which appear to be responses to them. In this setting we analysed the circumstances in which increased disincentives might be required and hypothesised three sets of such cases. We then proceeded to look at how exemplary damages would have to be interpreted to deal correctly with each class. This allowed us to make sense of the broad factors which the Quebec Civil Code indiscriminately invites the courts to take into consideration in setting exemplary damages. Our analysis allowed us to specify which factors would be appropriate in which circumstances.

Our last example concerned the very broad concept of good faith. It has given rise to a wealth of scholarship, analysing it both historically and systematically. This literature distinguishes two broad uses: good faith as justifiable of ignorance of a title defect and good faith as not exploiting one's contract partner in circumstance where he is vulnerable. The distinction makes immediate sense in an economic analysis because the incentive problems in the two cases are quite distinct. In the first case looking at the incentives quickly made us see the analogy with the economics of trading costs of precautions against the cost of the risk of mishaps, which is the core of the economics of civil responsibility, part of our second example. The calculus of care applies here to the question of how much information one should acquire about potential defects. The economic analysis, relying on common sense generalisations about relative costs, appears to make good sense of the legal analysis.

In analysing the second meaning of good faith, we were quickly led to reciprocity as the basis of contract, which game theory allows us to elucidate. Analysis of the incentive logic pointed us to the idea of asymmetries which one party might exploit at the expense of the other. Good faith would be a corrective for such circumstances. This invites the query of how other institutions might deal with that problem. We quickly found a host of specific institutions dispersed throughout the Civil Code. A comparison of these institutions leads to the conclusion that good faith must be treated as a background concept to be used only where more specific institutions cannot be found in the Code. Good faith closes the Code system, providing open-ended support for corrections in novel circumstances outside the purview of all those more specific institutions.

The Pattern

The pattern of the economic analysis of law appears to be this. Flesh out the incentive structure for the institution to be analysed and for close alternatives. For a change in a legal rule, this should point you to the expected effects (impact analysis). Applied to existing institutions, it brings out the apparent rationale of the institution. From here, examine what factors may interfere with the workings of the institution: transaction costs, asymmetries and other 'perversities' such as free riding, public goods, moral hazard, hold-outs.[21] Look at further institutions as attempts to correct these transaction costs. Determine whether these attempted corrections are themselves subject to further perversities or otherwise entail costs which may interfere with their corrective mission and may leave the initial problem untouched or require themselves yet further correction.

Once we have come this far, the power of the economic analysis as a tool for generating educated guesses about legal institutions may run out. To go further, we have to engage in empirical analysis. This commits us to specify our hypothesis in more precise, and often mathematical, form and to collect data and analyse them. Here we are likely to have to borrow more tools from economics. We are engaging in more precise but also more time-consuming and more painstaking scientific work. There is a substantial and growing literature of such studies. But the bulk of economic analysis of law is still engaged in the earlier steps of the approach, that is looking for remarkable insights in the law, by generating educated guesses about the effects, the rationale and the coherence of legal institutions.

Lest you think that this is a letdown, allow me to reply by asking the economist's standard question: what is the alternative? One alternative is standard positivist legal analysis. Since you are as familiar as I am with this approach, I merely point out that economic analysis, as we saw, usually joins the lawyer's conclusions from a standard legal analysis, and often the justice considerations, but places them on clearer and more tractable footing. It also allows one to see analogies across fields of law, which might remain hidden to a more traditional approach. If, as a lawyer, you take the view that consequences of legal rules and decisions matter, then positivist analysis alone cannot provide the answers. You must then add to your tools as a lawyer an approach which can do field work.

Several such approaches are proposed. The economic analysis of law is only one of them, competing with sociology of law, anthropology of law and, in a more specialised area, criminology. Perhaps these approaches are complementary. At all events, their acceptance will come about only if lawyers can be persuaded that the benefits to them are well worth the costs.

What are the costs? To practice economic analysis of law as we now know it, one has to be acquainted with micro-economic analysis, with game theory and with public choice, that is the analysis of the political order by means of the rational choice model on which micro-economics too is based. Besides these three sets of tools, it also pays to be familiar with the economic analysis of a number of core legal institutions, such as the due care model sketched earlier in the context of the exemplary damages, but also private and common property rights, the economics of risk and insurance, and so on.

On the benefit side, economic analysis of law, even with modest recourse to these tools, allows you, I hope to have shown, to generate a broad range of plausible guesses about the impact of legal rules and about their rationales. It provides these services across the gamut of different fields of law.[22] Although I use the terms 'guesses', I submit that many of the insights offered here have considerable intuitive appeal: conclusions of economic analysis often and rather systematically coincide with the lawyer's sense of justice and make sense of legal concepts which the wisdom of earlier generations of lawyers has bequeathed to us. Moreover, at a number of key points, the conclusions of the economic analysis of law have found support in empirical studies.[23]

CONCLUSION

From the foregoing, I proffer the conclusion that the economic analysis of law has much to say to lawyers of all shades of practice and academe. But, you might wonder, if economics lays bare the foundations of law, is law really applied economics in disguise? This question has given rise to considerable debate since about 1980.[24] It focused on Posner's thesis that the common law is economically efficient. If true, it would mean that the basic structure of law could be derived from economics and the days of law as an autonomous discipline would be numbered.[25] There are problems with the efficiency of law thesis, not least that no convincing theory has been formulated to account for it. Moreover, the efficiency judgements on which Posner relies are frequently of the sort that refer to common sense and hence not as readily amenable to rigorous testing as he assumes.[26] Some plausibility is bought here at the cost of some testability.

All the same, it is rewarding to investigate what in a given situation might be the efficient rule or whether an existing rule is efficient. As David Friedman puts it, 'it converts the study of law from a body of disparate doctrines into a single unified problem, where the same arguments (...) help make sense of a wide variety of legal issues.'[27] This perspective on law and economics should be even more appealing to civilian lawyers than to common lawyers, living as they do under Civil Codes whose abstract principles have been articulated which would more clearly express the economic logic implicit in the law. For civilian lawyers, law and economics is interesting in that it permits 'a non-dogmatic (in the sense of academic lawyers) knowledge of legal regulation'.[28] All in all, economic analysis of law is a powerful instrument of doctrinal analysis, an indispensable tool for legal policy making and a first class way of linking legal analysis to empirical studies.

NOTES

1. This effect has been found in numerous empirical studies in different countries. (See for instance Cousineau, 1991, pp. 144–165; M. & R. Friedman, 1980, pp. 237–38; Hirshleifer, 1984, 350–355; Rhoads, 1985, p. 102; Deere et al., 1995, pp. 232–237; Deere et al., 1995; Deere et al., 1997, pp. 2–28).

2. As in fact they do (see for instance Baird, 1980; Cheung, 1979; Cheung et al., 1996, pp. 224–243; Hirsch, 1979, Chap. 3; Klappholz, 1987a or 1987b; Lehrer, 1991a, b).

3. Cooter & Ulen, 1996; Friedman, 2000; Posner, 1998; Schäfer & Ott, 1995; Bouckaert & De Geest, 1999 (forthcoming); Mattei, 1997; Newman, 1998.

4. For instance art. 1150 of the French Civil Code and art. 1613 CCQ (Civil Code of Quebec) (accessible at http://www.droit.umontreal.ca/doc/ccq/en/index.html).

5. In a different context, this is one of the lessons of the Coase theorem (Coase, 1960, 1988).

6. Arts. 899, 1902, 1968 CCQ.

7. Revised Statutes of Quebec, c. P-40.1, sct. 272.

8. Revised Statutes of Quebec, c. C-12, art. 49.

9. *United States v. Carroll Towing Co.*, 159 F.2d 169, 173 (2d Cir. 1947).

10. Artt. 1478 and 1479 CCQ.

11. Calabresi was the first person to draw attention to this point, although he makes it in more complex form. (See Calabresi, 1970).

12. To be precise, if the damage is D and the chance of being caught and convicted is p, the judge should impose total damages of 1/p*D, of which D are compensatory damages and (1-p)/p*D exemplary damages. The term (1-p)/p is the exemplary damage multiplier. In practice its use would have to be simplified. Polinsky & Shavell, 1998, 892 propose a table in 10% steps at p. 962. For a 10% chance of being caught and convicted, the multiplier would be 9.

13. See (Charpentier, 1996).

14. The new Code is being put into force piecemeal. See *New Netherlands Civil Code – Patrimonial Law / Le nouveau Code civil néerlandais – Le droit patrimonial* (trilingual edition) (translated by P. P. C. Haanappel and E. Mackaay) Kluwer, Deventer, The Netherlands and Boston, MA 1990; *New Netherlands Civil Code – Patrimonial Law/ Le nouveau Code civil néerlandais – Book 8 – Traffic Means and Transport/ Livre huitième – Du transport et des moyens de transport* (trilingual edition) (translated by P. P. C. Haanappel and E. Mackaay) The Hague, Kluwer Law International, 1995; *Netherlands Business Legislation*, translated by Peter Haanappel, Ejan Mackaay, Hans Warendorf and Richard Thomas, The Hague, Kluwer Law International, 1999.

15. Crépeau & Charpentier, 1998.

16. Examples in the Quebec Civil Code: 932, 958 (possessor in good faith entitled to reimbursement of expenses made to property being reclaimed by its owner; has a rentention right for the reimbursement); 1559 (payment in good faith to the apparent creditor is valid); 1714 (reimbursement of price to purchaser in good faith of a stolen

object); 2163 (principal bound towards third persons who relied in good faith on the appearance of a mandate).

17. 6 and 7 (rights to be exercised in accordance with good faith); 1375 (good faith to govern the conduct of parties to an obligation at all stages of its existence); 1420 (nullity of a contract may only be invoked by party in good faith who suffers damage from its continuing existence).

18. Posner, 1998, p. 103.

19. On this matter, see in particular Sugden, 1986, 1998a, 1998b; Mackaay, 1988, 1989.

20. Katz 1998 in particular has insisted on the correction of such asymmetries as a major function of the law.

21. This perspective is taken in Katz, 1998. Or again 'I believe that many of these intuitions ultimately rest on notions of contracting or market failure, in particular, on externalities, coercion, and information failures. Although these concepts themselves are highly problematic, as I elaborate in later chapters, at least they direct our inquiry at particular sources of potential infirmities in the classes of transactions where the commodification concern is commonly raised. In this respect, I follow Gauthier: "Morality arises from market failures. The first step in making this claim good is to show that the perfect market, were it realized, would constitute a morally free zone, a zone within which the constraints of morality would have no place". [Morals by agreement 84]' (Trebilcock, 1993, p.29).

22. If you are not persuaded, have a look at the texts mentioned earlier by Posner, Mattei and Schäfer/Ott, and at the *Palgrave Dictionary of Economics and the Law*.

23. For an impressive survey of such empirical work in the field of accident law, see Dewees et al., 1996. Dewees, Don, David Duff and Michael Trebilcock, *Exploring the Domain of Accident Law – Taking the Facts Seriously*, New York, Oxford University Press, 1996.

24. Symposium: Change in the Common Law: Legal and Economic Perspectives, (1980) 9 *Journal of Legal Studies* 189–427; Symposium on Efficiency as a Legal Concern, (1980) 8 *Hofstra Law Review* 485–809 en 811–972, Posner's reply: Posner, A Reply to Some Recent Critics, (1981) 9 *Hofstra Law Review* 775–794; Symposium: The Place of Economics in Legal Education, (1983) 33 *Journal of Legal Education* 183–369.

25. Posner, 1987.

26. Posner, 1988.

27. Friedman, 2000, ch. 19 http://www.best.com/~ddfr/Laws_Order/laws_order_ch_19.htm.

28. [. . .] présente l'interêt de permettre l'accès à une connaissance non dogmatique (au sens de la pratique des juristes universitaires) de la régulation juridique.

REFERENCES

Deere, D., Murphy, K., & Welsh, F. (1995). Employment and the 1990–1991 Minimum-Wage Hike. *American Economic Review*, *85*, 232–237.

Baird, C. W. (1980). *Rent Control: The Perennial Folly*. Washington DC, Cato Institute.

Bouckaert, B., & De Geest, G. (Eds) (1999, forthcoming). *Encyclopedia of Law & Economics*. Cheltenham, U.K. and Ghent, Belgium, Edward Elgar and the University of Ghent.

Brenner, R. (1980). Economics – An Imperialist Science? *Journal of Legal Studies, 9*, 179–188.
Calabresi, G. (1970). *The Cost of Accidents*, New Haven: Yale University Press.
Charpentier, E. (1996). Le rôle de la bonne foi dans l'élaboration de la théorie du contrat. *Revue de droit de l'université de Sherbrooke, 26*, 300–320.
Cheung, S. (1979). Rent Control and Housing Reconstruction: The Postwar Experience of Prewar Premises in Hong Kong. *Journal of Law and Economics, 22*, 27–53.
Cheung, S. (1996). Roofs and Stars: The Stated Intents and Actual Effects of a Rent Ordinance. In: L. J. Alston, T. Eggertsson & D. C. North (Eds), *Empirical Studies in Institutional Change* (pp. 224–243). New York: Cambridge University Press.
Coase, R. (1980). The Problem of Social Cost. *Journal of Law and Economics, 3*, 1–44.
Coase, R. (1988). Notes on the Problem of Social Cost. In: R. H. Coase (Ed.), *The Firm, the Market and the Law* (pp. 157–185). Chicago: The University of Chicago Press.
Cooter, R., & Ulen, T. (1996). *Law and Economics* (2nd ed.). New York: Harper Collins.
Cousineau, J.-M. (1991). L'effet du salaire minimum sur le chômage des jeunes et des femmes au Québec: une réestimation et un réexamen de la question. *Actualité économique, 67*, 144–165.
Crépeau, P.-A., & Charpentier, E. (1998). *Les Principes d'UNIDROIT et le Code civil du Québec: valeurs partagées?/ Principles and the Civil Code of Québec: Shared Values?* Scarborough, Carswell.
Deere, D., Murphy, K., & Welch, F. (1995). The Minimum Wage Revisited. *18 Regulation – The Cato Review of Business & Regulation*.
Deere, D., Murphy, K., & Welch, F. (1997). *The Minimum Wage Debate* (special issue), *Journal of The Institue of Economic Affairs, 17*, 2–28.
Dewees, D., Duff, D., & Trebilcock, M. (1996). *Exploring the Domain of Accident Law – Taking the Facts Seriously*. New York: Oxford University Press.
Friedman, D. D. (2000). *Law's Order*. Princeton: Princeton University Press; http://www.best.com/~ddfr/Laws_Order/laws_order_ToC.htm
Friedman, M., & Friedman, R. (1980). *Free to Choose – A Personal Statement*. New York: Harcourt Brace Jovanovich.
Hirsch, W. Z. (1979). *Law and Economics*. New York: Academic Press (2nd ed.: 1988).
Hirshleifer, J. (1984). *Price Theory and applications*. Englewood Cliffs, N.J.: Prentice-Hall (3rd ed.).
Katz, A. (Ed.) (1998). *Foundations of the Economic Approach to Law*. New York: Oxford University Press.
Kirat, T. (1999). Économie du droit, Paris: La Découvert, p. 4.
Klappholz, K. (1987a). Rent Control. In: J. Eatwell, M. Milgate & P. Newman (Eds), *The New Palgrave – The World of Economics* (pp. 598–603). New York: W. W. Norton.
Klappholz, K. (1987b). Rent Control. In: J. Eatwell, M. Milgate & P. Newman (Eds), *The New Palgrave – The World of Economics* (pp. 219–224). New York: W. W. Norton.
Lehrer, K. (1981). *Rent Control – Myths and Reality*. Vancouver: The Fraser Institute.
Tucker, W. (1991). *Zoning, Rent Control and Affordable Housing*. Washington, DC: Cato Institute.
Lehrer, K. (1991). *The Landlord as Scapegoat*. Vancouver, B.C.: The Fraser Institute.
Mackaay, E. (1988). L'ordre spontané comme fondement du droit – un survol des modèles de l'émergence des règles dans la société civile. *Revue juridique Thémis, 22*, 347–383.
Mackaay, E. (1988). L'ordre spontané comme fondement du droit – un survol des modèles de l'émergence des règles dans la société civile. *Revue internationale de droit économique, 3*, 247–287.
Mattei, U. (1997). *Comparative Law and Economics*. Ann Arbor: University of Michigan Press.
Newman, P. (Ed.) (1998). *The New Palgrave Dictionary of Economics and the Law*. London: MacMillan.

Polinsky, A., & Shavell, S. (1998). Punitive Damages: An Economic Analysis. *Harvard Law Review, 111*, 869–962.

Posner, R. (1988). Conventionalism: The Key to Law as an Autonomous Discipline. *University of Toronto Law Journal, 38*, 333–354.

Posner, R. A. (1987). The Decline of Law as an Autonomous Discipline: 1962–1987. *Harvard Law Review, 100*, 761–780.

Posner, R. (1998). *Economic Analysis of Law* (5th ed.). New York: Aspen Law & Business.

Rhoads, S. (1985). *The Economist's View of the World – Government, Markets, & Public Policy*. Cambridge: Cambridge University Press.

Schäfer, H. B., & Ott, C. (1995). *Lehrbuch der ökonomischen Analyse des Zivilrechts* (2nd ed.). Berlin: Springer-Verlag.

Sugden, R. (1998a). Conventions. In: P. Newman (Ed.), *The New Palgrave Dictionary of Economics and the Law*, Vol. 1 (pp. 453–460). London: MacMillan.

Sugden, R. (1998b). Spontaneous Order. In: P. Newman (Ed.), *The New Palgrave Dictionary of Economics and the Law*, Vol. 3 (pp. 485–495). London: MacMillan.

Sugden, R. (1986). *The Economics of Rights, Co-operation & Welfare*. Oxford: Basil Blackwell.

Trebilcock M. (1993). *The Limits of Freedom of Contract*. Cambridge, MA: Harvard University Press.

THE NEGOTIATION OF DISPUTED RIGHTS OR HOW THE LAW COMES TO ECONOMICS

Evelyne Serverin

INTRODUCTION

The law is a long-standing guest of economics. Economic theories, whether they deal with the action of agents from an institutional or an individual aspect (Kirat, 1999), always leave some room, however small, for legal mechanisms. The two sectors most propitious for this meeting of law and economics are *trade* and the *treatment of disputes*.

Economists found it necessary to refer to the law as necessary when considering the circulation of goods. It is apparent at a very early stage that trade could not be considered from a purely material aspect, and that transfers primarily concerned *rights* attached to things. John R. Commons, the founder of institutional economics, was the first to link the law to economics via trade, in considering that every transaction involved two transfers, one relating to assets and the other their legal control (Commons, 1938: 129). Ronald Coase also discovered the legal aspect of trade (Coase, 1960), a "discovery" whose scope he emphasised in 1988 by siding with the lawyers, who "think of what is bought and sold as consisting of a bundle of rights", against the economists, who "think . . . as they do of factors of production as physical units" (Coase 1988: 11).

Law and Economics in Civil Law Countries, Volume 6, pages 43–60.

ISBN: 0-7623-0712-9

As well as the legal aspect of assets, economists have had to take into account the legal rules applicable to the settlement of the disputes that arise between persons over the allocation of rights. In this regard, too, the role played by the law varies according from one economic theory to another.

According to institutional economists, in transactions between equal parties, the court has a central role in resolving conflicts of interests (Commons, 1938: 132–133). Commons considered that the law allows the transformation of customs into working rules for the period and in the sector considered (Commons, 1931: 651). It is therefore essential to know about judicial decisions in order to know these working rules which form one of the categories of the joint action.

Economic analysis of the law is also aware of the role which the courts play in resolving disputes over the allocation of rights. In his 1960 article *The Problem of Social Cost*, Coase gave several examples of disputes over the allocation of rights in relation to nuisance, and took pains to study the precedents laid down by the courts. Unlike institutional economists, however, these economists tend to dispute the efficiency of court action in the allocation of rights. In their view the agents are *prima facie* the ones most capable of finding efficient arrangements and court action is justified only where private arrangements are too expensive.[1] *An alternative* is thus offered between two methods of dispute resolution: judgment or direct arrangement between the parties. More than towards a structure based on rules and precedents, the Coase approach opened the way to a theory of *negotiation and agreements over rights*. It is the latter approach that still serves today as a point of support of a significant body of work by microeconomists on out-of-court dispute resolution.

The legal aspect of negotiated settlements has not been explored as fully as it ought to have been, however. The institutionalist approach has not opened the way to substantial developments in dispute settlement procedures, since court decisions were primarily regarded as a means of imposing sanctions in the context of a collective action. For its part, economic analysis of the law, which places the emphasis on out-of-court settlements, has dealt with questions of legal disputes as problems of private decisions and bargaining.

The purpose of this article is to further the understanding of the methods and procedures whereby *the law is introduced into the sphere of settlements and negotiations*. In doing so, the author will compare the categories employed in legal economics with negotiations and settlements (Part I) and with the legal categories to be found in out-of-court settlements, taking as a basis the French legal system (Part II), and conclude that there is no rupture between law and settlement.

THE NEGOTIATION OF DISPUTED RIGHTS IN LEGAL ECONOMICS: A PROCEDURE INVOLVING THE ALLOCATION OF RIGHTS

For Coase and his supporters, the negotiation of rights is primarily an *alternative* procedure to the allocation of rights. This procedure has three particular features:

- it *competes with* the allocation of rights by the court;
- it involves *individual agents* (or parties); and
- it concerns subjective rights.

Three categories of disputed rights have been seen by economists as capable of being appropriated by bargaining: the right to exercise certain activities, the right to take court proceedings and "potential" rights.

The Acquisition of the Right to Exercise Certain Activities

As observed above, the idea that these rights may be the subject of "bargaining" was proposed and developed by R. Coase, in connection with two specific situations: the conditions governing the allocation of radio frequencies (Coase, 1959) and damage caused by polluters (Coase, 1960). The first example, which concerns competition in the allocation of a market, may be ignored in favour of examples taken from the law relating to nuisance caused by industrial or commercial activities. In this sphere, American law offered a number of solutions, which according to Coase were inefficient.

The Legal Doctrine of Nuisance

At the end of the nineteenth century the American courts treated industrial pollution disputes as disputes between "occupiers" of adjoining properties. The doctrine of "nuisance" then in force in the United States protected entrepreneurs in their use of land, as against private homeowners objecting to the former's' activities.[2] In order to encourage the intensive use of land, the American doctrine was obliged to abandon the English concept known as "uninterrupted enjoyment", which recognised that an occupier had an "easement of light and air".[3] By the end of the century "every State except three [had] rejected this easement" (Friedman, 1985: 413). In order to regulate industrial activity, American law very quickly framed land law with regulations, in particular by devising "zoning". According to an observer of the development of American law, "the restrictive covenant and common-law nuisance doctrine were together not strong enough to hold the forces of change at bay in big cities. The 20th century tried zoning. New York City had the first comprehensive zoning ordinance (1916). From this beginning, zoning became an almost universal feature of the land-use law of the cities. Planning and controls were used to monitor the growth of the city, to preserve the character of the neighbourhoods, to stop any downward slide of land values, to counterbalance the iron laws of the market" (Friedman, 1985: 678).

The Invention of the Right to Pollute

In Coase's view, the problems of pollution could not be efficiently dealt with either by the courts or by regulation, but only by direct negotiation between the parties concerned. His theory of "social cost" was developed in two stages.

- Disputes arising over pollution are not regarded as giving rise to problems of liability but to problems of the allocation of rights: the right to graze a herd, the right to erect certain buildings, the right to emit polluting substances, etc. According to Coase, the function of the courts is to determine which of two competing, *but prima facie equal*, rights is to prevail. Thus, a court which finds against an occupier who considers that he has been harmed by a polluting activity is deemed to confer on his opponent a veritable right to pollute. Once established, this right will be freely used by the person holding it: "Just as the possession of the right to build a factory on a piece of land normally gives the owner the right not to build on that site, so the right to emit smoke at a given site can be used to stop smoke being emitted from that site (by not exercising that right and not transferring it to someone else who will)" (Coase, 1988: 12).
- Next, Coase examines the legitimacy of court action in the procedure of the allocation of rights. The argument maintained in *The Problem of Social Cost* is that, in an ideal world in which the costs of a settlement would be nil, that allocation of the rights in question must be determined not by either a government (the example of the allocation of radio frequencies) or a court (examples taken from the common law on various problems associated with pollution), but by the market. In fact, "If rights to perform certain actions can be bought and sold, they will tend to be acquired by those for whom they are the most valuable either for production or for enjoyment. In this process, rights will be acquired, subdivided, so as to allow those actions to be carried out which bring about that outcome which has the greatest value on the market" (Coase, 1988: 12). The market would prove more efficient than any other authoritarian form of allocation. Thus between 1960 and 1988 Coase consistently maintains that, in such a world, it makes no difference to

which of the parties the court initially allocates the rights. Whatever the court does, the outcome will always be the same, since "[i]t is always possible to modify by transactions on the market the initial legal delimitation of rights. And, of course, if such market transactions are costless, such a rearrangement of rights will always place if it would lead to an increase in the value of production" (Coase, 1960: 15). Without going into detail on the disputes to which this claim that the initial allocation of rights "fails to make any difference" has given rise,[4] the author draws attention to the role played in the reasoning by the assertion that there is competition between *individual* and *prima facie equal* subjective rights, between which a problem of "*preference*" arises. In the examples given by Coase, the problem is dealt with in terms of competition between subjective rights having the same rank, between individuals: the "right to pollute" competes with the "right to breathe clean air"; the "right to cultivate" with the right to "graze a herd"; the "right to operate a factory" with the right to "build consulting rooms", etc.

This formulation by "pairs" of opposing interests implicit in the early works of R. Coase has been generalised under the word "entitlement". According to Calabresi and Melamed, the problem of "entitlement" arises whenever a State is faced with conflicting interests: "Hence the fundamental thing that law does is to decide which of the conflicting parties will be entitled to prevail. The entitlement to make noise versus the right to have silence, the entitlement to pollute versus the entitlement to breathe clean air, the entitlement to have children versus the entitlement to forbid them – these are the first order of legal decisions" (Calabresi & Melamed, 1972: 1090).

The Acquisition of the Right to Take Court Proceedings

In the logic of a market without transaction costs, the involvement of the courts is considered harmful. As soon as such costs are found to exist, however, court proceedings become a necessary evil. The economist then becomes a critic of the action of the courts, which he enjoins to "understand the economic consequences of their decisions" (Coase, 1960: 19). Two lines of research open up from that analysis. The first, which the author does not propose to pursue here, consists in studying the economic rationality of decisions, which were presumed to be efficient, and in any event more efficient than settlements (Priest, 1977). The second concerns the conditions of court action, by identifying a specific time for bargaining: relating to the rights to take action, in which what is at stake is the costs of the proceedings.

The Time for Bargaining

The time for bargaining is the period between the initiation of the action and delivery of the judgment. Although it is the decision to initiate proceedings that causes this period to begin to run, neither the reasons for that decision nor the nature of the rights involved are included in the analysis. According to Cooter and Rubinfeld, "[a] rationally self-interested person makes this decision [i.e. whether or not to enforce his claim in court], by solving a sequential game that balances immediate costs (hiring a lawyer, filing the claim) against benefits expected in the future (the proceeds from settlement or victory at trial)" (Cooter & Rubinfeld, 1989: 106). The decision to take action is therefore left to each party considered individually. The nature of legal claims, like the position of the parties in the trial, are not affected by the fact that the bargaining procedure has commenced.

The Rights Forming the Subject-Matter of the Bargaining

The subject-matter of the bargaining is also altered: it is not the principal claims that are at stake, but the parties' right to act. According to Deffains, "applying the rules of the market, an agreement reached in the event of a dispute consists in the dropping his complaint in return for payment from the defendant. In other words, *the defendant buys the claimant's right to take proceedings.*" (Deffains, 1997: 61) This bargaining may cover rights of all kinds, in particular those which, according to economists, are very difficult to negotiate before proceedings are commenced owing to the high costs of a settlement. That is so of actions in negligence. This argument has been supported by a number of writers (for example Calabresi and Melamed (1972), Haddock and McChesney (1991) and Hirsch (1979), who in that regard contrast the rules of property, which are open to negotiation ab initio, and the rules on negligence, which only permit bargaining before the court: "If we were to give victims a property entitlement not to be accidentally injured we would have to require all who engage in activities that may injure individuals to negotiate with them before an accident, and to buy the right to knock off an arm or a leg. Such pre-accident negotiations would be extremely expensive, often prohibitively so. . . . And, after an accident, the loser of the arm or leg can always very plausibly deny that he would have sold it at the price the buyer would have offered" (Calabresi & Melamed, 1972: 108–9).

What is at Stake in the Bargaining Procedure

Every court action gives rise to costs, which economists consistently assume to be high, although, as writers recognise, there is no means of measuring them (Cooter & Rubinfeld, 1989). Bargaining in the interest of settling a dispute principally concerns all the foreseeable costs for each of the parties. The "costs of a trial" become a burden to be avoided, *in the common interest* of each of the parties. Cooter and Rubinfeld have summarised what is at stake in the bargaining procedure by considering it as "... a bargaining game whose cooperative solution corresponds to a settlement out of court, and whose non-cooperative solution corresponds to an adversarial trial. In settlement negotiations, as in any bargaining game, the interests of the two parties diverge with respect to division of the surplus, but converge with respect to an efficient resolution of the dispute. A legal dispute is resolved efficiently when legal entitlements are allocated to the parties who can bear them at least cost, and the transaction costs of dispute resolution are minimized" (Cooter & Rubinfeld, 1989: 1069–1070). As thus presented, the rights involved in the dispute form part of what is at stake as "contested titles", on Coase's model of the allocation of rights. The reference to the allocation of the title gives the impression that the parties claim competing rights, and that it is the choice between beneficiaries that is at stake in the negotiations. However, it is not simple to define the nature of what is initially at stake. Is it the substantive right or the costs of the procedure? It is difficult to accept that the right in issue is the substantive right. Where a dispute is not over ownership of an asset but over the compensation of a harm, it is difficult to see what the *common stake* is, since *it is only the claimant's claim that is in issue.* In reality, the common stake can be reduced to the costs of the proceedings. The interest of a negotiated settlement "is in principle to release a surplus corresponding to the total costs that the parties would have had to bear had the case gone to trial" (Deffains, 1997: 61). The situation of bargaining before the court is reduced to an exchange between parties who are both in the same situation of seeking to avoid costs. This situation clearly does not mean that the parties are given equivalent information, or even a comparable negotiating capacity (Kennan & Wilson, 1993). Numerous models incorporate, in varying proportions, the subjective characteristics of individuals: aversion to the risk, pessimism or optimism in assessing the risk, asymmetry of information,[5] strategic behaviour.[6] However, this scenario disregards the unequal positions of the parties in regard to the utility of court proceedings, since economists ignore legal variables.[7] As thus reduced, the exchanges may have the tools of microeconomic modelling applied to them, as may be seen from the numerous publications on the subject dedicated to them (Spier, 1992).

The Acquisition of "Unmatured Tort Claims"

More recently, the same bargaining logic has been applied to rights which have not yet come into existence, known to legal economists as "unmatured actions". As defined by Cooter , "the term 'Unmatured Tort Claim' (UTC) refers to tort claims, like the pedestrian's, based on accidents that may occur in the future" (Cooter, 1989: 383). That title conceals a series of propositions tending to authorise potential victims (pedestrians, for example) to sell their right to a future claim against the *driver* or his *insurer*. For the victim, the consideration for a sale of that nature is that he can obtain better insurance at a better cost. Overall, efficiency is ensured by a saving in costs of proceedings: "The law, however, prohibits the transfer of the right to recover in tort before an accident occurs, and instead provides machinery for resolving disputes after they arise" (Cooter, 1989: 395). It follows that "Premiums for insurance against tort liability must include the cost of processing claims through the transaction structure prescribed by law" (Cooter, 1989: 395). By means of a transaction known as a "sale" of rights of action, what is envisaged is a transfer of the burden of insurance, from the driver (third-party insurance) to the victim (accident insurance) (O'Connell, 1977). In the model suggested, everyone should be able to carry out such a transaction, within a framework of negotiations subject to judicial supervision: ". . . courts would require a bargain between the parties over the sale of UTCs. The bargaining requirement, already explored extensively in the general literature on contracts, would guarantee that exchanges are voluntary" (Cooter, 1989: 387).

On the basis of these examples alone, it is found that in economic theory disputed rights may form the subject-matter of bargaining where considerations of efficiency take precedence over the desire for legal realism. The tendency to regard "negotiated settlement" and "judicial settlement" as radically opposed to one another obscures the analysis, by precluding consideration of the rules which apply to the *production* and *validation* of exchanges over disputed rights.

THE NEGOTIATION OF DISPUTED RIGHTS IN THE CONTEXT OF FRENCH LAW: A MECHANISM FOR THE APPLICATION OF THE LAW

From a legal point of view, bargaining between the parties to a dispute raise questions which are ignored by legal economists. The negotiation of rights implies the determination of the legal characteristics of ownership of the disputed right. The settlement of disputes by agreement presupposes an examination of the rules applicable to measures of settlement.

The Ownership of the Disputed Rights

In a situation involving opposing claims, it is necessary to determine whether all the rights are negotiable, and if so on what conditions, and whether the rights to bring proceedings are transferrable.

Disposable Rights

What, in legal terms, does it mean to be the "holder of a right"? That is a classic question for legal writers, who approach it from the viewpoint of subjective rights. As commonly defined, a subjective right "represents an asset which is appropriated by the individual concerned, on which he may rely in accordance with the law" and "of which he may dispose, either in favour of a third party by transferring it, or, where he is unable to do so, by relinquishing it" (Roubier, 1964, p. 85). It is according to this criterion of the "disposability" of rights that legal writers have drawn a distinction between subjective rights, which, like the right of property, can be appropriated, and legal prerogatives, which, like the citizen's individual rights or rights deriving from marriage or affiliation, do not form part of the assets of the person concerned.

Although writers are not always agreed as to precisely what rights come within one category or the other, it is generally accepted that certain rights (such as those relating to personal status,[8] public office or freedoms) cannot be disposed of.

In addition to cases where they cannot be disposed of, many rights conferred by measures adopted in the public interest, in order to protect certain categories of persons (consumers, borrowers, workers), can be disposed of only on certain conditions. The first condition to be satisfied if a right of that kind is to be disposed of that it has "become part of the assets" of the person concerned, that is to say that the event which causes the right to come into existence has occurred (for example, notice terminating a tenancy in the case of the right to continue to occupy the premises). The situation envisaged by economists of a "sale" of rights which have not yet become part of a person's assets is therefore not legally admissible. Furthermore, the conditions of validity of the legal measures whereby these rights are disposed of (essentially settlement and renunciation) are strictly controlled by the Court of Cassation, and the considerable body of case-law on the subject gives an indication of the legal interest attaching thereto.[9]

Abandonment of the Right of Action

Economists tend to treat a pre-trial agreement as the result of a *sale by the claimant of his right of action* in order to save the costs of the proceedings. But what is meant, in legal language, by a right of action and by abandonment of the right of action?

Confusion frequently arises between the *right of action* and the *substantive right* claimed in the court proceedings. As defined in Article 30 of the New Code of Civil Procedure, an action is simply "the right, for the person making a claim, to adduce argument on the merits of that claim so that the court can declare it well founded or ill founded" and, for the opposing side, "the right to dispute the merits of that claim". In other words, although the right to bring an action is generally regarded as a subjective right, it is distinct from the right which the claimant claims as against the defendant. The right to bring an action is exercised, not vis-à-vis the defendant, but vis-à-vis the court, which must hear and determine the action if it is not to be guilty of a denial of justice (Motulsky, 1964: 223).

To what extent may the right of action, as thus defined, be relinquished? As we have seen, economists consider that it can be sold, *to the defendant*. However, although in legal terms a right of action may conceivably be sold to a third party (in the form of the assignment of a debt, for example, as provided for in Article 1689 et seq. of the Civil Code), it is impossible to imagine a sale for to the defendant, which would be tantamount to authorising the defendant to turn the action against the claimant. Although a sale to the defendant is inconceivable, however, it is perfectly lawful for the parties to *abandon the right of action*. It is possible to disclaim a right of action, either unilaterally or by agreement, by means of various procedural measures listed in Article 384 of the New Code of Civil Procedure (NCCP): "as well as being terminated by the judgment, the proceedings are terminated, incidentally to the action, where the claim is settled, where it is admitted or where the action is discontinued . . ." The effect of such steps is to terminate the court's duty to determine the claim, and, in addition, to prevent the initial claim from being able to succeed.[10] Admittedly, such acts of abandonment on the part of the claimant (discontinuance of the claim), the defendant (admission of the claim) or both (settlement) *may* be the consequence of bargaining over the disputed right. However, the right of action as such cannot be directly transferred. The objection may be raised that the outcome is the same, and that matters proceed *as though* the right of action had been surrendered, but there is an essential difference: the fact that the claimant agrees to drop the claim, even in return for financial consideration, cannot have the effect that the right of action is transferred to the defendant's assets. To the contrary, the loss of the right of action resulting from such steps means that *the rights claimed cannot subsequently be recognised in law*, whether they were the subject of a financial arrangement of whether the person claiming them renounced them without consideration. In other words, owing to the loss of the right of action, the substantive right itself is abandoned. As such, however, this right is not an essential element of the validity of the act of renunciation.

Rules Applicable to Measures of Settlement

A right which is disputed is always *uncertain*, since it is necessary to have recourse to a specific legal measure in order to determine the principle and the amount of the right. Various legal measure are ascribed by law with the power to determine a dispute effectively. Some of these measures are imposed by an authority, such as a judicial decision or an arbitral award. However, disputes may also be settled by agreement, by means of a specific contract, namely a settlement, which applies to the substantive rights in issue, while the prospects of reaching such a settlement depend on the position of the parties.

The Settlement as a Legally Effective Means of Resolving the Dispute

The specific measure whereby the parties agree to settle a dispute is a special contract, a settlement contract, the cause and legal effect of which are precisely defined by law.

The settlement, as regulated by Title 15 of Book III of the Civil Code which bears that title, has its *legal basis* in the *existence of a dispute*, either present or foreseeable, which it is designed to terminate. Article 2044 of the Civil Code defines a settlement as "a contract whereby the parties terminate a dispute which has arisen or prevent a dispute which is yet to arise". Although disputes are not defined in the Civil Code, they may be regarded as being sustained by the failure to determine claims, either because they are disputed in principle or because the amount is contested. Thus, in a dispute arising as a result of an accident, the issue to be resolved may be the very existence of liability (in the absence of a guarantee or where there has been contributory negligence of the part of the victim, etc.) or the quantum of damages. The "rights" on which victims rely are thus weighed down by "disputes yet to arise", the very ones which under Article 2044 of the Civil Code constitute the "legal ground" the settlement agreement. Thus, any out-of-court settlement will tend to be classified as a settlement, purely because it relates to an uncertain claim. Does that mean, however, that a settlement cannot be validly concluded unless *the very existence* of a right is in doubt? That was the position envisaged by those who drafted the Civil Code, who did not perceive that it was possible to determine by settlement a right which was certain: "there would be no settlement if it did not have as its subject-matter a doubtful right". Where a known right is sacrificed the relevant act is not a settlement but a sale or a gift (Bigot de Préameneu, 1803). However, that analysis has not withstood the ascent of the negotiated settlement in the sphere of the most firmly established subjective rights. Legal writers have had to abandon the concept of "doubt" inherited from the Civil Code in favour of the concept of "dispute", placing the negotiated settlement where there are rights to be claimed.[11] As a result, the scope of agreements has increased: instead of being confined to disputes for which no legal solution exists,[12] the negotiated settlement is chosen where rights can be claimed with sufficient prospects of success.

A negotiated settlement produces a legal effect of its own: it prevents an *effective* return to the court on the facts forming its subject-matter, owing to the *binding authority* which it is recognised as having. Under Article 2052 of the Civil Code, a negotiated settlement has the same authority as a judgment: "as between the parties, a negotiated settlement has the authority of a binding decision delivered at last instance". The scope of this effect is defined in Article 1351 of the Civil Code, which provides that "the subject-matter claimed must be the same; the claim must be based on the same legal grounds, it must be between the same parties, and brought by them and against them in the same capacity". In procedural terms, this binding authority acts as a bar to admissibility, that is to say, a ground for declaring a claim inadmissible, without any examination of the merits (Article 122 of the NCCP).[13] Where these three identities exist, the parties can no longer be heard by the court and, consequently, the terms of the agreement cannot be re-examined.

Negotiated Settlements Linked with Substantive Rights

Whereas negotiated settlements are readily conceived as a model of "extra-legal negotiation", they are now most common in areas where clearly defined substantive rights exist. That is the case of road traffic accidents, where the victim is recognised as being entitled to compensation, but the "value" of the right to compensation following an accident remains to be determined. The central object of the negotiation will therefore be *that which has not been determined*, which in all cases, even the least disputed, is the quantum of damages. In that context, the negotiated settlement will compensate for the doubt existing in regard, not to *the existence of a right*, but of *its value in the case in point*. In the context of mechanism set up by the Law of 5 July 1985, a negotiated settlement is merely a procedure for the *enforcement* of the obligations of the insurer. A procedure of negotiation is established, together with a strict formal procedure. The negotiation procedure must "mimic" a trial, observing, in particular, the *audi alteram partem* principle. Negotiated settlements conducted in this sphere are therefore *framed by legal requirements*. Far from being conflicting with one another, negotiated settlement and trial tend to come within the common framework of procedures for the determination of rights.

Incentives to Negotiate

Although a negotiated settlement is a procedure for the "implementation" of a right, it none the less remains that the right in question belongs to *just one party*. It follows that the parties have not got the same interest in negotiating. In any dispute there is an *asymmetry of interest* in obtaining a negotiated settlement. As we have seen, that consideration is generally ignored by legal economists. That position depends directly on the state of the (essentially procedural) rules governing mutual relations between the parties. Although they have *equal* legal guarantees, the parties may be in different positions in procedural terms in relation to the negotiation process, and will have unequal prospects of obtaining compensation.

The importance of this initial position may be illustrated by two examples, taken from the law on negligence, where the obligation to take action has been moved from one party to the other: compensation for physical injuries resulting from road traffic accidents (Serverin, 1997) and compensation for victims of infection by the hepatitis C virus (Serverin, Munoz-Perez & Bedu, 1996).

(1) In an action in negligence brought by a victim against the negligent party and his insurer, the general rule is that the victim must take the necessary action. The Insurance Code provides that a person seeking compensation is to submit a claim, either on a friendly basis or through the courts, to the insurer (Article L. 124–1 of the Insurance Code).[14] In the case of road traffic accidents causing physical injury, this principle has been reversed. The Law of 5 July 1985 transferred the obligation to take action, and the insurer is now responsible for making a compulsory offer of compensation, which must be made to "a victim who has suffered physical injury" (Article L. 211–8 of the Insurance Code). The obligation thus placed on the insurer may be analysed as *an obligation to enter into negotiations with the victim*. The insurer can no longer simply await a claim: he must play an active role in the compensation process. The victim is not obliged to take action to obtain compensation, but does not lose the right to act, in order to obtain a judgment on the merits or to obtain interim orders, in civil proceedings and in criminal proceedings, at any level of the procedure. This requirement to make an offer is particularly effective in terms of the opening of files: the annual proportion of physical injury cases in which the insurer offered compensation (with or without payment of sums) was thus estimated at 75% in 1994 (Serverin, 1997: 134). Of all the cases closed during the same year, the proportion settled by negotiated settlement was 95%.[15]

In the structure of the compensation mechanism, negotiated settlement and judgment are treated as being *equivalent*: both procedures allow cases of accidents causing physical injuries to be dealt with within the legal framework established by the Law of 1985.

(2) The situation is quite different for victims infected by the hepatitis C virus as a result of blood transfusions. The profile of that infection is typical of public health problems coming under what is customarily called

"therapeutic risk". In this sector, apart from cases of HIV infection, there is no compulsory offer procedure. In an inquiry commissioned by the Ministry of Justice in 1996, the author showed that this situation directly influenced the structure of associated claims: first, claims were few in comparison with the numbers of infected persons identified (a total of 550 over six years, out of 400,000 victims); second, no proposal for a negotiated settlement had been made by the insurers. That may come as a surprise when it is clear from its case-law that the Court of Cassation is very favourably disposed towards victims, who have not been required to establish negligence on the part of the transfusion centre in order to be awarded damages. However, the fact that the insurer is under no obligation to negotiate means that the victims are required to initiate legal proceedings, which only a tiny number of them do. This situation is in stark contrast with that of victims of road traffic accidents, where the offer is automatic, and where the court merely ensures the proper functioning of the negotiated settlement mechanism.

CONCLUSION

These last two examples may provide us with matter to conclude on the role of the law in negotiations, and also on the scope for rules which economists might allow in their analysis of dispute resolution.

As we have seen, the incentives to negotiate depend on the *obligation to act* inherent in the parties' positions. Since, in addition, the prospects of negotiating also depend on the existence of substantive rights, then negotiations assume the aspect of one of a number of procedures for the *application of the right.*

Therefore, what meaning is to be ascribed to transactions involving "bargaining over rights"?

- If these bargaining procedures are conceived as procedures for the *allocation* of the rights in issue, so that efficient solutions are thereby possible (the rights are allocated to whichever of the parties places the highest value on them . . .), then they clearly correspond to a mythical transaction, which does not exist in any legal system. The allocation of the rights which may be observed at collective level is never the result of the *aggregation* of bargaining between individuals over competing subjective rights. This allotment of rights is more surely the result of the centralised procedures for allocation devised by the regulatory authorities.
- But if "bargaining over disputed rights" is taken to mean all the *legally valid* operations carried out in respect of those rights, then it is necessary to

recognise both their legal reality and the significant role which they play in achieving a more precise understanding of the processes for the implementation of the right. Particular attention must be paid to the role which, an accordance with legislation and case-law, the parties themselves must play in implementing certain rights, without any procedure being involved, and indeed without any dispute. In order to give a more precise meaning to the actual concept of bargaining, it would be necessary to conduct empirical research into the sectors of legal relations concerned by such processes, in particular by negotiate settlements. Where such research has been carried out, the conclusions drawn have been largely counter-intuitive, as regards both the subject-matter and the scope of negotiations. The empirical analysis of certain negotiation mechanisms and their implementation has made it possible to see bargaining as a *form of implementing the right*, not necessarily very remote from the outcome of judicial proceedings. By comparing the levels of compensation awarded by the courts and those reached by negotiated settlement in road traffic accident cases, the author has found that there is a common ground of assessment, resulting in very similar amounts of compensation, between what are readily regarded as "alternative" procedures. The conclusion might of course be drawn that there is no point in initiating court action when the outcome is very similar to what the parties themselves are likely to reach; but that would fail to take into consideration that the results of negotiated settlements have been obtained within frameworks of action that are strictly delimited by rules of all kind: rules on the allocation of the rights under negotiation; procedural rules governing the conduct of negotiations; and rules defining the conditions of validity of the measures of settlement.

Such procedures, by their scope, form part of a *legislative policy* on compensation. It is inconceivable that equivalent effects could be obtained solely by spontaneous arrangements. Far from being an alternative to the law, bargaining provides a means of involving individuals in implementing the rules, thus extending the sphere of influence of those rules beyond the circle of members of the legal professions.

NOTES

1. For Coase, "The reasoning employed by the courts in determining legal rights will often seem strange to an economist because many of the factors on which the decision turns are, to an economist, irrelevant" (Coase, 1960: 15).

2. For the history of the doctrine of nuisance, see Kurtz, 1976.

3. According to this concept, "(. . .) a landowner whose land had always had a pleasant, open view had a right to keep things that way" (Friedman, 1985: 413) and therefore to object to any undesirable development.

4. R. Coase himself repeated this thirty years later, in his *Notes on the Problem of Social Cost*, but only to reassert the validity of the analysis previously carried out in terms of the maximisation of rights by agreements concluded on the rights (Coase, 1988: 157–185).

5. Among current works which emphasise the asymmetrical nature of information, see, in particular, Spier, 1992. This study develops a model of sequential negotiation with asymmetric information, from the inception of the dispute to the termination of the proceedings, via the listing of the case.

6. In particular with B. Deffains, who develops different models of strategies of offer according to the parties' information. See Deffains, 1997.

7. Except on the prospective form, as in the conclusion of Cooter and Rubinfeld, who stress that ". . . the insights needed to improve strategic bargaining theory may be *inspired partly by law's institutional detail*" (Cooter and Rubinfeld, 1989: 1094 – emphasis added).

8. Article 311–319 of the Civil Code: "Actions relating to affiliation cannot be renounced".

9. The Court of Cassation requires, in particular, for the renouncement of a right an "unequivocal manifestation of the intention to renounce it" (Extended Chamber, 26 April 1974, D. S., J., 249, annotated by Boré; JCP, 1975, II, 18157, submissions of Gegout). On all these points, see Dreifuss-Netter, 1985, *Les manifestations de volonté abdicatives*, Paris, LGDJ.

10. Where a party merely abandons the proceedings, without renouncing the right of action, he is not prevented from subsequently resuming the proceedings. This applies to acts which terminate the "main" action, such as where the action lapses, where the proceedings are discontinued and where the writ lapses (Article 385 of the NCCP).

11. "Two persons are in dispute when one claims that the right directly protects his interest in conflict with the other's interest and the latter challenges the claim, or where, although he does not challenge it, he does not meet it . . . It seems clear that the necessary and sufficient condition for judicial action to be possible is that the parties have the power to provoke it. There must be a right of action." (Boyer, 1947: 38 et seq.).

12. The assertion that it is "small disputes", which are "very different [in nature] from those heard by the courts" (Commision Haenel and Arthuis Report, 1994: 13), that are dealt with in out-of-court procedures, is a commonplace that sustains the descriptions of an alternative justice.

13. Article 122 of the NCCP defines an objection to admissibility as "any submission for a declaration that the opposing party's claim is inadmissible, without an examination of its merits, on the ground that the party is not entitled to act, whether because he lacks *locus standi*, or he has no interest in taking part in the proceedings, or the claim is time-barred, or the period is pre-determined, or a final decision has been taken."

14. This article provides that "in liability insurance, the insurer shall not be liable unless, following the injurious event provided for in the contract, a friendly or judicial claim is made to the insurer by the injured third party."

15. The opening of a negotiation procedure does not necessarily lead to compensation, since under the applicable rules the right to compensation is reduced, or even cancelled, where the victim has been negligent.

REFERENCES

Bigot de Préameneu (1803). *Exposé des motifs du projet de loi relatif aux transactions, Code civil contenant la série des lois qui le composent avec leurs motifs*. Paris: Garnery, p. 143 et s.

Boyer, L. (1947). *La notion de transaction*. Toulouse: Sirey.

Calabresi, G. (1965). The Decision for Accidents: an Approach to No-Fault Allocation of Costs. *Harvard Law Review*, *78*(4).

Calabresi, G., & Melamed, A. D. (1972). Property Rules, Liability Rules, and Inalienability, one View of the Cathedral. *Harvard Law Review*, *85*, 1089–1128.

Coase, R. (1959). The Federal Communications Commission. *The Journal of Law and Economics*, October, 1–40.

Coase, R. (1960). The Problem of Social Cost. *The Journal of Law and Economics*, October, *III*, 1–44.

Coase, R. (1988). *The Firm, the Market and the Law*. Chicago and London: University of Chicago Press.

Commission Haenal et Artuis (1994). *Propositions pour une justice de proximité*. Paris: La Documentation française.

Commons, J. R. (1931). Institutional Economics. *American Economic Review*, December: 648–657.

Commons, J. R. (1938). The problem of correlating law, economics, and ethics. *Recueil d'études sur les sources du droit en l'honneur de François Gény*. Paris: Librairie du recueil Sirey, t.3.

Cooter, R. (1989). Toward a Market in Unmatured Tort Claims. *Virginia Law Review*, *75*, 383–411.

Cooter, R. D., & Rubinfeld, D. L. (1989). Economic Analysis of Legal Disputes and their Resolution. *Journal of Economic Literature*, *XXVII*, 1067–1097.

Deffains, B. (1997). L'analyse économique de la résolution des conflits juridiques. *Revue Française d'Economie*, *XII*(3), 57–99.

Friedman, L. M. (1985). *A History of American Law*. New York: A Touchstone Book, Simon & Schuster Ed.

Haddock, D. D., & McChesney, F. S. (1991). Bargaining Costs, Bargaining Benefits, and Compulsory Nonbargaining Rules. *Journal of Law, Economics and Organization*, *7*(2), 334–354.

Hirsch, W. Z. (1979). *Law and Economics: An Introductory Analysis*. New York: Academic Press.

Jolibois, C., & Fauchon, P. (1996). *Quels moyens pour quelle justice?* Paris: La Documentation française.

Kirat, T. (1999). *Economie du droit*. Paris: La Découverte, coll. Repères.

Kennan, J., Wilson, R. (1999). Bargaining with Private Information. *Journal of Economic Literature*, *31*, 45–104.

Kurtz, P. M. (1976). Nineteenth Century Anti-Entrepreneurial Nuisance Injunction-Avoiding the Chancellor. *William & Mary Law Review*, *17*(4), 621–670.

Motulsky, H. (1964). Le droit subjectif et l'action en justice. In: *Archives de Philosophie du droit*, Tome IX, "Le droit subjectif en question" (pp. 215–227). Paris: Sirey.

O'Connell, J. (1977). Transferring Injured Victims' Tort Rights to No-Fault Insurers: New Sole Remedy Approaches to Cure Liability Insurance Ills, U. Ill. L. S: 479–788.

Priest, G. L. (1977). The Common Law Process and the Selection of Efficient Rules. *Journal of Legal Studies*, *6*, 65–82.

Roubier, P. (1964). Délimitation et intérêts pratiques de la catégorie des droits subjectifs. In: *Archives de Philosophie du droit*, Tome IX, "Le droit subjectif en question" (pp. 83–95). Paris: Sirey.

Serverin, E, Munoz-Perez, B., & Bedu, C. (1996). Six années de traitement juridictionnel des demandes en réparation des dommages causés par des contaminations virales non V.I.H., Report for the Ministry of Justice, 174 pages.

Serverin, E. (1997). Les accidents corporels de la circulation, entre transactionnel et juridictionnel, Report for the Ministry of Justice, Saint-Etienne, multigr., 205 pages.

Spier K. E. (1992). The Dynamic of Pretrial Negotiation. *Review of Economic Studies*, *59*, 93–108.

Troplong (1846). Du cautionnement et des transactions: commentaire des titres XIV et XV et du Livre III du Code civil, Paris: Charles Hingray éditeur.

LEGAL SYSTEMS AND ECONOMIC ANALYSIS: HOW RELEVANT IS AMERICAN LAW AND ECONOMICS FOR THE UNDERSTANDING OF FRENCH *JURISPRUDENCE*?

Thierry Kirat

INTRODUCTION

It seems that there is a considerable gap between the universal-type categories of economic analysis and those appertaining to national or regional legal systems (Mattei, 1977). This statement prompts us to question the Law and Economics discipline which is broadly based on American common-law. I intend here to deal with this problem in reference to the problem of coordination of judicial decisions in the United States and France. There is a considerable amount of literature in the field of Law and Economics in America concerning the common law and *stare decisis*. This literature has also been the result of the meeting between a discipline (micro-economic theory) and a context (American common law). What then is its heuristic value and its application within the context of French private law?

I will attempt to answer this question by beginning with the idea that case-law and *jurisprudence* are the products of legal systems which establish the

Law and Economics in Civil Law Countries, Volume 6, pages 61–78.

ISBN: 0-7623-0712-9

particular ways in which the decisions of the courts are coordinated. Following this, I will examine the relevant areas of economic analyses in the original context (case law and the rule of precedent in the USA) and in French private law. I aim to show that the paths chosen for jurisprudential regulation require theories which are suited to the object under study.

AMERICAN CASE-LAW AND FRENCH *JURISPRUDENCE*

The study of jurisprudential regulation raises the question of how the courts contribute to the production of rules of law. A comparative analysis should question the ways in which the judiciary contributes to the production of legal rules as well as the conditions under which the courts are bound by past decisions. One must take account of the grip of a judicial system which defines the position of the jurisdictions in the production or application of law, clarifying the power of the precedent within the jurisprudential process (MacCormick & Summers, 1997).

The Contribution of the Courts to the Production of Legal Rules

The courts contribute to the production of legal rules in two different ways:

- a direct normative type of process through which the courts have the power to act upon the existence of a rule – opposing its application, declaring its nullity or anti-constitutionality;
- an indirect process through which the supreme courts exercise control over the way the ordinary courts interpret the statutes (Serverin, 1999).

These are the characteristics of jurisprudential systems in the two countries. In the USA, the judicial system uses direct procedures to contribute to the production because of the judicial power of control of unconstitutionality of statutes.

The Supreme Court in America acts directly upon statutes either by putting them into practice or by refusing to apply them because of their unconstitutional nature. In France this is not the role of the Cour de Cassation but of the Conseil Constitutionnel. French civil courts, whether they be lower or appeal courts – and even the supreme court – do not have such prerogatives: their vocation is to apply the legislation under the control of the Court of Cassation which supervises the interpretations made by lower judges. Indeed it is the supreme jurisdiction which provides a certain uniformity to the interpretations of the law; its rulings have a much wider effect than the case before the supreme judges.

Indeed, the lower courts are very heedful of the permanent jurisprudence delivered by the Court of Cassation so much so that when arriving at their decisions they take into account the "odds" of their decisions being overruled by the higher civil court. This subtle mechanism may be likened to a specific variety of judicial precedent that Troper and Grzegorczyk qualify in the following manner: "The decision of a lower court will be confirmed if it applies statutes or principles as they have been interpreted by the precedent of a higher court" (Troper & Grzegorczyk, 1994: 113).

Stare Decisis and Legal Precedents

Defined in absolute terms, the rule of *stare decisis* forces judges to treat similar cases in a similar manner. The aim of the rule is to provide a certain regularity in the solutions brought to similar disputes. This is a particularly important issue in common law systems: the binding precedent rule provides a certain legal stability, predictability and safety, all of which are guaranteed in the continental legal systems via a codification of the rules (Goodhart, 1934; Zander, 1998). Certain traits are peculiar to common law and to civil law:

(1) in common law, the coordination of court rulings is sought via institutional processes aimed at establishing regularities: either by a mandatory respect of precedents or by forcing the judges to explain why they have not conformed to the precedents by using *distinguishing*;

(2) in countries of civil law, responsibility for coordination does not fall to the judges. It is assumed through three institutional factors:

- codification means that the judges share the same rules;
- the Court of Cassation has a very strong influence in terms of control of lower courts;
- there is no mechanism ensuring the stability of lower court decisions except their motivation in law. A French judge is under no obligation to place his decision in a long line of decisions given for similar cases.

France does not have the principle of binding precedent in the sense that the "Code Civil" forbids the courts to interfere with legislation and to make rules ("It is prohibited for judges to decide by way of general provisions and rules on the cases that are brought before them" – Article 5 of the Civil Code). This provision goes a long way to explaining the special feature of the jurisprudence system in France appertaining to case law: the Highest Court ensures a certain uniformity in the interpretation of the law by the lower court judges hence making a significant contribution to the structuring of "a series of institutional procedures and adjustments furthering the adherence to previous decisions under certain conditions" (Serverin, 1999: 6). The Highest Court tends to produce tendencies or a consistency of interpretation expressed by the notion of "persisting jurisprudence" (*jurisprudence constante*). Should the French judge not consider himself to be totally tied down by previous decisions emanating from his jurisdiction or from other courts, he nevertheless attempts to understand the tendency inherent in decisions already rendered on a particular point (Zander, 1999): 234): "In France, the judicial precedent does not, ipso facto, bind either the tribunals which established it nor the lower courts; and the Court of Cassation itself retains the right to go back on its own decisions. (. . .) The practice of the courts does not become a source of the law until it is definitively fixed by the repetition of precedents which are in agreement on a single point" (Lambert & Wasserman, 1929: 14–15).

In the USA, even if the binding nature of the precedent is less pronounced than in Great Britain (Zander, 1999), the rule of *stare decisis* is nevertheless of unquestionable importance. Macey believes that the American precedent has no generalised binding nature but that it may be explained by the preferences of the judges: "(. . .) the form of precedent practised in U.S. courts can be explained in large part by reference to the individual preferences of judges who subscribe to the doctrine" (Macey, 1998: 68). However, there does exist a principle of precedent forcing a Present day judge to adhere to a previous decision even if he considers it to be mistaken (Kornhauser, 1998).

It is nevertheless important to clarify the types of relationships that the Present judge may have with the Prior judge who created the precedent. Kornhauser (1998) has identified five types:

(1) the Present judge may be a member of the court which has decided upon the former case;
(2) the Present judge may be in office in a court lower to that having decided upon the Former case;
(3) the Present judge may be in office in a court higher to that having decided the Former case;
(4) the Present judge may be in office in a court having no hierarchical relationship with the court which decided upon the Former case;
(5) the Present judge may be in office in a court have no relationship with the court which decided upon the Former case.

In the three last cases, the judge is not obliged to refer to the precedent. Cases 3, 4, and 5 thus indicate a situation where there is no mandatory precedent whereas in cases 1 and 2 there is an obligation to refer to the precedents. The nature of the precedent nevertheless varies in both cases: in case 1, the precedent is horizontal whereas in case 2 it is vertical.

In fact, the existence of a *stare decisis* is organized via the institutional framework of jurisdictional activity and the structure of the legal system. According to Kornhauser (1998), in the USA the District Court judges are under no obligation to adhere to the former decisions of the judges of the same court. However, they are required to adhere to the decisions of the Supreme Court and the Appeal Court for their circuit. Hence, the District Court judges are in a vertical and not horizontal *stare decisis* situation. This is not the case of the Court of Appeal judges who are required to follow a vertical and horizontal *stare decisis*. The influence of the vertical *stare decisis* should not be under-estimated because, as Macey remarks: "Appellate review in hierarchical judicial systems has the obvious benefit of overcoming the problem of conflicting precedent and achieving standardization" (Macey, 1998: 72).

Two Forms of Jurisprudence: Decisional Regularities and Interpretative Regularities

A comparative analysis of systems brings to light two types of consistency borne by the forms of regulatory jurisprudence in the two countries: regularities in *decisions* and regularities in *interpretation* which tallies with the distinction drawn between the Anglo-American case-law method and French *jurisprudence*. The first type relate to the material dimensions of the legal solutions that the courts apply to disputes. These are based upon both the permanent nature over time and the diffusion of the *ratio decidendi* of the decision which creates the precedent.

The *ratio* of the decision which takes on the force of a precedent indeed produces either a horizontal or a vertical effect depending upon the position of the court in the judicial hierarchy as to the uniformization of former decisions. This is in line with the principle of "treating all cases alike". In this instance we talk of decisional consistency because they are *decisions* which take on the form of a precedent: the decisions of the Future judges are required to follow the decisions of the Prior judges.

The second regularities, those concerning *interpretation,* are located within a framework of strict legal hierarchy and legislated law; the lower courts do not create rules, they concern themselves with applying positive, legislative law to legal cases. In America the precedent deals with *cases* which are a "mixture" of material or behavioural facts and positive rules, whereas in France *jurisprudence* is based solely upon the rule with no reference whatsoever to the factual dimension of the disputes.

We draw a distinction similar to that of Troper and Grzegorczyk (1997: 126) who deal with "precedents of solution" and "precedents of interpretation" in order to highlight the predominance of the second type in the French legal system. The lower court judges have wide scope for decision within this system on all the aspects of the decision which do not come within the field of motives in law. In the words of Lambert: "(. . .) all that he [i.e. the judge, TK] need do is to preface his judgement by the traditional formula "with reference to (*vu*) section 1121", "with reference to section 1134", "with reference to section 1382 of the Civil Code". These are some of the most usual screens adopted, and it matters little whether there is any actual connection between the question raised and the text quoted. In many a case *the reference is a pure formality*, and the judge has to find the reasons for his decision elsewhere. And before deciding to act on his own initiative or personal opinion, *he looks for precedents* in the decisions of the courts above him or of his own predecessors" (Lambert, Pic & Garraud, 1926: 14 – emphasis added).

According to Lambert, the French judiciary has a precedent that he thought is more dependent upon the practices of the lower court judges than upon institutionalised mechanisms. However, the jurisprudential regulation *stricto sensus* is to be found at quite a different level: it is due to the Court of Cassation which oversees the way in which lower court judges interpret the statutory rules and which thereby homogenises the terms of legal motives rather than the motives of the decision.

Consequently, because of the absence of a binding precedent mechanism, lower judges' decisions reveal a marked tendency toward dispersion particularly on the material level, beyond any legal solutions *stricto sensus*.[1]

DIFFERENT AVENUES IN THE APPROACHES TO THE ECONOMIC ANALYSIS OF JURISPRUDENCE

The economic analyses of common law have gone down several avenues which seem to us to be complementary: the function of the court, the choice of rules,

[1] E. Serverin (1997) in her study on road accident victims reveals significant differences in the amounts of compensation awarded by the courts in metropolitan France. The combined effects of a lack of any mandatory scale, of the freedom of the judges in appreciating the facts, in the name of the sovereign power of the lower court judge and the lack of any manner of regulation regarding the material aspects of the decisions all unite to explain this dispersion.

the production of precedents and legal decision making. The underlying motive is always that of seeking out regularities in legal regulations.

The question of jurisprudence indeed requires the regularity of decisions to be analysed. American economic analyses examine three levels at one and the same time:

(1) the regularities affecting the production of one particular judge or court over time thereby creating stability of legal and material decisions over time;
(2) the regularities observed at a global level in the judiciary and which provide a consistency in material and legal solutions;
(3) those emanating from the highest court when they monitor the way in which the lower court judges solve the cases before them.

It remains to be seen whether these three levels are simultaneously vital elements for the production of jurisprudence. It would appear to the case for the USA when we examine the effect of the mandatory precedent mechanisms upon the production of regularities at these three levels. It would also appear that the French system of private law prompts us to draw a distinction between two objects: *jurisprudence* stricto sensus and decision-making by the lower court judges. We now wish to reveal the light thrown onto this field by the economic analyses of case-law process.

Theorising on the Functions of the Common Law Courts in America

We would like to highlight two theories of common law: the first questions the functions of court activity whilst the second deals with the selection and evolution of legal rules.

The Settlement of Disputes and the Creation of Rules

Landes and Posner (1979) show that the common law courts have two roles: settling particular disputes *stricto sensus* and creating law in the form of legal precedents. The authors justify the existence of institutional justice via this double function. Indeed, even though a private and competitive market for legal services appears capable of providing the first of the two, as is the case with arbitration, its ability to carry out the second appears dubious as the creation of a precedent is a positive external effect, prompted by a judge and which will be of benefit to other judges and to those going before the courts in the future. The private production of legal precedents, short of ways to internalise the external effect, may well turn out to be socially under-optimal.

Landes and Poster conclude that the private justice market is limited to the responsibility for only one of the two functions – the settlement of disputes – which justifies the parties paying private judges and not the State. But is it economically rational and efficient to separate the two functions by making the legislative organs responsible for creating rules, for example, whilst private judges deal with the settlement of disputes? Such a separation is not desirable as long as there are economies of scope between the two functions: the creation of precedents is thus a by-product of the activity of dispute settlement. In the presence of economies of scope, legal services may be provided at a minimum cost by a multi-product "firm", that is to say by the Anglo-American model of justice.

When applied to French law which does not recognise the judge's legislative powers, nor does it possess mandatory precedents, the argument of Landes and Posner should lead us to believe that as French justice is exclusively devoted to the settlement of disputes *stricto-sensu,* it could be part of a private organisation rather than a public one. However, the French judiciary is part of the public justice service, paid for by the State budget which employs civil service magistrates. The decisions of the lower court judges are not supposed to create external effects beyond the interest of the parties concerned by the case.

Should there be externalities and aspects of public goods in the decisions, these phenomena are only to be found when dealing with supreme courts whose jurisprudence takes on the dimension of a producer of legal information which have the character of public goods.

Litigation as a Rule-Changing Mechanism

Rubin (1977) in his analysis of the efficiency of common law considers it necessary to link this question to the trial which is an exclusive moment in the evolution of rules. This proposition appears acceptable for the case of France *on condition that the trial is less directly a source of rule modification than the stakes of interpretations.* Rubin offers to link these two connected problems: (a) the efficiency of common law, and (b) the decision to settle or to litigate.

His demonstration is an attempt to show that efficiency is the result of an evolutionary mechanism driven by maximising decisions of those under the jurisdiction of the court and in no way by the "wisdom of the judges". Rubin believes that:

- resorting to a trial is even more likely when the rules in force are inefficient,
- a settlement is even more likely when the rules in force are efficient,

- the predominance of transactions lessens the incentive to future litigation and increases the probability that efficient rules will persist.

Three scenarios should be taken into account when analysing why parties resort to a trial:

(1) in the first, the two parties are equally interested by the precedent, be it in terms of confirming it or disagreeing with it depending on the position of each party;
(2) in the second, only one party is interested as in the case of disputes where one actor is repeatedly present in legal proceedings (e.g. an insurance company) along with one occasional actor (a private individual);
(3) in the third case, no party is interested in contesting the precedent.

In the first case and with the two parties being interested, Rubin's analysis postulates that if a rule in *t* is inefficient then legal activity will be activated and will last as long as is required – from *t+1* to *t+n* – so that the party having an interest in the inefficient rule being questioned will win their case. In the instance of only one party being interested, i.e. with one repeatedly present player and one occasional player, this virtuous mechanism fades out. The result is an evolution of the precedent in favour of the most persistent player and the emerging rule may be either efficient or inefficient. In the third case where neither party sees an interest in the rule evolving, no-one will activate the recourse to a trial and the prevailing rule, even if inefficient, will remain.

The analysis of Priest (1977) extends that of Rubin who shows that common law has a tendency toward efficiency by referring to a process of efficient rule selection. But whereas Rubin emphasises the interest that the parties may have in prompting the judiciary to produce a precedent that may be applied in similar cases in the future, Priest considers that the driving force behind litigation in court is more the cost of inefficient rules than the search for a precedent.

Indeed, Priest contends that disputes settled in a context of inefficient rules is more costly for the parties than if the rules were efficient. This implies that the stakes of the dispute will be even higher as a court ruling based upon an inefficient rule will be given for the case. For example, in a liability suit, if the marginal cost of reducing the likelihood of accident (through care and attention, maintenance of a vehicle) is higher for one party than for the other, placing liability on the party with the highest marginal cost is inefficient: the result will be an increase in accidents or accidents of a more serious nature because the higher the cost of avoiding them, the lower the will be the amount of investment made to avoid them. The motive behind prompting the legal system to get rid of these inefficient rules lies in cost.

The demonstration of Priest begins with the idea that the proportion of efficient rules in force at a given moment *t* is a function of:

- the stock of efficient rules in *t*–1,
- the relitigation rate of efficient and inefficient rules,
- the judicial bias towards efficiency (i.e. of the percentage of efficient rules produced by the judges).

The argument is that if the relitigation rate and the judicial bias are constant over time, then the percentage of efficient rules will attain equilibrium. At this level the proportion of efficient rules will be greater than that of the inefficient rules promulgated by the judges at any given period. Priest arrives at a double conclusion. First of all, the tendency for legal rules to be efficient over time is independent from both judicial bias and the methods for judicial decision making: it is a property of the jurisdictional process of common law: "Efficient rules "survive" in an evolutionary sense because they are less likely to be relitigated and thus less likely to be changed, regardless of the method of decision. Inefficient rules "perish" because they are more likely to be reviewed and review implies the chance of change whatever the method of judicial decision" (Priest, 1977: 72). Secondly, the tendency toward efficiency in the properties of the process of common law allows us to get around the delicate question of the psychological foundations of individual judges; it enables us to locate the origin of decisional regularities in the institutional characteristics of the jurisdictional system.

There is an interesting possible application for these models in French law, to the extent that *they emphasise the behaviour of those under the jurisdiction of the court and the way this is translated when it comes to challenging the rules.* Jurisdictional activity, appeal court and high court activity are in fact motivated by the interests at stake in the interpretation of the law and in the drawing up of legal solutions. Litigation is in fact powered by an economic engine: "the interest of the parties is at the heart of jurisprudence in two ways: in the selection of the questions of law which are the object of the means for an appeal; in the interpretation of the rulings given concerning this legal issue. The diffusion of the rulings thus plays a major role, not regarding the judge (who can make a ruling without referring to any precedent) but regarding the parties who will act in accordance with the interpretations already given by the Highest Court and also by trying to obtain their interpretation in their favour." (Serverin, 1999: 11). However, these analyses provide us more with a theory of the active behaviour of those concerned when faced with the rules than with a theory of the coordination of the production of court decisions.

The Production of Precedents and Stare Decisis

Important developments in economic analysis have been devoted to the production of legal precedents and to the existence of a principle of *stare decisis* in non-evolutionary frameworks. Following a general description, we aim to examine their relevance in French system of jurisprudential regulation.

Legal Precedents as a Legal Stock of Capital: Landes and Posner

Landes and Posner (1976) consider a precedent to be an accumulation of the judges' experience, a crystallisation of decisions which tend to produce one and the same rule and which is likely to be adhered to in the future. The authors believe the body of legal precedents created in the past to be a stock of capital generating a flow of information. This depreciates over time with the occurrence of new events which could not be foreseen by those having created the precedent. Landes and Posner define this stock of legal capital as "the set of precedents that have accumulated from judicial decisions in prior decisions ($t-1$, $t-2$, etc.)" (Landes & Posner, 1976: 262). This stock generates a flow of services that may be defined as information concerning the types of behaviour which may be subject to a penal or civil sentence and the importance of these sanctions. The stock of legal capital existing in t is a function of the investment and of the depreciation during all previous periods. The depreciation of the stock of precedents is directly linked to the loss of its informational content over time depending upon the changes in society. The monetary equivalent of informational services of the stock of precedents is an increasing function of two variables: firstly the stock of capital and secondly the number of users. Moreover, the production of new precedents by the legal profession is costly, the marginal cost increasing with the investment made.

The optimal production of precedents is that which maximises the current value of the difference between the value of the flow of services and the investment costs for each period. The conditions determining the stock of legal capital are defined taking account of the marginal product of the legal services given by the stock, the marginal costs of the capital investment and the depreciation of the stock. Landes and Posner conclude that "(. . .) the stock of legal capital will be greater, the greater the value of its marginal product and the lower its marginal user cost (. . .)" (Landes & Posner, 1976: 265). The notion that the stock of legal capital is all the greater when its product exceeds its cost is acceptable for the French system, on condition that we consider this stock as being provided by the rulings and the precedents of the Court of Cassation. As jurisdictional activity is not synonymous with regulation by *jurisprudence*, the hypothesis that the courts indiscriminately contribute to the size of the stock of capital is not plausible. In this sense, the Landes and Posner model arrives at the conclusion that legislative activity is the cause of the depreciation of legal capital and leads to the size of the optimal stock being reduced. In the case of France, however, the size of this stock is positively linked to legislative activity and only marginally to the production of jurisprudence by the Court of Cassation. The reason for this is that, contrary to the USA, there are no barriers between the fields of legislation and the judiciary nor is there competition between the two. On the contrary, they are complementary and based upon a division of labour: the legislature is responsible for issuing positive rules and the judiciary for putting them into practice and interpreting them under the watchful eye of the Court of Cassation. Seen in this light, "A precedent has not an unlimited lifetime; its influence decreases with time and this is the reason why there is from time to time a new decision, that shows that the rule is still in force" (Saluden, 1985: 197).

It can be understood that the life expectancy of court-made is limited and that they will depreciate under the influence of legislative innovation and changes in jurisprudence, but it remains very difficult to appreciate the relative weight of this.

Stare Decisis and the Preferences of the Judges

Kornhauser gives the following definition of *stare decisis*: "this principle 'requires' that a judge, having determined that a Present case should be governed by a Previous decision, adheres to this decision even if he considers it to be a bad one" (Kornhauser, 1989: 66). He then raises the question of how a judge is forced to adhere to a ruling he considers to be bad. He highlights four sources of discrepancy between the opinions of the Present and of the Prior judges:

(1) Changes in values: in this instance, the Present judge and the Prior judge settle similar cases. Kornhauser defines the similitude in liability law for example, by the fact that careful behaviour, the costs and profits of those in conflict (e.g. a pedestrian, the driver of a car) are identical for both parties and that the liability in force is strict or based upon negligence. With the similitude of cases, defined here in *material and not legal* terms, the Present judge considers that the Prior judge decided the case wrongly due to the values of the first being different from those of the second. The disagreement over values may indeed affect two dimensions: either "substantial" values, that is to say the objectives and aims of the judge and of the legal system; or "formal" values which determine when two cases are "equivalent" and may be the cause of a disagreement

over the similitude of cases. The techniques brought into play are those checking whether the precedents have been respected or conversely, those of *distinguishing*.

(2) Changes in the world: in this case Kornhauser retains the hypothesis of an agreement between the Present judge and the Prior judge about substantial and formal values. The agreement regarding the former leads them to accept that the correct legal rule should be one minimising the sum of accident costs and prevention costs, which is a principle of the maximisation of social welfare. The "right" rule can not thus be defined in absolute terms: it is contingent to the costs of being careful, to the technology appertaining to accident prevention and to the value of the profit linked to a particular behaviour (e.g. using a vehicle or walking). If these values alter over time, a rule initially deemed to be "good" may turn out to be "bad" in $t+1$. Here again, the reference to the cases is made from a material point of view.

(3) Improvements in information: even if the values of the world remain unchanged over time, differences in preference may arise between the Present and the Prior judge. They may be attributed, in the decision interval, to the existence of a learning process by which the Present judge improves his understanding of the world and his information in comparison with his predecessor.

(4) Imperfect decision making: if the three parameters above remain constant, a source of discrepancy between the judges lies in the fact that mistakes can be made by one or other judge and that this will lead to incorrect decisions.

The effects of *stare decisis* do indeed deserve discussion. The question which must be asked is that of knowing what part of a previous decision can attain the statute of precedent: either the result of the decision, the rule contained in this decision or, finally, the logic or reasoning leading to this decision becoming a precedent. But in absolute terms "the characteristics of the institutional structure of the legal decision influence the way in which judges deal with former cases" (Kornhauser, 1998: 509). Among these characteristics we find the problem of the unitary nature or collegiality of adjudication. Kornhauser here identifies four court models (Kornhauser, 1989):

(1) the court having only one, immortal judge who hear every case that arises in his jurisdiction (unitary model);

(2) the court with one, mortal judge who deals with the cases in his jurisdiction during his working life only, so that not every case will be decided by the same judge (sequential model);

(3) the court having several co-equal judges, each dealing with a specific case (panel model);
(4) the hierarchy of courts each having one infinite-lived judge (hierarchical model).

The principle of *stare decisis* can be explained with reference to the stability and predictability of the rules created and imposed by the judicial institutions. If we admit that the rules serving as a basis for the coordination of the agents and for the selection of an equilibrium are of legal origin, it then becomes possible to highlight the consequences of the four models described upon the quality of the coordination.

The quality of the coordination process suggests that jurisdictional activity chooses an equilibrium and that it then keeps to it. According to Kornhauser (1989), if an initial decision has selected an equilibrium, the judges may consider that coordination is preferable to an absence of coordination and thereby adhere to the precedent formed by the initial decision. This argument in favour of *stare decisis* is a particularly important element of the panel model as it reduces the uncertainty of the decision (and hence of the rules to be followed) inherent in the fact that the deciding judge is drawn toward the panel in quite an unpredictable manner. This argument loses its importance, going as far as becoming irrelevant in the unit and hierarchical models: in the first one, the need for a principle of *stare decisis* does not make itself felt as the judge applies his preferences, his values and his information to all the disputes on which he must give a ruling in a consistent manner over time. The judge restricts himself to his own methods and preferences which are stable over time. In the hierarchical case, the highest court oversees the stability of the rules of jurisprudence. Finally, in the sequential model, the stability of the rules depends above all upon the life span of the judges: "(. . .) if each judge presided for an extended period she might consider the abandonment of *stare decisis* desirable if her preference for one equilibrium over the other were sufficiently strong" (Kornhauser, 1989: 80).

Kornhauser's court models are heuristic and somewhat unrealistic. It is not easy to find applications for them in the French legal system which brings together various elements of these models at different levels of the judicial hierarchy. Certain jurisdictions have one sole judge (e.g. the judge for family affairs) but the vast majority have the principle of the collective decision. The absence of any *stare decisis* in the unit model does indicate *in fine* regularities of a judge making routine decisions. However, the stability of decisions in the sequential model can be explained more by the diffusion of the jurisprudential rules emanating from the Highest Court than by the life expectancy of the judges. It is difficult to apply Kornhauser's categories because he does not deal with the question of the stability of solutions on jurisdictions in their entirety i.e. the system taken as a whole. In fact, decision coordination in France is not the responsibility of the judges: three instances can be highlighted:

(1) the stability of routine decisions over time which, strictly speaking, do not come under *jurisprudence*;
(2) there is no homogenisation mechanism at the inter-tribunal level in France, which explains the wide dispersion of legal solutions or of the material results of the lower courts;
(3) the Highest Court plays the role of common reference for the coordination of decisions, taking account of the adaptation of lower court decisions to what the judges expect will be the attitude of the supreme court.

The Legal Decision in Imperfect Information

Heiner, in an original article ponders on the existence of a *stare decisis* in a context where the judges would benefit from imperfect information and possess an imperfect ability to deal with this information (Heiner, 1986). He applies a decisional model of incomplete information to the legal decision and to *stare decisis*, considering that the legal decision is not in line with the optimization. He creates a Bayesian decision model in which he distinguishes between the decisions based upon rules and those being "flexible optimization". The latter correspond to the decisions made by judges capable of gathering information and of acting accordingly. If we note *rd* as the conditional probability of making an optimal decision *d* in reply to optimal information and conversely *wd* as the conditional probability of a non-optimal decision being made in reply to non-optimal information, the ratio $\rho = r_d/w_d$ represents the reliability index of the decision. For an optimal decision-maker, $\rho = \infty$ because $r_d = 1$ and $w_d = 0$.

However, for those judges not belonging to this category and for whom $\rho < \infty$, behaviour can not be with a view to optimization: it is based upon rules, procedures and routines. Due to this "(. . .) we have a formal characterisation of a variety of well-known phrases such as "habits", "rules of thumb", "routines", "administrative procedures", "traditions", "norms", and so forth. Each one refers to some kind of limitation on agents' flexibility to make different decisions or to use information. (. . .). agents with bounded reliability ($\rho < \infty$) (. . .) will benefit from using rules and procedures that can be followed without necessarily being aware of the broader social objectives indirectly promoted or hindered by their decisions" (Heiner, 1986: 236).

Heiner shows that legal reasoning by analogy is a basis for stability providing that the judge's information is local or, in other words, that the information required for a case t is similar to that used in the past to settle a case $t-n$. Should the information not be local, the capacity of the judges to make consistent – and globally coherent in the jurisdictions overall – rulings is weakened. Consequently, "(. . .) just in the case in which judges cannot reliably use all information (thereby preventing long-term developments in the law from being the intended result of prior decisions), the legal systems will evolve procedures that tend to perpetuate the influence of past cases on future ones (thereby producing more stable and predictable changes in the law than would otherwise occur)" (Heiner, 1986: 246). Heiner's conclusion tallies with that of Macey who believes that "(. . .) judges generally employ precedent precisely because it enables them to avoid having to rethink the merits of particular legal doctrine" (Macey, 1998: 70).

Taken overall, these considerations encourage us to see the legal decision as a form of rationality located in a particular legal context which informs the decision via procedures and the organisation of legal activity. In other words, the face of the legal decision which, in the case of France may be that of decisions made within a given jurisdiction over time, is that of limited rationality based upon routines and procedures that have developed through the experience of judgement. The "intra-tribunal" decisional regularities which exist separately from a binding precedent may be considered as the expression of routines and procedures set in place by the judges and which, over time, ensure there is a stability of legal and material solutions in litigation. But here again we must distinguish between decisional routine and *jurisprudence* in the case of France.

CONCLUSION

Two conclusions can be drawn from this analysis:

(1) in the American system the precedent is decisional. It is the reason for the ruling (the *ratio decidendi*) which takes on the force of a precedent in a context noted for the absence of any hierarchical control over what the courts produce. Furthermore, the fact of whether a present decision adheres to a precedent is in itself the object of discussion by the judges. The American precedent is a decisional regularity which spreads from court to court, thereby consecrating the stability of a legal solution.

(2) there is no binding precedent in France. *Jurisprudence* expresses the stability of the interpretation of the law provided through the control of

the Court of Cassation. Regularity is not centred around legal solutions as much as around the interpretation of the positive rules by the lower courts.

The definition given by M. Saluden may help us arrive at a final conclusion: she states that "jurisprudence is a mechanism which, by reproducing the practices of judging and of selecting them via the hierarchy, ensures the creation of legal rules" (Saluden, 1985: 198). Hence, it is in the combination of "practices of judging" and of selection by the Court of Cassation that the regulating pattern of French *jurisprudence* is to be found, whereas the main feature of American case-law is that "the reproduction of the practices of judging" is almost entirely constitutional. It is thus understandable for the American economists of law to examine the preferences of the judges, the legal decision and the control of the Supreme Court whereas in the case of French private law these objects have been separated into two: on the one hand there is the legal decision and on the other, jurisprudence *stricto sensus*. Indeed, the important question of decisional regularities, the work of the lower courts, means that we may put forward the hypothesis stating that judges have routines and habits in thought and action. This appertains to the study of the legal decision, which is not the same as *jurisprudence* in the meaning that the French system gives to the word.

REFERENCES

Cooter, R., & Kornhauser, L. (1980). Can Litigation Improve the Law Without the Help of Judges? *Journal of Legal Studies*, *IX*(1), 139–163.

Goodhart, A. L. (1934). Precedent in English and Continental Law. *Law Quarterly Review*, *50*, 40–65.

Heiner, R. A. (1986). Imperfect Decision and the Law: On the Evolution of Legal Precedent and Rules. *Journal of Legal Studies*, *XV*, 227–261.

Kornhauser, L. A., & Sager, L. G. (1993). The One and the Many: Adjudication in Collegial Courts. *California Law Review*, *81*(1), 1–59.

Kornhauser, L. A. (1989). An Economic Perspective of Stare Decisis. *Chicago-Kent Law Review*, *65*(1), 63–92.

Kornhauser, L. A. (1992a). Modeling Collegial Courts. I: Path-Dependence. *International Review of Law and Economics*, *12*, 169–185.

Kornhauser, L. A. (1992b). Modeling Collegial Courts. II. Legal Doctrine. *Journal of Law, Economics and Organization*, *8*(3), 441–470.

Kornhauser, L. A. (1998). Stare decisis. In: P. Newman (Ed.), *The New Palgrave Dictionary of Economics and the Law*, Vol. 3 (pp. 509–513). Macmillan.

Lambert, E., Pic, P., & Garraud, P. (1926). The Sources and the Interpretation of Labour Law in France. *International Labour Review*, *XIV*(1), 1–36.

Lambert, E., & Wasserman, M. (1929). The Case-Method in Canada and the Possibilities of its Adaptation to the Civil Law. *Yale Law Journal*, *39*(1), 1–21.

Landes, W. M., & Posner., R. A. (1976). Legal Precedent: a Theoretical and Empirical Analysis. *Journal of Law and Economics*, *XIX*(2), 249–307.

Landes, W. M., & Posner, R. A. (1979). Adjudication as a Private Good. *Journal of Legal Studies*, *VIII*(2), 235–284.

Macey, J. R. (1998). Precedent. In: P. Newman (Ed.), *The New Palgrave Dictionary of Economics and the Law*, Vol. 3 (pp. 68–74). Macmillan.

MacCormick, D. N., & Summers, R. S. (Eds) (1997). *Interpreting Precedents. A Comparative Study*. Adelshot: Ashgate & Dartmouth.

Mattei, U. (1997). *Comparative Law and Economics*. Michigan University Press.

Priest, G. L. (1977). The Common Law Process and the Selection of Efficient Rules. *Journal of Legal Studies*, *VI*(1), 65–82.

Rubin, P. H. (1977). Why Is the Common Law Efficient? *Journal of Legal Studies*, *VI*(1), 51–63.

Saluden, M. (1985). La jurisprudence, phénomène sociologique. *Archives de philosophie du droit*. Paris, Sirey: 191–205.

Serverin, E. (1985). *De la jurisprudence en droit privé. Théorie d'une pratique*, Lyon: Presses Universitaires de Lyon, coll. "Critique du droit".

Serverin, E. (1993). Juridiction et jurisprudence: deux aspects des activités de justice. *Droit et Société*, *25*, 339–349.

Serverin, E. et al. (1997). *L'accident corporel de la circulation, entre transactionnel et juridictionnel*, CERCRID-University of Saint-Etienne, report to the Direction des affaires civiles, Ministry of Justice, Paris.

Serverin, E. (1999). Le phénomène jurisprudentiel comme un des aspects de la production du droit par les tribunaux. Paper presented at the TACIS worskhop, Moscow, 25th–26th November.

Troper, M., & Grzegorczyk, C. (1997). Precedent in France. In: D. N. MacCormick & R. S. Summers (Eds), *Interpreting Precedents. A Comparative Study* (pp. 103–140). Adelshot: Ashgate & Dartmouth.

Zander, M. (1999). *The Law-Making Process*. Coll. Law in context (5th ed.). Butterworths.

DID THE COMMON LAW BIASED THE ECONOMICS OF CONTRACT . . . AND MAY IT CHANGE?*

Eric Brousseau

INTRODUCTION: THE RISE OF THE ECONOMICS OF CONTRACT

Over the last 25 years, the notion of contracts has become essential in economics. Indeed, by focusing on contractual relationships researchers have become able to analyze more effectively the features of decentralized economies. Previously the sole available concept was the walrasian market that is quite irrelevant in many situations, despite its strength. As is now well known, the notion of centralized markets without transaction costs is inappropriate for the analysis of many bilateral situations (such as R&D alliances, sub-contracting or distribution channels, etc.) and even market equilibria. (Markets are out of equilibrium, or reach only second best equilibria when information asymmetries and transaction costs are taken into account: see, for example, the developments of New-Keynesian economics reported by Mankiv, 1990; Romer, 1991). This new concept has led to the development of several theoretical frameworks – particularly the Incentives Theory (IT), the Incomplete Contract Theory (ICT) and Transaction Cost Economics (TCE) – that are essential today in the updating of many theoretical and applied analyses (see Brousseau & Glachant, 2000).

Law and Economics in Civil Law Countries, Volume 6, pages 79–105.

ISBN: 0-7623-0712-9

These developments in the economics of contracts have had a marked influence in Law and Economics thinking, especially in the U.S. Regulatory and antitrust legislation had been primarily concerned with the earlier development of the economics of contracts: as to whether franchising public utilities or specific vertical contractual arrangements could be considered efficient, or second-best solutions to coordination problems (see Williamson, 1985; OCDE, 1994; Joskow, 2000). But as shown in the New Palgrave of Economics and the Law (Newman, 1998) or in the Encyclopaedia of Law and Economics (Bouckaert & De Geest, 1999), economic thinking has latterly also strongly influenced the more detailed regulation of contract: default rules, contract breach and remedies, contract interpretation, etc. More precisely, economic analysis has enabled researchers to systematically analyze the consequences (especially in terms of incentives) of alternative contractual practices and regulations, and to evaluate the conditions in which some rules are more efficient than others. As is usual in Law and Economics, economic reasoning can be contradicted because it often relies on very restrictive assumptions, and because it does not take into account all issues of a social nature. (Clearly efficiency should not be the sole criteria of Law design!). Nevertheless, it is undeniable that economic reasoning has enabled a more systematic analysis of the consequences of alternative contractual regulations.

Conversely, legal thought has substantially influenced economic analysis of contracts. Researchers such as Schwartz, Goldberg and Macneil are often quoted in economic papers either in support of certain assumptions or to establish a parallel between results drawn from economics and those resulting from legal reasoning. In some instances, legal thinking has strongly influenced economic concepts.

By contrast, in Civil Law Countries, and especially France, the economics of contracts can be considered as totally separate from the legal doctrine of contracts. French researchers specializing in the economics of contracts seem to be influenced primarily by theories that have been developed in the U.S. Evidently, economic theory is not restricted either historically or nationally: economists develop theories aimed at describing universal phenomena. However, when it comes to notions deeply grounded in an institutional framework together with its legal system, historical and national aspects have a marked effect. For instance the concepts relevant for a U.S. lawyer – bilateral contract vs. unilateral contract, express contract, implied contract – are quite different from these prevalent in Roman-Germanic law – commutative contracts, contracts with or without payment, etc. More generally, the structure of legal thought is quite different on both sides of the Atlantic Ocean (and even of the Channel). European economists working on contracts most usually invoke

U.S. legal concepts when they refer to actual contracts or legal notions. This explains why legal researchers in Civil Law do not incorporate economic reasoning when they are working on contracts, and why the large body of legal doctrines relating to contracts in Civil Law countries do not make reference to economics. This arises partly because most of these legal doctrines are much older than contract theories and even economics, and also because many European Law researchers do not understand how contractual issues are addressed by economic thought. The concepts and issues on which they focus are quite different from those of economists. It may also be added that in the French institutional framework, historical and organizational features make for a clear separation between legal and economic researchers. This organization obviously favors mutual misunderstanding.

Whatever the causes, it is evident that in Civil Law countries, and especially in France, cross-fertilization of legal and economic thought does not really exist in respect of contracts. The aim of this paper is to query this situation. More precisely, I would like to address the relevance and the utility of dialogue between the two disciplines. Are the economics of contracts compatible with the development of Civil Law doctrine? Can the Civil Law doctrine enrich the economics of contracts?

To answer these questions, I will first consider how the U.S. legal framework influences the economic reasoning on contracts. This will enable me to demonstrate how the economics of contracts could assist in the development of legal doctrines. I will then suggest how Civil Law doctrine could enrich the economics of contracts.

Two basic arguments will therefore be developed through this paper. First, in a quasi-Veblenian spirit, I will argue that economic thinking relating to contracts and to institutions depend inherently on the legal systems theoreticians have in mind. Indeed legal doctrine and the features of the institutional environment deeply impact on contracting practices, and even on the "spirit" of contractual commitments, because to be valid and enforceable, contracts must necessarily correspond to the institutional environment to which they refer. For various reasons, the present economics of contracts is deeply rooted in the U.S. legal framework. Second, I will argue that despite this situation, cross-fertilization is possible between U.S.-centric economics of contracts and Civil Law doctrine. Indeed, the two systems generate general analytical categories and normative criteria (efficiency, equity, etc.) that are relevant for analysis and comparison of the two legal structures. Moreover, due to globalization, there is increasing hybridization and competition between legal systems, raising questions of compatibilities and cross-fertilization among the various legal systems and their practice.

HOW ACTUAL INSTITUTIONS INFLUENCE ECONOMICS

To better understand how economic reasoning on contracts could enrich legal doctrines in Civil Law countries, and vice-versa, it is essential to recognize the strong influence of the U.S. legal framework on the economics of contracts. Three examples will enable a better understanding of how researchers are influenced by the their individual legal institutions. This is not surprising, but there are consequences even on the very abstract concepts economics is dealing with. Economic reasoning has been strongly influenced in the U.S. context by problems relating to contract design and enforcement. We will thus indicate that the questions raised by Civil Law doctrine are slightly different from the major issues addressed by the economics of contracts. This will lead us to show that contracts under U.S. legislation have a quite different status from those under Continental legal doctrines.

Three Examples of the Influence of Common Law on the Economics of Contracts

The first example shows how economics in general, and the incentive theory in particular, consider contracts. In the language of the economist, a contract is a bilateral agreement aimed at organizing a transaction by designating mutual obligations for both parties without pre-existing constraints. A "standard" contract for the economist is a complete contract concluded between two parties, which enforceability is guaranteed by a third party, acting in the capacity of a benevolent and neutral arbitrator. The role of the third party is neither to determine that the contract is in conformity with the legal framework, nor to interpret the ambiguities in the contract, but to oblige the parties to behave according to their commitments. Clearly this simplified description of a contract can be refined: the third party can be considered as non-benevolent; his ability to supervise (verify) can be considered limited; etc. Nevertheless, the contract of reference in economics is a complete contract concluded without any constraint by two parties and guaranteed by a third party. The contract is so perfect and so neutral that the two parties never need recourse to the third party. Since the contract is complete and since the third party guarantees that its wording will be scrupulously applied, both parties are incited to perform it. In that sense, the contract is both the unique means of co-ordination and the means to completely solve co-ordination problems.

Obviously, this modelization of a contract is far removed from actual contractual practice under U.S. or British law. It is for instance obvious that judges have to interpret contracts in Common Law countries. Most of the Law and Economics debates related to contracts consider the approach of judges to the interpretation of the real intent of the contracting parties. However, our argument is that this simplified description of contract is closer to the concept of contract under Common Law, especially U.S. Law, than the Roman-Germanic view of contracts. In Civil Law countries, contracting is performed under the Law. The Law is considered as the principal means of inter-individual co-ordination: contracts are tools enabling parties to complete the general rules in order to customize co-ordination rules to their specific situations. In Common Law countries, co-ordination is based on bilateral agreement with the Law acting simply as a means to facilitate contract settlement or to set aside excess negative externalities of private practice. In a sense the stock phrase: "In U.S. Law whatever is not forbidden is authorized, while in French Law whatever is not explicitly authorized must be considered forbidden" reflects appositely the present state of contractual practices within the two legal frameworks. Freedom of contracting is recognized on the two shores of the Atlantic, but in continental Europe there are significant constraints under codified law in comparison with the U.S.

In the same vein, it is to be noted that a contract is by definition bilateral and reciprocal in economics (in the sense that it states bilateral obligations). This is true under U.S. Law, but it is quite different in French Law. In the French system, a contract can be unilateral. In the U.S., contracts refer to a specific type of Civil Code contracts: synallagmatic contracts (*contrats synallagmatiques*). Additionally, in the U.S. contracts also refer to a specific category of French contract: the "*contrat d'adhésion*". Under U.S. legislation a contract results from a proposition made by one party that is accepted or rejected by the other. In the French system this "take-it-or-leave-it" method of concluding a contract is a specific type and refers to the notion of "joining" contract. Under French Law there is no distinction between the offeror and the offeree, whereas in economics as in U.S. Law there is a party – the "principal" – who proposes various contractual schemes to the other – the "agent". The focus of economics on a specific type of contract is not surprising since commercial transactions are generally the center of interest, and also the essential aim of economists was not (initially) to study in depth the economics of contractual practices, but the features of a decentralized market economy. This bias needs to be borne in mind.

The second example of the institutional influence on the economics of contracts can be found in Incomplete Contract literature. This literature is organized around confrontations and recombination between two basic models developed by Hart and Moore (1988) and Aghion, Dewatripont and Rey (1994) (quoted as H&M and ADR). The central issue addressed by the theory is the design of an optimal contract when it is impossible to make enforceable ex-post a commitment in respect of a variable that is essential for successful completion of the transaction, because that variable, for instance a specific investment, is not verifiable by a third party (see further in the next section). Such a contract should implement a *default option* and a *renegotiation mechanism.* The default option states the minimum conditions of exchange aimed at inciting one of the parties to behave (invest) optimally, because the option guarantees a desirable return on the investment. The renegotiation provision enables the second party – who is not protected by the default option – to adapt the conditions of exchange to the ex-post situation. There is necessarily a period between the date of commitment and the date of exchange. During this period, the circumstances of the parties may change, with the evolution of the situation. Ex-post, with a review of the situation and the investments of the parties, the optimal conditions of exchange – i.e. the price and the quantity that generate the largest collective surplus – may be different from those stated in the default option. By allocating the right to decide what should be the ex-post conditions of exchange to the second party, an incomplete contract implements incentives inducing this party to behave (invest) optimally, since he will be able to receive a surplus generated ex-post and therefore make a return on initial investment.

The main difference between H&M and ADR is in the enforceable default option. For us, it is strongly linked to the assumptions of the authors as to the behavior of judges and courts. Hart and Moore have in mind the American legal system in which extended renegotiations of contract provisions is considered a factor of efficiency. In U.S. law, the present will of contractors is preferable to the past, because if the parties reach a new agreement it takes into account the evolution of the mutual situation, and therefore guarantees an outcome superior to any previous mutual commitment. On the other hand, it seems that ADR have in mind the French legal system. While this is a simplification (since there are many exceptions), French courts are more reluctant than U.S. ones to authorize contracting parties to renegotiate their commitments. They more systematically apply specific performance principles (*exécution en nature*), that oblige the parties to observe their initial contractual commitments (even if both parties were to agree to renegotiate). Under Civil Law doctrine, such a principle is a good guarantor of the fairness of the agreement. It is implicitly recognized that a contract creates some irreversibilities that one of the parties could try to exploit ex post, to gain an unfair advantage in renegotiating the contract. Whatever the reasons, by forbidding ex-post renegotiations and by obliging observation of the initial contract, French courts substantially increase the credibility of contractual commitments. Parties can safely consider ex-ante commitments as secure, therefore the agreement provides them with the incentive to optimally invest ex-ante, even though the ex-post lack of flexibility can generate sub-optimal ex post level of exchange in a changed situation. The U.S. flexibility is an effective method of optimally adapting agreements to ex-post conditions. However, since any component of the agreement can be ex-post renegotiated, the parties will not take the initial commitments for granted, and they will ex-ante limit their implication in the cooperative process. To sum up, the H&M vs. ADR types of contract seem to reflect the differences between the U.S. and the French legal systems. Obviously, neither of the two models is aimed at describing a specific legal framework, but even unintentionally they do so.[1]

The third example of the influence of the U.S. legal framework on the economics of contract can be provided by the Transaction Costs Theory (TCT). In his analysis of incomplete contracts, Williamson (1991, 1996), is very much influenced by Macneil's analysis of relational (or neoclassical) contracting that draws directly from an analysis of U.S. legal practices (Macneil, 1974). Macneil's main conclusion is that incomplete contracts are less costly and more robust than complete contracts (in certain circumstances). Incompleteness enables contractors to economize on ex-ante negotiation and contract design costs. It also reinforces the credibility of commitments since commitments can be adapted to many contingencies arising ex-post but unforeseen ex-ante. This flexibility of commitments prevents the parties to breach them, because they know that they will be able to find compromises that will take into account both parties' interest. While it has to be taken into account that the analyses of Macneil and Williamson are not recognized by all American Law researchers and practitioners, it is clear that U.S. case-law recognizes the efficiency and at least the legality of incomplete contracting. This is quite different from French doctrine. Until the mid 1980s, incomplete contracts were considered as legally void.[2] This was for instance the case for a long term distribution contract in which prices were not fixed and for which one of the parties (the supplier) had a unilateral right of decision over the mutually agreed price. Even today, contracts in which unilateral rights of decision are implemented are considered with suspicion by the doctrine and by practitioners.

While these three examples clearly point out that the U.S. legal practices have a marked influence on economic thinking as concerns contracts, they do not prove at all that economic concepts are irremediably biased, nor can it be reasoned from these examples that economics has no application in the analysis of French law. What does emerge is that the issues and their causes addressed by economic thinking on contractual practice are principally based on U.S. legal practice.

Equity and Contract Formation at the Heart of Civil Law Reasoning

To go further, it is interesting to note that the questions raised by French legal thought on contracts are quite different from those that are crucial in the Common Law framework. Textbook and doctrinal debates are concentrated in Civil Law countries, and at least in France, on two central issues: *Contract formation* and *Equity* (see, for instance, Malinvaud, 1992). Both relate obviously to building guidelines for the judiciary system for contract interpretation and translation into judgements where conflicts occur. In fact, the main point is not to interpret the contract because contracts are supposed to be quite complete (see above and note 2) in the sense that they must set down detailed obligations when general default rules do not apply. The essential question addressed by the doctrine is the validity of the contract – the unavoidability of the contract – *because the main objective of a contract is to generate legally binding commitments*; i.e. to implement obligations that can be made enforceable by the judicial and administrative bodies of the State.

Pursuing this theme, the question of contract formation is essential to determine if the parties had the ability to commit themselves in an arrangement, to assess if the contract really reflects the free will of the parties, and if mutual commitments are in accordance with the legal framework. In the Civil-Law framework, laws are supposed to primarily organize relationship among people in order to avoid negative externalities and to ensure public order. Therefore, contractual arrangements can be made only where law does not specifically apply. To guarantee that within these limited conditions, contracts really reflect the free will of the parties, civil legal doctrine is much concerned with the process through which mutual consents are expressed. The formality of the procedure is supposed to guarantee that neither of the parties accepts commitments against his free will. Lastly, the capability of the parties to commit themselves is carefully examined. Since contracts will be ex-post enforced as they are written (by limiting the capacity of the judge to interpret them), the capability of the parties to actually enforce their commitments has to be checked ex-ante. Indeed, the contracting capabilities of certain individuals is restricted either because of their situation (mental disorder, youth, or even indebtedness) on the grounds of protection against themselves, or because they are not allowed to commit third parties (their family, their company, etc.).

Equity makes reference to the Christian notion of commutative justice. To be valid, any type of exchange has to be "fair" in the sense that it shall not generate illegitimate enrichment. Contracts are not supposed to modify the distribution of wealth that existed ex-ante between the parties (see Ghestin, 2000). This holds closely to the moral philosophy of both Aristotle and Thomas of

Aquina according to which the sole legitimate source of welfare is labor. Market exchange is considered as a practical way of reallocating the fruits of labor among members of society, and exchanges that result in the obtainment of rents by one member of the society is considered as immoral (and implicitly inefficient). Consequently, judges assess the fairness of the terms of the exchange. In case of conflict, they analyze the contract conditions: does the agreement result from a process in which one of the parties was able to obtain conditions (especially price) far superior to those obtainable from any other fair third party? The judge has therefore to intervene if errors, cheating or even violence has occurred during the negotiation and acceptance of the arrangement. While control of the conditions of contract formation also exist in an Anglo-Saxon legal framework, the requirement for conformity of contracts to the principles of social justice is a particular specificity of Roman-Germanic legal systems. In addition to the analysis of the conditions of contract formation, French judges also assess if there is equivalence between the inputs from each of the parties.[3]

- First, it is essential to note that this notion applies only to disequilibra existing at the beginning of the contract (*lésion*), but not to disequilibria that arising ex-post because unpredicted events have occurred (*imprévision*). Put another way, if an ex-ante disequilibrium exists because one of the parties was able to exercise an influence on the other or because one of the parties benefited from private information, the contract can be considered as void (or alternately as opening a right to compensation in favor of the disadvantaged party). However, if a contract that was signed in certain market conditions results in unfair conditions of exchanges following a significant modification of the environment that was unforeseeable ex-ante for both parties, then it still remains valid.
- Second, the notion of equivalence is obviously very difficult to assess for a judge because in practice he is required to determine what is a "fair" price. There are obvious difficulties when goods or services are scarce and specific: "market prices" cannot be applied since there are no markets for such goods. In practice, the judge tries to assess what is the actual meaning of "fair" price or "fair" conditions of exchanges in the whole set of a specific situation. There is therefore a complex set of laws describing the minimal contractual conditions in case of ship rescue (L. 29/04/1906), provision of seeds or fertilizers (L. 8/07/1907 and L. 10/03/1937), financial loans (L 18/12/1966), etc. There is also a wide set of laws describing "exorbitant provisions" (*clauses abusives;* especially L 10/01/1978). The principal aim of these laws are to protect the weaker party in all "non-negotiated" contracts, typically for contracts an individual customer (implicitly) signs when he buys

goods or a service. These contracts are qualified as "joining contracts" (*contrats d'adhésion*) and focus especially on the rules applying to liability, guarantee of ex-post quality, etc. Generally, they are codified in a document called "general sales conditions" that is supposed to be available to every customer, and that is usually non-negotiable. The "general sales conditions" are precisely the quasi-contract that is heavily regulated to guarantee fair exchange conditions to consumers.

- The third category of cases in which equity matters in contract governance refers to the "advantages that are unjustly derived from a situation". These cases have to be contrasted with situations in which advantages are deliberately and unfairly accrued arising from opportunistic behavior. In this instance, there is an unjustified transfer of wealth between the two parties. For example, those members of a family employed in a commercial activity without remuneration, or if an agent in a company enables the owner to considerably increase the value of its stocks. In both cases, a French judge will consider that the effort made by one of the parties opens rights to compensation because what was actually done by one of the party for the benefit of the other exceeded the obligations initially existing between the parties.

Efficiency at the Heart of the U.S. Legal Reasoning . . . and of Economics

By contrast, it is clear that the legal perception concerning contracts is quite different in Common Law tradition. It would obviously be erroneous to argue that moral considerations do not matter in this legal system. . . . just as it would be wrong to consider that efficiency is not taken into account in Civil Law doctrine.[4] However, it is evident that Common Law practices, especially as regards the U.S., focus on quite different questions when it comes to the matter of contract. Contract is considered as a basis of social relationship in Common Law doctrine and legislative and judicial powers are not "naturally" allowed to interfere in contractual relationships. Such powers are considered as support in facilitating contracting, not as a superior social overriding structure that would be entitled to determine what would be preferable for both parties, with a restrictive contractual practice. Consequently, legal thought focuses on the expression of the free will of the agents (to ensure that they agree on mutual commitments), on the impact of these commitments on their individual wealth (while negative externalities can obviously matter), on the current state of their mutual interest (rather than on their past agreements). *In fine*, what really matters in Common Law tradition is the current mutual interest of contractors. If they agree on any kind of re-interpretation or re-negotiation of contractual arrangements, judges should ratify these agreements, because they must favor the implementation of the most efficient solution. This is obviously in line with the philosophy of enlightenment, which considers society as the convergence of free individuals endowed with irremovable fundamental rights. Each citizen is the most able to know how to use (and even to void) these rights. Consequently, neither the State, nor any third party is entitled to assess in the place of free contractors whether they are right or wrong to contract or to transact as they do. Contractors are supposed to be rational. That apparently unfavorable contracts are concluded may be ascribed to some aspect which is not visible to an observing third party. Even if it is considered that not all contractors are efficient decision makers, it can be argued that the re-allocation of economic resources resulting from an unequal contract leads to a more efficient distribution, because valuable resources go to the brightest decision maker, resulting in better uses. The combination of competition and responsibility is consistent with the fact that human beings benefit from fundamental non-voidable rights, and guarantee the most efficient use of resources.

The efficiency perspective is essential in North American legal theory, both because it fits in with the philosophy of liberalism forming the base of the social contract on this continent, and because it is a pragmatic way to solve theoretical debates. This perspective is obviously one of the causes of the strong cross-fertilization between the economics of contracts and legal thought and is an explanation for the heavily influence of economics on U.S. legal practice and legal categories. (In addition to the fact that, since World War II, the greatest number of economists, and probably the most active in terms of scientific publication, has been that of the researchers that have been trained or work in the U.S.)

However, the American influence on economic thought relating to legal categories (whether of contract, liability rules or legal procedures) is also due to the particular role of theory in the Common Law system. As pointed out by Hatzis (2000), because the Common Law leaves many questions open and does not state ex-ante what is legal or not, because the law in action results from the decentralized interpretation of basic principles by judges, legal uncertainty is potentially wide. Common Law therefore requires theoretical debates to enlighten and uniformize judges' decisions. In addition to the focus of Common Law and economic thought respectively on the question of efficiency, this is probably one of the major reasons for both disciplines mutually influencing each other. Economics also provides legal thinking with a consistent method to analyze the consequences of legal practice. Theoreticians can predict the reaction of a population of rational agents to a legal rule, and assess the attainment of an equilibrium that is efficient. The contributions by Coase (1960)

Becker and Stigler (1974), or Posner (1986) typically illustrate this. Obviously economics can be (and is) contested as being an element for judges' decisions (Barnett, 1999), but beyond doubt economic categories have had an influence over the last forty years. Conversely, legal cases and practice provide economics with categories that impact upon the way problems are analyzed. Since economists have been mainly mobilized to interpret cases and categories raised by U.S. legal practice, these categories have become common ground for economists. Damages or liability rules are good examples.

It could well be asked why the relationship between economics and Civil Law categories and problems is not stronger. This is largely because in the Civil Law framework, the uniformization of practice and applied legal thinking has traditionally occurred through doctrinal debates. Indeed many of the debates that occurred in the U.S. over the last forty years have already existed for decades in Civil Law countries. Civil codes evolved under the influence of legal practice and practical problems raised by the evolution of the social order. For instance, liability rules evolved rapidly after the industrial revolution, with the introduction of the liability without fault category (*responsabilité sans faute*) aimed at ensuring financial compensation in favor of the victim of an accident due to the use of equipment made mandatory by a contract; typically the use of a machine-tool linked to an employment contract (see Jamin, 2000).

This said, it must be remembered that many doctrinal debates in Civil Law countries do not escape the logic of economics. For instance, Ghestin in France had a strong influence over doctrinal evolutions in favor of incomplete contracting, as in long term distribution contracts between oil companies and retailers in which the providers fixed prices unilaterally. Ghestin demonstrated that a unilateral mechanism of price determination could be upheld because of the advantages in terms of ability to adapt to changing market prices, while avoiding costly renegotiations, as long as market power was not exercised by petroleum products providers (either because of competition from alternative providers or because of control by the antitrust authorities). While law researchers such as Ghestin do not often refer to economic thinking, their reasoning parallels that of economics. Mackay is a good example of a legal scholar who explicitly links economic reasoning to Civil Code doctrinal debates.

Thus, in that codified law does not escape from economics reasoning, it is wholly relevant to perform an economic analysis of Civil Law doctrines. First, this is a good approach to a critical assessment of prevalent Civil Law doctrine with a view to suggesting potential improvement of codes and practice. Second, it constitutes an appropriate method for advancing the evolution of economic analysis of contracts. Indeed, Civil Codes and associated practice can reveal problems and solutions that are relevant for the economic analysis of co-ordination in general.

Put another way, while the economic analysis of contract is much influenced by Anglo-Saxon categories and practices, the use of economic reasoning to analyze contractual problems is a potentially promising method to enrich doctrinal debates concerned with the evolution of Civil Codes.

WHAT CAN BE LEARNT FROM THE ECONOMICS OF CONTRACT

At the outset, it is essential to remark that despite the strong influence of the legal framework on the theories of contracts, these theories were neither developed primarily to deal with legal problems nor to contribute to legal thought. Economists develop contractual theories to get a better understanding either of market co-ordination (Incentive Theory) or of organizational co-ordination (Transaction Costs Theory and Incomplete Contract Theory). Indeed, economists are essentially interested in developing theoretical tools to analyze the functioning of economic systems composed of markets and organizations. Actual markets are very different from the walrasian markets – i.e. systems able to display prices and to centralize all the resulting bids from the supply and the demand in order to fix price of equilibrium; see Walras (1874) – because they are decentralized and rely on bilateral contracts. Organizations result from the establishment of specific incomplete contracts which implement a hierarchical link between two parties (Coase, 1937; Williamson, 1975). Studying contractual relationships – the causes and effects of alternative contracting practices – was an effective method for economists to achieve a better understanding of the real functioning of our economies. However, by deepening the analysis of contractual practices, economists have been able to demonstrate the usefulness of economics in the analysis of contractual relationships and their legal implications. Many types of contractual relationship – e.g.: labor contract, vertical restrictions, sub-contracting, long term contracting, etc. – have been submitted to contract theory analysis both to renew insights into the manifold problems of industrial organizations (labor economics, organizational economics, etc.), and also to explore further the economic analysis of contracts.

We will try to establish here that some results drawn from the economic analysis of contracts could be useful in enlightening some doctrinal problems in Civil Law. In addition to the fact that economic reasoning can demonstrate in certain circumstances the efficiency of alternative legal doctrines, it is important to note that we are today in a context in which the combination of globalization of the economy, of acceleration in technical change, of the increasing intangibility in production call for an evolution in Civil Law. In certain circumstances, this law is neither well adapted to current conditions, nor able to sustain competition by alternative legal frameworks. It seems important therefore there be an acceptance of the economic aspect, in that it also influences the evolution of these alternative frameworks.

On the lines of the preceding section, my demonstration will focus on three examples which do not attempt to be exhaustive. My main objective is to indicate the usefulness and the richness of economic reasoning through the presentation of three topics which seem relevant for the legal analysis of contract in the context of Civil Law. First, in the economic analysis of contract, contracts are above all commitments that enable parties to limit future risks and therefore incite them to "invest" into a relationship that would not otherwise occur. The central question is therefore to make those commitments credible. Second, economic thought insists on the idea that it is quite difficult, and sometime impossible, to formulate complete contracts. Moreover, complete contracts can cause a result exactly opposite to that anticipated. Flexible contracts may therefore be considered as favoring more robust commitments than those in a complete contract. Third, contractual standards prescribed by the law can be considered both from the perspective of reducing transactions costs – since they limit the scope of negotiation of the contracting parties (and additionally their chances of making mistakes) – and from the perspective of increasing those costs – since the general solutions implemented are poorly adapted to the specific co-ordination requirements of the contracting parties. This in turn leads to consideration of the complementarities existing between the private, specific and informal institutions, and the public, general and formal legal framework.

Contracts as Commitments

In the absence of uncertainty, contracts would serve no purpose. Economics of contracts as a whole is based on the fact that contracts are commitments aimed at solving problems generated by uncertainty. There are two types of uncertainties in an economic exchange. First, the precise features of the goods or services exchanged are unknown by (at least one of) the parties. In the absence of a mechanism providing the economic agents with complete and free information on the features of the goods or services transacted there will be risks of error or fraud. Second, since most exchanges do not occur instantaneously, the incentives for both parties evolve between the time they reach agreement and the time the transaction is completed.

Since agents are self interested and rational – even if it might occur that their rationality has limits, and that they sometimes behave in an altruistic manner – uncertainty generates potential mistrust between the contracting partners. Each economic agent may fear to be a victim of the opportunistic behavior of the other not delivering ex-post what was specified ex-ante. And this can result in unequal incentives. Two parties who attempt to maximise their own advantage at the expense of the other in completing an exchange will either not enter into the exchange, or will fail to "invest" at the optimal level. Thus, economic agents who doubt the other will therefore decide to limit their risks by reducing their investment and efforts. This is a rational response to uncertainty: agents diversify their portfolio of risks and consequently limit their "investment" in each transaction.

Two types of remedies to this problem of incentives raised by uncertainty can be imagined: institutional and contractual. Economists point out that the institutional solution cannot be complete and unique, since that would entail the existence of perfect institutions. Such theoretical institutions would enable perfect transparent information between the parties and also systematically suppress opportunistic behavior. In short, this would suppose an ability to measure everything, a capacity to observe any transaction and the means to penalize each instance of untoward behavior. This presupposes two important assumptions. Firstly, the formulation of a perfect institutional framework, either by totally rational and benevolent designer, or by a selection process systematically eliminating inefficient institutional elements. Secondly, the supposition that such an institutional framework would have no cost. Where institution intervention is costly, the social cost of any marginal deviation should be less than the expenses involved to prevent it. Clearly, it is economically inefficient to forbid all deviant practices, and there will be many situations in which institutions cannot solve co-ordination problems. It therefore follows that the only definite solution for co-ordination problems arising from uncertainty is a contractual one. In that context, contracts are commitments aimed at guaranteeing the reciprocal input of each party within the transaction. By credibly assuring the other party of the nature and the value of the input into the transactional process, each of the parties incites the other to efficiently "invest" into the transaction, making for a positive return on the "investment".

On this aspect, economics highlights the "verification" constraint. The credibility of a contract is heavily dependent upon the means of enforcement by the third party. Whereas a contract is usually a bilateral commitment, the guarantee of its enforcement in the last resort is almost always ensured by the intervention of a third party. Without this third party – that can be a judge, a private arbitrator, or the institutional framework – contracts would need to be completely self-enforceable, ensuring both parties of the possibility to invoke a guarantee which makes preferable continuation of performance as opposed to breach. Such a guarantee is logically inconsistent in situations in which non-performance is more profitable as, for example, when the contracting parties are in a zero-sum or "winner-takes-all" game. A third party is therefore essential to ensure that the parties observe their commitments, even when enforcement of an initial commitment is against the interest of at least one of the contracting parties. If it is assumed that a third party is essential for the enforcement of contractual commitments, it must also be assumed that this third party has limitations in his capability. This is the consequence of the imperfection of the institutional environment (see above). The third party ("judge") who is responsible for guaranteeing contract enforcement in the last resort is the symbolic representation of the institutional framework. It may be supposed that he may be constrained by a limited capability to verify (or observe, or measure) certain variables which are relevant for the transacting parties. These variables therefore cannot reasonably form part of the contract. It would be meaningless to evoke such variables because the judge would be unable to verify ex-post if the parties had actually observed their performance. Through the concept of verification the economics of contracts indicate the impact of the institutional environment – more precisely, the enforcement mechanisms – on contract formation. This concept leads to two general conclusions.

First, it can be stated that contract formation depends upon the institutional framework in force. More precisely, implementable and efficient contracts depend upon the supervision ability of the third party responsible for their enforcement. As reported by Brousseau and Fares (2000) and by Fares (2000), the Incomplete Contract Theory can largely be interpreted in this perspective. In order to guarantee that the contracting parties will efficiently "invest" in a transaction where significant variables cannot be predefined, the optimal contract will incorporate renegotiation terms that will incite at least one of the parties to optimally invest because he will be able ex-post to adjust the "level" of exchange (i.e. the effective terms of the exchange) in the light of the current situation taking into account the investments of the two parties. The other party could however be the victim of this ability to adjust the level of exchange. As a protection, a default option guaranteeing a minimum level of exchange needs to be implemented. If well designed, this default option should incite optimal investment by this second party. Default options are, however, dependent on the capability of the applicable institutional framework to enforce them. Indeed, where judges are unable to prevent renegotiation – open or concealed – of the default option the contracting parties will not invest optimally. Renegotiation of the default option ruins the credibility of the contract. A party will not optimally invest ex-ante if it is recognized that the default option may be renegotiated ex-post. Preventing renegotiation of the default option is crucial, whilst very difficult to attain. And to do so the enforcing authority must have access to the details of the transaction. This is indeed the only way to ensure that the default option can be enforced. It is therefore clear that where the judge is prevented from observing (verifying) what is really happening, the ability of the potentially injured party to implement the optimal default option will be bounded; i.e. the option that should incite the parties to "optimally" invest on the non-contracted aspects of the transaction would be un-implementable.

Second, leading on from the above, is the question of the institutional framework. In other terms, the ability of the parties to implement an efficient default option is dependent on two criteria of the judge responsible for contract enforcement in last resort: his attitude towards renegotiation and his supervision capability.

- A judge who authorizes renegotiation of the default option – on the grounds that the parties have agreed to renegotiate and should therefore be allowed to renegotiate fully including the default option[5] – destroys the credibility of such an option. It is therefore important that the parties contract under a jurisdiction which prevents renegotiation of the default option. When a choice is possible, a judge under a Civil Law regime should be preferred as opposed to an Anglo-Saxon jurisdiction. Parties can also prefer to designate independent arbitrators versed in Civil Law. Obviously the assurance of ex-ante optimal incentives has to be balanced with the ability to efficiently adapt to a given ex-post situation.
- A judge empowered to enter into the details of the transaction would favor the implementation of a default option, which would lead to optimal level of investment by the parties. A more codified jurisdiction should therefore be preferred to a Common Law regime. Contractors may also choose to have recourse to independent specialized arbitrators if they consider that they would be more appropriate than public ones. In a sense, this is what happens when arbitration is chosen as the way to solve disputes. Specialized bodies such as industry federations may also perform arbitration.

Thus the extent of the credibility of contractual commitments is dependent on the supervision capability offered by the institutional framework agreed. However, this capability will always be partly manipulatable by the parties. Indeed, contractors can choose (to a certain extent) the type of institution that legislates their agreement in last resort.

Flexibility as a Guarantee

Whereas enforcement by a third party may in certain instances be unavoidable, it is not necessarily efficient. The process of enforcement (public or private), whilst enabling the benefit of an external coercion to oblige the recalcitrant party to honor his commitments, can be inefficient. Dispute resolution is costly, takes time (because inquiries and assessments have to be made), and can fail to achieve an equitable result (because circumstances prevent the judge from fully ascertaining the situation and thus preclude his ability to make any decision to or to arrive at a correct decision). Given these "enforcement failures" (see Williamson, 1975, 1985) it may be preferable to implement contracts that are (to a certain extent) self-enforcing. Both parties will prefer to perform the contract rather than to breach it. A major conclusion emanating from economic literature over the last twenty years is the importance, in that respect, of contractual incompleteness.

If it is assumed that the scope of forecasting by contracting parties is limited – to foresee all the solutions to a complex problem is costly; see Simon (1947) – and also that they face radical uncertainty – some of the problems that they will face in the future cannot be imagined ex-ante; see Knight (1921) – then it must be conceded that they cannot set-up ex-ante contracts that will precisely describe the optimal actions to be taken in all future states of their particular situations. Additionally they cannot reasonably restrict their future freedom of action, because there will be a high probability that such ex-ante restriction of their ex-post freedom of action will prevent their subsequently making optimal adjustments. Extremely detailed, inflexible contracts tend to create situations in which at least one party will be incited ex-post to breach: he will prefer to pay damages rather than perform the contract. This would not be a problem if damages assessed by adjudicating institutions were consistently perfectly computed and victims of breach fully compensated. Since courts, arbitrators and other adjudicating bodies are human institutions, necessarily with imperfections, it follows that perfect assessment of damages occurs only in rare instances. In certain cases such as sunk investment or sunk transfer (e.g. a transfer of know-how to the other party) damages do not fully compensate the victim because the situation created cannot be reversed. Overly detailed, inflexible contracts cannot therefore be considered as offering efficient protection to the parties involved in a transaction. Because they can anticipate that the contract might be breached in the future, contracting parties will not optimally "invest" ex ante. This is why, to be efficient, a contract has to be flexible in certain respects. Both parties should be allowed to revise ex-post their commitments in order to adjust to new situations as they unfold (see Goldberg & Erickson, 1987, Crocker & Masten, 1991).

If initial commitments are susceptible to future revision, little purpose is served in attempting to draft rigorously complete contracts. Contracts need to be understood as being the vehicle for framing future ex-post renegotiations in order to minimize ex-ante contracting costs (Coase, 1937) together with ex-post enforcement and decision costs (Williamson, 1985; Hart & Moore, 1988; Aghion, Dewatripont & Rey, 1994). This is put into effect with allocation of decision rights to the parties, functionally equivalent to implementation of what is usually termed *authority* and *renegotiation mechanisms* (see Brousseau, 1993). In each case, the parties agree ex-ante to ex-post follow the steps laid down in a decision mechanism which can be unilateral or bilateral. Both mechanisms rely on the implementation of an authority/subordination principle. The sole difference is the way decision rights are allocated. The optimal choice depends upon the allocation of cognitive capacities and information between the two parties. Unilateral decision avoids duplication of effort but can be inefficient in the situation where the two parties have disparate decision-making or information capabilities, and where the most correct decision requires concertation of those disparate capabilities. Otherwise stated, the optimal allocation of decision rights is dependent on the trade off between decision and maladaptation costs.

The above two sections reinforce the idea that contracts should above all be understood as the structure for solving problems raised by uncertainties as to the quality of the goods to be exchanged and future situations which will arise. Contracts need to set out credible obligations which incite both parties to optimally "invest" in the transaction process. This calls for a judicious mix of flexibility and rigidity. Contractual obligations have to be flexible in order to incite the parties to ex-post honor their undertakings, sure in the knowledge that they will be able to adapt them as unanticipated situations arise. But at the same time the obligations need to be rigid in order to guarantee a minimum amount of exchange that will protect the investments of (at least one of) the parties.

Concurrently, as noted before, the contracting capabilities of the parties are significantly conditioned by the attitude and the capabilities of the enforcement institutions. Optimally they should authorize ex-post renegotiations and contractual incompleteness, while forbidding renegotiation of the default option. It is clear that the achievement of this dual objective is by no means evident, due to the difficulty in separating out the default option provisions distinctly from the overall contract provisions. By widely allowing renegotiation U.S. Law and courts preclude the incorporation of efficient default options, in contrast with French Law and courts which do not empower a sufficient level of ex-post adjustment by severely limiting renegotiation and contractual incompleteness.

Contractual Standards

In his synthesis of Law and Economics literature on the regulation of contractual practices, Schwartz (2000) identifies five main domains of possible state intervention: enforcement, vocabulary, interpretation rules, default rules, contract settlement procedures. He then argues that courts and legislature ought to be considered as two "levels" of State intervention and that an analysis of the scope and relevancy of State intervention in these various areas should take into account the type of public body providing these facilities. According to Schwartz, the main finding in the literature is that State intervention should be as light as possible and should prefer ex-post intervention at court level as against ex-ante intervention at the legislative level. Indeed legislatures create rules that are necessarily general and abstract, calling for the ex-post intervention of courts in order to interpret those rules. Second, general rules can be inappropriate to specific situations, generating maladaptation costs.[6] Third, State intervention is justifiable if and only if instrumental in creating obvious benefits such as reduced transaction costs, solution of externality problems, long-term sustainability of competition, etc.

According to Schwartz, only four sub-fields are concerned in practice by this types of proven benefits: Enforcement has definitively to be provided by public institutions both because a State solely can dispense legitimate violence and also because decentralized enforcement without a central court of ultimate appeal would degenerate into conflicts, social disorder and inefficiencies (because of more imperfect enforcement). Making available vocabulary – or a measuring system in the North-Barzel analytical framework (North, 1990, Barzel, 1989) – to facilitate the writing of contracts and avoid misunderstanding between contracting parties is also a function that can be efficiently performed by a central body, because there are gains to benefit from a single standardized interface. However, Schwartz reasons that the providing of interpretations should remain decentralized to enable a fine adaptation to the local specificities of each situation. Default rules can be provided by the State, but only for those default rules aimed at forcing information disclosure leading to the increase of communal and social welfare. The purpose is to prohibit the exploitation of information asymmetries that would generate negative results for both parties. Fourth, State intervention in the contracting process is also considered as legitimate when it aims to reduce fraud and to avoid the exercise of monopoly power generated by the contract itself (lock-in effect). Thus Law and Economic literature concludes that providing interpretation, supplying the parties with default rules which have objectives other than that of solving specific information asymmetry problems (e.g. arriving at a fair compromise or solution of co-ordination failures), or regulating contracting processes to favor the emergence of efficient or fair solutions should not be exercised by the State because of the risks of inefficient performance.

These conclusions correspond very closely with those of the recent developments of New Institutional Economics (e.g. Brousseau & Fares, 2000). Inter-individual co-ordination is extremely personalized. Reliance on a general solution mechanism – i.e. standardized contractual provisions completed by generic bodies such as courts – leads to maladaptation costs. Nonetheless, these general solutions, by avoiding the design of specific co-ordination rules and supervision procedures, enable contracting parties to benefit from economies of scale, scope and expertise as regards transaction costs. Also, the parties concerned can have the reassurance that these general rules with their enforcement provisions will be effective, in that they have been formulated by specialists, and in that they survived a selection process. In practice contracting parties rely both on general solutions provided by the applicable institutional framework and specific solutions formulated at bilateral level having regard to the best trade-off between maladaptation and transactions costs. From recent applied and theoretical literature on contracting practice it appears that the terms of this trade-off are not exclusively determined by the features of the transaction, on the one hand, and the characteristics of the general institutions of the society, on the other. In addition to public and governmental institutions (that are imposed), and the bilateral contract (specifically formulated), economic agents can create collective rules and governance mechanisms aimed at solving problems that are specific to a particular population (such as an industry, a certain business community, etc.). The resulting private institutions – typically a body incorporating standardization and certification committees, or an industry federation regulating the practices of its members, or a business community with a declared deontology, etc. – enables more precise trade-off between maladaptation and transactions costs: the parties are provided with "ready to use" coordination solutions that are less general and abstract than those of the public and governmental institutions. An efficient institutional framework is therefore an appropriate mix of public and private institutions.

It is to be noted additionally that private institutions are able to emerge and evolve at a quicker pace than public institutions (see Brousseau, 2000). In a dynamic context, this is an essential way to achieve greater efficiency.

Lastly, one of the essential advantages of the collective solutions provided by private institutions is that they are non-mandatory: economic agents are free to apply them or not. This is an effective means of circumventing maladaptation costs incurred by the formulation at collective level of mandatory generic solutions.

Thus the propensity of Civil Law to provide contractual standards over a wide range is called into question. In order to protect weak parties this Law has many standard contracts – e.g. housing rental contracts – together with standards and mandatory contractual provisions. Moreover, private dispute resolution mechanisms and individual standards are not considered legitimate ways for the resolution of co-ordination problems. They can be provisional or temporary, but public opinion and administrations in Civil Law countries frequently adjudge that the most legitimate way to solve collective problems is through public institutions because the State will assure the strength viability and neutrality (benevolence) of the solutions implemented. Maladaptation costs as well as flexibility constraints are therefore not taken into consideration.

CONCLUSION: CIVIL LAW AND ECONOMIC REASONING

In this paper, I argue that economic reasoning in regard to contracts can stimulate evolution of doctrinal debates in Civil Law countries. Whereas Anglo-Saxon liberal ideology and the U.S. institutional framework undoubtedly have a major influence on economics as a whole and economics of contract in particular, economics nevertheless underlines the inescapable fact that contracts are essential to overcome problems resulting from uncertainty in a world of imperfect institutions (otherwise there would be no reason for contracts to exist). And also, contracts need to be incomplete and partly non-renegotiable. Incomplete contracting is an effective method for achieving efficiency and for ensuring performance where future events are either (too) costly to forecast or impossible to foresee. Non-renegotiable default options are the sole means to guarantee to the parties a minimum level of return on their "investment" in the transaction. The Civil Code should therefore evolve to integrate the complex requirement for both flexibility and rigidity in contracting practices. The notion of incomplete contracts should be more explicitly and widely recognized as should be the identification of default options and their non-renegotiability. It is true, however, that the high propensity of Civil Law court to enforce specific performance is a factor that enables contracting parties to ensure the imposition of default options: in this respect Civil Law doctrine is in harmony with economic thought.

Another important conclusion that can be drawn from what has been developed above relates to the institutional design. Civil Law tends to not recognize the usefulness of private institutions. Since private institutions are partly informal – and therefore uncodified – and relate to private order, they are at best ignored by the doctrine. But there is also a strong school of thought that rejects the principle of private order – for instance the *lex mercatoria* – because it would be the expression of private interests as opposed to the public Law, which derives from the collective interest as well as superior moral principles. Economic thought considers that the design of efficient collective rules and astute enforcement of contracts (which need to be flexible, with non-renegotiable default options) make for the solution of manifold coordination problems at an "intermediary" level as regards the scope of public and collective bodies and the scope of inter-individual arrangements. Non-mandatory standards and collective rules designed at industry or regional level, in addition to alternative dispute resolution mechanisms – administrative non-jurisdictional entities (such as regulatory commissions arbitration tribunals) – should also be more explicitly recognized both by the doctrine and by the positive Law. They form a useful complement to the general public rules (contract and liability laws) and courts. The guiding philosophy should be to regulate the resulting composite framework, not to contest or ignore it. Whilst the adoption of non-State rules and the development of private enforcement agencies can be justified by the quest for increased efficiency, they also risk being subverted for the exercise of monopolistic power. Public institutions should therefore be involved in the strengthening of certain non-State standards and enforcement institutions – for instance by recognizing them as participating in a collective effort for enhancing the efficiency of co-ordination, by recognizing the significance of their assessments and decisions, etc. – because this will help to avoid duplication of effort and guarantee that efforts will be made by the most appropriate (efficient) bodies. However at the same time, public institutions should control these private arrangements to suppress collusion and rent capture. Indeed, the coasian enthusiasm for the efficiency of private institutions relies on the idea that competition among institutions precludes the capture of rents (in the longer term). Public institutions therefore have the remit to maintain the viability of the competitive process and to sanction private institutions which run counter.

It must be stressed that Civil Law doctrine is not based solely on philosophical and moral principles. Efficiency considerations have systematically influenced the construction of the doctrine over the centuries. Consequently, the existing doctrine and practices should be more deeply investigated to obtain a fuller understanding of their underlying economic rationality; and this could well have an impact on economic thought. Three examples in illustration.

As described above, the Civil Code prescribes extremely detailed, elaborate constraints regarding both contract formation and the contractual equilibrium between the parties. This is because equity considerations – in the sense of the Aristotelian-Christian moral of commutative justice – have a profound influence on Civil legal doctrine. In that context, rather than considering efficiency and fairness as being contradictory, it can be reasoned that fairness and equity impact favorably on efficiency. If a contract is considered fair and equitable by the signatories (because a third party and a procedure guarantee a fair and equitable result in the last resort), it will become more legitimate for both parties. Therefore, the propensity not to honor commitments should decrease. While this is only an insight, the impact of Civil Law doctrine (about fair contracting) upon the beliefs of economic agents, and therefore on their propensity to behave opportunistically should be investigated. The fact that there is a far greater incidence of judicial disputes in the U.S. than in France, for instance, may not be not proof, but is at least a good indication, that the equity aspect is an important element in the legitimacy of contractual commitments and is a significant factor in deciding their enforcement.

Second, it is clear that in Civil Law the preference is for ex-ante prevention as opposed to ex-post compensation for damages. The existence of a variety of mandatory contractual standards together with the *a priori* exclusion of many types of arrangement is due to a preference for avoidance, to the greatest possible extent, of ex-post complex conflict resolution and also for more firm control of non-reversible situations. There is clearly a trade off between the maladaptation costs arising from multiple restrictions on the freedom to contract as against the private and social costs caused by inefficient contracting, compounded by the restricted rationality (or lack of information) of the parties. It is certain that there are many instances where the trade-off is in favor of prevention. This should be better documented: for instance by comparing, case by case, the application of U.S. Law with the outcome under French Law.

Third, and in the same vein, the trade-off between maladaptation costs generated by standard, non-customized rules and the transaction costs induced by specific bilateral arrangements should also be analyzed in greater detail. Again, a comparison between France and the U.S. should enable researchers to better understand the factors favoring the implementation of public mandatory contractual standards and the areas in which they would generate inefficiencies. Such comparative Law and Economics would serve to promote the evolution of both the Civil Code and Common Law in achieving enhanced efficiency.

NOTES

* Useful comments were provided by the members of the workshop "Contracts and Institutions", GENI, Universities of Paris 1 and Paris X, especially Camille Chasserant, Bruno Chaves, Pierre Garrouste and M'hand Fares. I thank the participants in this workshop. Usual caveats apply.

1. The conclusion must not be drawn from this example that the U.S. legal framework is the only one permitting economic analysis of contractual practice. The ADR model

demonstrates that practices under alternative legal frameworks may also be reflected. However, the contrast between the two models is a reasonable proof of the influence of a legal framework on theoreticians in the way they think a "decontextualized" theory.

Most typically, the two models highlight the extent to which respective judges examine transaction details. It is argued here that an Anglo-Saxon judge cannot be considered less rational than a French one, but it is nonetheless true that he does not seek to concentrate on transaction details for "at will" contracts that are self-enforcing, i.e. where the two parties need to agree ex-post on the way in which the contract will be performed. Judges do not intervene in the enforcement of "at will" contracts, but prefer to authorize renegotiation between the parties.

2. It needs to be made clear, however, that incomplete contracting is not totally impossible under French Law. The legal doctrine recognizes that in certain circumstances – as in labor agreements – implementation of an authority/subordination principle is unavoidable. The Civil Code is nevertheless reluctant to authorize incomplete contracting – especially in the case of price agreements, and the majority of contracts have to be as complete as possible. This is linked with the necessity to ensure equity in contractual relationships (see the following sub-section).

3. Commutative Justice needs to be contrasted with Distributive Justice, which determines the attribution of gain between economic agents. Further, various norms of distributive justice exist (from Pareto to Rawls). In a sense, U.S. legal doctrine also refers to a norm of justice that is essentially distributive and heavily influenced by efficiency – Paretian – considerations. Ethical considerations are therefore present in U.S. legal doctrine, but since the norm of justice is different from that prevalent in Europe, the effect is slightly different.

4. Comparison between Civil Law doctrine and Common Law Theory is difficult in that there are many open questions within the two legal frameworks. At the risk of over simplification solely the dominant doctrine and theory of the two legal systems are discussed.

5. Since the default option formulated ex-ante is based on the probability of various situations foreseeable at that point, the later real situation ex-post is generally not optimal. This explains the acceptance of renegotiation of the default option ex-post, even by the party whose investments are protected by the default option.

6. Maladapation costs make reference to rules that are inappropriate to specific situations or that are insufficiently precise. Such costs could be considered as referring to different categories of transaction costs; for the purposes of this paper it is assumed that they are in a single category. In fact, in both cases enforcement of the rule leads to sub-optimal results (or efficiency losses). Non-enforcement of the rule leads to the generation of decision costs. Maladaptation costs signify a solution established ex ante which is not conducive to efficient ex-post modification, thus leading to efficiency losses or the requirement for decision, as against ex ante negotiation costs borne by the parties in respect of co-ordination solutions that will be efficient ex post.

REFERENCES

Aghion, P., Dewatripont, M., & Rey, P. (1994). Renegotiation Design with Unverifiable Information. *Econometrica*, *62*, 257–282.

Akerlof, G. A. (1970). The market for lemons: quality, uncertainty and the market mechanism. *Quarterly Journal of Economics*, 488–500.

Barnett, R. A. (1999). The Richness of Contract Theory, *Michigan Law Review*, *97*(6), 1413–1429.

Barzel, Y. (1989). *The Economics of Property rights*. Cambridge University Press.

Becker, G. S., & Stigler, G. J. (1974). Law enforcement, Malfeasance and Compensation of Enforcers, *Journal of Legal Studies*, *3*, 1–18.

Bessy, C., & Brousseau, E. (1998). Technology Licensing Contracts Features and Diversity. *International Review of Law and Economics*, *18*, 451–489.

Bouckaert, B., & De Geest, G. (Eds) (1999). *Encyclopaedia of Law and Economics*. Aldershot: Edward Elgar.

Brousseau, E. (1993). *L'économie des contrats; technologies de l'information et coordination inter-entreprises*. Paris: PUF.

Brousseau, E. (2000). What Institutions to Organize Electronic Commerce: Private Institutions and the Organization of Markets. *Economics of Innovation and New Technology*, *9*(3), 245–273.

Brousseau, E., & Fares, M. (2000). The Incomplete Contract Theory and the New-Institutional Economics Approaches to Contracts: Substitutes or Complements? In: C. Ménard (Ed.), *Institutions, Contracts, Organizations, Perspectives from New-Institutional Economics* (pp. 399–421). Edward Elgar Pub.

Brousseau, E., & Glachant, J.-M. (Eds) (2000a). *Economics of Contracts in Prospect and Retrospect*, Special Issue, *Revue d'Economie Industrielle*, *92*.

Brousseau, E., & Glachant, J.-M. (2000b). Economie des contrats et renouvellements de l'analyse économique. *Revue d'Economie Industrielle*, Special Issue: *Economics of Contracts in Prospect and Retrospect*, *92*, 23–50.

Coase, R. H. (1937). The Nature of the Firm. *Economica, NS4*, 386 405.

Coase, R. H. (1960). The Problem of Social Cost. *Journal of Law and Economics*, *3*, 1–44.

Crocker, K. J., & Masten, S. E. (1991). Pretia ex machina? Prices and process in long-term contracts; *Journal of Law and Economics*, *34*, 69–99.

Fares, M. (2000). *Contrats Incomplets Cadre de renégociation et engagement de long terme*, Doctoral thesis. Université de Paris 1.

Gazzaniga, J.-L. (1990). Domat et Pothier. Le contrat à la fin de l'Ancien Régime. *Droits, Revue Française de Théorie Juridique*, *12*, 37–46.

Ghestin, J. (1990). La notion de contrat. *Droits, Revue Française de Théorie Juridique*, *12*, 8–24.

Ghestin, J. (2000). Le contrat en tant qu'échange économique. *Revue d'Economie Industrielle*, Special Issue *Economics of Contracts in Prospect and Retrospect*, *92*, 81–100.

Goldberg, V. P., & Erikson, J. E. (1987). Quantity and price adjustment in long-term contracts: a case study of petroleum coke. *Journal of Law and Economics*, *30*, 369–398.

Grossman, S. J., & Hart, O. D. (1986). The costs and benefits of ownership: a theory of vertical integration. *Journal of Political Economy*, *94*(4), 691–719.

Hart, O., & Holmström, B. (1987). The Theory of Contracts. In: Bewley (Ed.), *Advances in Economic Theory*. Cambridge University Press.

Hart, O., & Moore, J. (1988). Incomplete Contracts and Renegociation. *Econometrica*, *56*, 755–786.

Jamin, C. (2000). Plaidoyer pour le solidarisme contractuel. In: M. Fabre-Magnan and C. Jamin (Eds), *Le Contrat au début du XXIe° Siècle; Mélanges en l'honneur de M. Jacques Ghestin*. Paris: LGDJ.

Knight, F. H. (1921). *Risk, uncertainty and profit*. New York: Harper & Row.

Macneil, I. (1974). The many futures of contracts. *Southern California Law Review*, *47*, (May), 691 816.

Malinvaud, P. (1992). *Droit des obligations; les mécanismes juridiques des relations économiques*. Paris: Litec.

Ménard, C. (Ed.) (2000). *Institutions, Contracts, Organizations, Perspectives from New Institutional Economics*, Edward Elgar Pub.

Newmann, P. (Ed) (1998). The New Palgrave Dictionary of Economics and the Law, MacMillan

North, D. C. (1990). *Institutions, Institutional Change and Economic Performance*. Cambridge University Press.

OCDE. (1994). *Les accords de franchise*, publication de l'OCDE.

Pareto, V. (1906). *Manuel d'Economie Politique*.

Posner, R. A. (1986). *Economic analysis of law* (3rd ed). Little Brown, Boston.

Poughon, J.-M. (1990). Une constante doctrinale: l'approche économique du contrat. *Droits, Revue Française de Théorie Juridique, 12*, 47–58.

Schwartz, A. (2000). Contract Theory and Theories of Contract Regulation. *Revue d'Economie Industrielle*, Special Issue *Economics of Contracts in Prospect and Retrospect, 92*, 101–110.

Shapiro, C., & Stiglitz, J. E. (1984). Equilibrium unemployment as a worker discipline device. *American Economic Review, 74*(3), 433–444.

Sérousi, R. (1999). *Introduction aux droits anglais et américain*. Paris: Dunod.

Simon, H. A. (1947). *Administrative Behavior, a Story of Decision Processes in Business Organization*. Macmillan.

Stiglitz, J. E. (1977). Monopoly nonlinear pricing and imperfect information: the insurance market. *Review of Economic Studies, 44*, 407–430.

Tallon, D. (1990). L'évolution des idées en matière de contrat: survol comparatif. *Droits, Revue Française de Théorie Juridique, 12*, 81–92.

Walras, L. (1874). *Eléments d'Economie Politique Pure*.

Williamson, O. E. (1985). *The Economic Institutions of Capitalism*. New York: The Free Press.

COMPARATIVE LAW AND ECONOMICS AND THE DESIGN OF OPTIMAL LEGAL DOCTRINES

Gerrit De Geest

INTRODUCTION

Legal Doctrines

A legal doctrine is a scientific theory on the law. It is a coherent set of concepts and rules that describes legal reality. A legal doctrine is the equivalent of a 'law' in natural sciences, like Newton's law of falling bodies. Such a 'law' compresses hundreds of observations into one formula. A legal doctrine compresses hundreds of cases and legislative articles into a set of rules that is as simple and clear as possible.

A legal doctrine can be judged from two perspectives: (a) The content: are the rules desirable, i.e. efficient? (b) The quality of the formulation: are the rules described in a simpler and more precise way than competing doctrines?

The Role of Law and Economics Scholarship in Finding Better Legal Doctrines

To date, law and economics scholarship has focused solely on the first perspective. The second is left to traditional doctrinists. Posner (1986: 85–88) for instance seems to defend the consideration doctrine, because it fulfills some useful economic functions.[1] The consideration doctrine is quite complex from

Law and Economics in Civil Law Countries, Volume 6, pages 107–124.

ISBN: 0-7623-0712-9

a technical point of view, which has led some scholars to propose to abolish it (Gordon, 1991). Posner does not delve into that debate – he just tries to prove that the common law is efficient. Yet comparative lawyers know very well that continental law leads in many cases to the same final results, albeit on the basis of different doctrines. Posner does not attempt to determine what the optimal formulation is.

Some comparative lawyers do try to select the doctrines that are superior from a technical point of view. This is especially the case for those groups of comparatists who are endeavouring to draft new European (civil) codes. The Lando commission (which has written a proposal for a new contract law code) is a well-known example (Lando & Beale, 1995). But a weak point of these scholars is their lack of methodology with respect to finding and choosing doctrines. In a sense they have no methodology: they select on the basis of intuition and – sometimes – compromise (in trying to please the lawyers of all legal families).

In this article, I will argue that searching for the optimal formulation is a task for law and economics scholarship as well. There are three major reasons why this is the case. First, since legal doctrines ultimately serve to save legal information costs, their merits should be weighed in terms of the saved legal information costs as well. Second, the psychology of creative thinking predicts that interdisciplinary scholars have the highest chance to come up with new legal doctrines. Third, and most importantly, what legislators and courts ultimately do is balance the advantages and disadvantages of rules. A theory that is focused on describing these advantages and disadvantages has increased chances in providing an accurate description of the legal reality.

This paper will start by giving several examples of economically inspired new doctrines. We shall then turn to discuss a number of methodological problems.

OPTIMAL DOCTRINES: EXAMPLES

Negligence: Reasonable Person vs. Learned Hand

In Belgium, France and many other continental countries, negligence is defined in terms of a 'reasonable person': the injurer is found negligent if he did not behave as a reasonable person would have. The 'reasonable person' concept goes back to Roman law, where the 'bonus pater familias' was the measure with which behavior was compared.

In current legal Belgian and French doctrine, the definition of 'reasonable person' is still extremely vague, even tautological. A reasonable person is not an average person. It is an ideal person, though not necessarily a superman. A reasonable person is someone who is always doing what he should do. And what should he do? What a reasonable person does. This is a circular definition that would never be accepted in natural sciences.

A competing definition of negligence comes from Learned Hand, the well-known American judge: negligence is not taking precaution when the precaution costs are lower than the expected accident costs. A reasonable person takes his own interests (saving precaution costs) as well as other parties' interests (saving accident costs) into account. The definition of a reasonable person is not tautological here. Rather, under this definition the reasonable person is a perfect altruist, who is concerned about other people's utility as much as about his own.

Faure and Van den Bergh (1987) have analyzed to what extent the Learned Hand formula is implicitly used by Belgian courts. They concluded that many cases could be reinterpreted this way. van Velthoven and van Wijck (1997: 163, 189) mentioned that in one decision the Dutch supreme court defined negligence in similar terms as Learned Hand.

Therefore, two competing legal doctrines seem to describe Belgian (and Dutch) negligence cases: the 'reasonable person' doctrine and the Learned Hand doctrine. Both are scientific theories that attempt to describe current law (*de lege lata*). What is the best doctrine from a scientific viewpoint? Clearly the Learned Hand doctrine. This is because it is based on defined concepts, in contrast to the reasonable person doctrine. Because of these definitions, the Learned Hand doctrine is falsifiable which is in contrast to the 'reasonable person' doctrine (if we cannot define a reasonable person, we cannot prove that courts do not apply this criterion).

Liability for Failed Negotiations: Reasonable Person vs. Misleading as to Chances and Amount at Stake

Who should bear the costs of failed negotiations? According to mainstream Belgian and French doctrinists, no one should bear the other party's costs, unless he (clearly) did not behave as a reasonable person. Again, this *culpa in contrahendo* doctrine is based on the non-defined concept of a *reasonable person*.

Wils (1993) developed a competing doctrine. It is an extremely simple one: you are liable only if you mislead the other party with respect to his chances or to the amount at stake.[2]

Suppose, for instance, that you asked a free offer from 50 competing constructors while you told each of them that you asked an offer to only 2 constructors. All competing constructors spend a substantial amount of time preparing the offer, believing they have a 50% chance to get the contract. In reality they have only a 2% chance. If they would have known their real chances, they would never have spent so much time in preparing the offer. The fundamental problem is asymmetric information (the buyer knows the chances better) resulting in wasted costs (more preparation costs are made than would have been if the buyer had to pay them). The solution is a legal duty to be honest, sanctioned by a duty to compensate.

Suppose that you enter a computer shop, falsely pretending that you plan to buy 100 computers for a non-existing firm. The seller will spend a lot of time to inform you about alternative computer systems. At the end you buy one computer for personal use. The waste of precontractual information costs is caused by the buyer misleading the seller with respect to the amount at stake.

This double rule explains Belgian case law quite well.[3] For instance, if the buyer is negotiating with several sellers and eventually signs a contract with one of them, he is obliged to inform the other candidates. If not, he is under a duty to compensate the useless costs made by one of them afterwards.[4] At the moment the buyer made a final decision, the chances of the other sellers to get the contract become zero. If they are not informed by the buyer, they are misled by him about their chances, which they believe are still substantial. The rule also explains why a party who starts negotiations with the sole goal of stealing know-how or trade secrets has to buy compensation: they falsely made the other party believe that their chances were higher than 0%.[5] Wils' doctrine is simple in other respects too. For instance, under Wils' doctrine, whether the misleading party was in bad faith is irrelevant. This way, serious evidence problems are avoided. Further, what party broke off the negotiations is also irrelevant. It is for these reasons that Wils' doctrine is by far superior to the traditional (tautological) 'reasonable person' doctrine.

Quasi Contracts: Unjust Enrichment vs. Imposed Transfers in High Transaction Costs Situations?

In France and Belgium (contrary to the USA)[6] the general term 'quasi contracts' refers to one of the basic categories of sources of obligations, including negotiorum gestio (*gestion d'affaires*), undue payment and unjust enrichment. There is an ongoing discussion whether the last doctrine – unjust enrichment – is the general one, of which negotiorum gestio and undue payment are applications. Many authors believe that undue payment is a specific case of unjust enrichment, while negotiorum is a separate category, with distinct rules.

Traditional Belgian legal doctrine (De Page, 1967, nr. 40.) awards compensation on the basis of unjust enrichment if four conditions are simultaneously fulfilled: (a) there is no enrichment; (b) another person has been impoverished; (c) there is a causal relationship between the enrichment and the impoverishment; and finally (d) there is no legal ground for the enrichment.[7] Compensation on the basis of negotiorum requires 3 main conditions to be fulfilled: (a) the intention to take care of someone else's interests (pursuing your own interests may not have been the primary purpose), (b) the voluntary nature of the act, i.e. the absence of any contractual or legal obligation (except for the legal duty to rescue of art. 422 bis and ter SW), (c) the necessary character of the act, i.e. the helped party may not have been able to take care for his own business (Kruithof and al., 1994: 610–613; Paulus, 33–43 who distinguished 6 main conditions).

Both traditional doctrines are extremely unclear. They are based on undefined concepts. More importantly, they do not explain why the legal system adheres to the requirement of a contract in some cases and allows coerced quasi contractual transfers in other cases.

De Geest (1994) and Bouckaert and De Geest (1995, 1998) have developed an alternative, more accurate doctrine, inspired by law and economics scholarship (especially Calabresi & Melamed, 1972). Quasi contractual transfers are to be considered as coerced exchanges of goods and services, wanted by one party (which they call the 'active party') and imposed on another party (the 'passive party'). They are not the normal method of exchange: a market economy is based on transfers that are agreed upon by both parties. Imposed transfers are allowed only if two conditions are fulfilled: (a) high transaction costs impede a normal contract, and (b) it is obvious to an outsider that the transfer is welfare enhancing.

Take for instance the case of the repaired roof, a standard example of gestion d'affairs. A person (the active party) takes the initiative to let someone else repair his neighbor's roof after a storm while his neighbor is away on holiday, where he can't be reached. The neighbor (the passive party) will have to reimburse the costs when he returns, whether he accepts it or not. The active party imposed a transaction upon his neighbor: a service (reparation of the roof) in return for money. Transaction costs were high due to time constraints. It is obvious to an outsider that repairing the roof is better than doing nothing at all.

Art. 646 of the Belgian/French Civil Code gives owners of land the right to force their neighbor to share the fencing costs. Neighbors are in a bilateral monopoly position toward each other as well. Therefore, the first condition (high transaction costs) is fulfilled. Is it obvious to an outsider that the exchange (the use of the fence in return for half of the price of it) is wealth increasing? Fences are one of the few things that are positively valued by nearly every owner. Obliging the beneficiary of a positive externality to pay a kind of 'tax' in return may be the only way to prevent free ridership.

Bouckaert and De Geest (1995) distinguished four fundamental sources of high transaction costs: (a) time constraints (urgent situations like in the repaired roof case); (b) incapacity (like in the traditional doctor-helps-unconscious-patient example); (c) errors (like in undue payment cases); and (d) serious bilateral monopolies (like in the fencing costs case).[8] With respect to the cases where it is quite *obvious to an outsider that the transfer is a Kaldor-Hicks improvement*, Bouckaert and De Geest (1995) made a distinction between the following categories of comparisons: (a) the life of one person versus a small amount of someone else's time (e.g. duty to rescue); (b) the market value of a property that was saved versus the repair or maintenance costs (e.g. *gestion d'affaires*, obligation of the creditors to contribute indirectly to the maintenance costs in bankruptcy law); (c) the value of a licence to the licensee versus the marginal cost to the inventor (compulsory licensing); (d) the value of goods to a consumer versus the marginal costs of a natural monopolist ('obligation to sell'); (e) the advantage of building against an existing wall versus the marginal costs to the owner (the right to make a wall common property); (f) the value of an entire parcel of land versus the value of a little piece of another parcel (e.g. the right to 'take' a way out); (g) the use of a fence to an owner versus 50% of the price.

This doctrine was inspired by law & economic theories, especially Calabresi and Melamed (1972), who made the distinction between property rules and liability rules. Long (1984) formulated a less elaborated legal doctrine on American restitution law. According to this doctrine a court should impose a 'hypothetical contract' when high transaction costs make an explicit contract impossible. Imposing such a 'hypothetical contract' results in a Pareto superior transaction.[9]

Misunderstandings Between Parties to a Contract: Five Separate Doctrines or One Least Cost Avoider Doctrine?

When parties are in the course of agreeing on the terms of a contract, misunderstanding can arise in many ways. Current Belgian law needs five doctrines to solve all forms of misunderstanding in contracts. De Geest and De Moor (1999) have recently proposed one unifying theory that covers all these aspects. We will briefly summarize the five traditional doctrines and then explain how one doctrine can do the same job.

(Excusable) Mistake Preventing the Contract.

One party believes he has bought lot of land A, while the other party is convinced to have sold lot of land B. In one recent case[10] the buyers saw a lot of building land, with a board on it, indicating "land for sale". They bought the land in a public sale, but later noticed that it was another lot and not the one with the board on. The court decided this mistake was excusable, and declared that no sale had taken place.

Mistake like this does not always lead to a nullified contract. The mistake should be 'excusable'. That criterion allows the court to decide who was responsible for the misunderstanding and to sanction the responsible party by not giving that party what he wants.

The Doctrine of Legitimate Expectation

One party signs a contract, without having read the contract before signing. He is convinced that clause A is included but did not check it. The other party is convinced that instead of clause A, clause B has been agreed upon, as is written in the contract. So there is a misunderstanding as to what clause has been agreed upon. Courts will in such cases normally decide that clause B is the valid one. The first party only has to blame himself: he should have read the contract. Though the starting point of Belgian contract law is the will theory, and that will is absent for the first party, courts will declare the contract valid on the doctrine of legitimate expectations: parties may reasonably expect that what is signed reflects the will of the one who signs.

Now suppose a contract has been signed by both parties, but there is an error in the wording. The seller wanted to sell a watch for 290 Euro, but erronously wrote 250 Euro in the contract. Or the seller wanted to sell a truck for 250,000 Euro, but erronously wrote 250 Euro. In the first case (a small error) courts will declare the contract valid. Though there was no 'meeting of minds' for 250 Euro (the seller had another price in mind), courts will argue that the buyer had a legitimate expectation that the price mentioned in the contract and signed by the seller reflected the seller's will. In the second case (a big error) courts will declare that no valid contract has been concluded, because there was no meeting of minds and because the error was so manifest that the buyer had no legitimate reason to believe that there was no error involved (Van Gerven, 1973: 301–307; Kruithof, 1991).

The Doctrine of Tacit Acceptance

The owner of a parking lot wants to be exempted from liability for car theft, so he places a large board at the entrance of the parking lot exempting him from liability. However, a consumer did not notice or read the board and believes that the parking contract includes no exemption clauses. There is a misunderstanding between both parties as to what has been agreed upon.

Belgian law will solve these cases under the doctrine of tacit acceptance, especially acceptance of standard term clauses. The basic idea is that offers can be accepted in more implicit ways. Case law has elaborated specific conditions. Boards with exemption clauses have to be large enough to be noticed without special effort, and the text should be clear enough to be easily read and understood. If a board was too small, courts will presume it has not been accepted by the consumer. If a board is large and clear enough, and the consumer did not react, the courts will presume that the consumer accepted the terms (Kruithof et al., 1994: 273–274).

Rules on the Interpretation of Contracts

Sometimes one party interprets a clause as A, while another party reads B in it. This different interpretation creates a misunderstanding as to what has been agreed upon. These misunderstandings are solved under the heading of rules on the 'interpretation of contracts'. One such rule is that contracts have to be constructed against the party that drafted it, like the insurance company (art. 1162 C. C. states that contracts have to be construed against the party that benefitted from the clause, but there is a tendency in Belgian case law to read this sentence as 'construed against the drafter'. Kruithof et al., 1994: 452).

The Doctrine of the 'Transformation of Rights' ('Rechtsverwerking')

This doctrine solves misunderstandings at a later stage of the contract, for instance whether a modification or prolongation has been approved.

In one case[11] the contract with a building contractor stated that the consumer had to pay the architect's fee directly to the architect and not to the builder. The consumer paid the fee instead to the builder. The architect knew this, but did not react, and consequently made the consumer believe that he agreed with this change. Later, the architect sued the consumer, but lost the case, on the basis of the doctrine of the 'transformation of rights': the architect had lost his right to require direct payment by his behaving in a contradicting way.

The Belgian supreme court (court of cassation) has later denounced the doctrine of the transformation of rights.[12] Some writers have (in our opinion correctly) argued that the doctrine still holds under Belgian law, in that several legislative rules and cases are an application of it.[13] The new unifying doctrine of De Geest and De Moor (1999) departs from the idea that a misunderstanding is a regrettable event. The legal system can reduce the number of misunderstandings by giving correct incentives to the parties who are in the best position to avoid them. In all of these kinds of cases, courts have to ask a simple question: which party was in the best position to avoid this misunderstanding?

The responsible party has to be sanctioned, by not giving him/her what he/she wanted, i.e. by nullifying a contract that the party wanted, or by declaring a contract valid that the party did not want. Let us analyze the former five cases in these terms.

In case (a) the misunderstanding as to what lot of land was sold, was created by the seller who placed the board 'land for sale' on the wrong lot of land. Most people would have believed that the board referred to the land on which it was placed, so the seller should have clearly indicated that it was another piece of land. A misunderstanding that is created by the fact that someone expected a different clause than the one in the contract he had signed and not read (case b), can in most situations be avoided by simply reading the contract before signing it. If a misunderstanding is due to an error in the wording of the contract, there were two possible solutions: the drafter could have been more careful, and the reader could have checked whether there was no error, by simply asking the drafter. If errors are small, it would be a waste to require readers to always double-check, since minor price reductions are common in a free market. If the difference between the normal price and the announced price is extreme (like a truck that is set for sale at a price of 250 Euro), then buyers should ask confirmation – which after all does not require too much effort from the buyer. Misunderstandings caused by not reading an exemption clause on a board (case c), can be avoided in two ways: the drafter can use bigger boards and the reader can check more carefully whether there are no announcements to be discovered. Noticing a small board would require too much effort from the reader. In that case it would be cheaper to buy a larger board. On the other hand, in a situation where the board is big and clear enough, the party with the least cost of avoiding a misunderstanding is the reader, as he/she can simply be slightly more observant when entering the premises. If unclear clauses are the source of the misunderstanding as to what has been agreed (case d), the least cost avoider is the drafter of the contract, who should have drafted the contract more carefully. Finally, in case e, the misunderstanding was caused by the fact that the consumer performed in a different, but parallel comparable congruent way (paying via the contractor instead of directly to the architect costs as much money) and the fact that the architect who did not accept this change, did not react. The least cost avoider of the misunderstanding was the architect, who simply should have objected.

The new doctrine of De Geest and De Moor (1999) is inspired by law & economics scholarship. Posner (1986: 88–90, also in the 1977 edition at 71–73) has briefly suggested that communication problem cases should be solved by looking at what party could have avoided the misunderstanding at least costs.

Cooter and Ulen (1988: 257–258), Van den Bergh (1991: 31–33) and De Geest (1994: 196–200) made similar, but brief, analyses. The idea that the legal system should sanction the party that could have avoided the misunderstanding at least costs is ultimately an application of the least cost avoider concept of Calabresi's work (1970) on tort law.

Let us now pay some more attention to the technical elaboration of the doctrine. De Geest and De Moor came to the conclusion that optimally it is not useful to make a further subset of rules on the distinction between the objects of the misunderstanding (like the subject matter, the nature of the contract, which clauses apply, how they are to be interpreted, etc.). It is much more fruitful to focus on the actual causes of misunderstandings. They found the following rules.

Misunderstandings Resulting from a Failure to Notice or Read Signs

Rule 1: A party who proposes a supplemental, non-default rule through a sign or notice must assure that it is posted in such manner that attracts attention or is in large font so that it is not necessary for the other party to take additional efforts to notice and read the sign. If, in such a case, the reader does not voice any reservations as to the content of the clause, he is to be regarded as having accepted the clause in a tacit manner.

Exception: When a signed document refers to information communicated through notices, it is sufficient that the other party can find the information upon request.

Misunderstandings Resulting from a Failure to Read the Contract Before Signing it

Rule 2: The party who signs a document without reading it, is responsible for misunderstandings, when the content does not correspond to his expectations.

Exception 2.1: Signed clauses are not to be considered accepted when the drafter made efforts to augment the signing-without-reading problem

Exception 2.2: The drafter (or offeror) of the contract stands in an agency or trust relation with the party that he signs for, in other words, the drafter was paid (direct or indirect) to read the contract.

Exception 2.3: When a contract revision or renewal contains significant modifications, which are not directly communicated, but rather, are implemented into the contract covertly, these changes are to be regarded as not accepted by the other party, regardless of the fact that this party has signed the contract.

Misunderstandings Resulting from Differing Interpretations of the Contractual Clauses

Rule 3: A party with an idiosyncratic definition of a word or concept, who neglects to explicitly communicate this to the other party, is to be held responsible for resulting misunderstandings.

Rule 4: The party that attaches a meaning to a text, other than that of the average third party (like a judge) is responsible for the misunderstanding, so that one has to express himself in a way so that the third party gets the correct impression on what has been agreed.

Rule 5: The drafter of a contract needs to formulate his proposal in a understandable and unambiguous manner. In order to provide the drafter with an incentive to do such, obscurities and contradictions are resolved to the detriment of the drafter.

Misunderstandings Resulting from Different Interpretations of the Spoken Language, the Context in Which the Contract was Made, and Forms of Non-Verbal Communication

Rule 6: Those who interpret spoken language, factual context or non-verbal signs of communication differently than the average bystander (without clarifying how it should be interpreted), are to be held responsible for consequential misunderstandings.

Rule 7: If someone acts in representation of or on the account of another party, this should be made clearly explicit by him/her. If he does not do this, he will be personally bound by the agreement.

Rule 8: When agreements are not put to paper and when no other type of evidence is produced, both parties are responsible for eventual misunderstandings and no legally binding contract is created.

Misunderstandings Resulting from Errors in the Wording of the Contract

Rule 9: When misunderstandings result from substantive errors in the wording of the contract, the drafter is to be held liable for relatively small errors and the reader for relatively large mistakes.

Misunderstandings Resulting from a Party Failing to React, or Late Reaction to Written Proposals to Amend or Clarify the Contract (Including Standard Terms and Conditions Made on Subsequent Invoices)

Rule 10: Forwarded/mailed contractual clauses on invoices should be read by the other party and when these conditions are not acceptable to this party, then he should communicate his disapproval. If he does not do so, he is responsible for eventual misunderstandings concerning the applicable clauses.

Rule 11: When a party has the intention to continue contractual collaboration but fails to communicate this intention or neglects to reply to correspondence on the subject, so that the other party has reasons to doubt such intentions, he will be held liable for ensuing misunderstandings.

Rule 12: When a representative or confidential agent in correspondence incorrectly specifies the intentions of the represented party, then the latter needs to correct this. If he omits to do so, the represented party will be held liable for the eventual misunderstanding.

Misunderstandings Resulting from a Failure to React to Proposals to Amend a Contract Issued Through Non-Verbal Communication

Rule 13: When one of the parties to a contract continues his deliveries (which benefit the other party) beyond the agreed period, although the other party does not desire continuance, it is up to the latter party to express this desire.

Rule 14: When a promisor performs the contract in substantial manner but differently than agreed upon, the creditor needs to take steps to voice his disagreement.

Rule 15: When a promisee consciously continues a contract, although he had the opportunity to terminate it because of non-performance by the debtor, then the debtor may assume that the creditor doesn't want to end the contract. It is up to the creditor to communicate his intention in an unambiguous manner.

Rule 16: When the creditor does not react immediately when the debtor does not perform on time, the debtor should not assume that the creditor wanted to give a period of grace with respect to time. The debtor should request for clarification.

Misunderstandings Resulting from Delays Incurred in Taking Court Action

Rule 17. When a debtor presumes that a delay is due to the creditor's desire to waive his right of recourse, while no other facts support this thesis, the debtor must in any event explicitly verify whether the creditor has such intentions.

Rule 18. A creditor who defers to follow suit and provides the creditor with additional indications that create confusion as to his true intentions, is to be held responsible for the misunderstanding.

What is the role of economics in this doctrine? The 18 rules as such contain no more economics than any other rule. But they are the result of an economic starting point: the idea that the number of misunderstandings can be reduced by holding responsible the least cost avoider of the misunderstanding. Because the doctrine focuses on the process of misunderstandings, a primary division is made in terms of the factual causes of misunderstandings. In contrast, traditional doctrinal analysis is primarily focused on the subject-matter of the misunderstandings (misunderstandings as to the subject-matter and nature of the contract, as to which clauses apply, as to the precise scope of a clause, as to the person seeking to contract; as to whether or not an offer had to be made, as to the period during which the offer is valid, . . .), which is less relevant.

The new, economically inspired doctrine is better from a pedagogical perspective as well. The central notion, 'misunderstanding' is something that everybody understands. The doctrine, its division and its 18 rules are much easier to explain to non-lawyers than the abstract traditional doctrines that it tries to replace.

METHODOLOGICAL AND NORMATIVE ISSUES

Criterions for a Good Legal Doctrine

A good legal doctrine is based on defined concepts, is as simple as possible, explains as much as possible as accurately as possible. These criterion do not differ from those criterion employed in scientific means in general.

The requirement of defined concepts is the major problem of 'reasonable person' doctrines. Legal concepts such as 'good faith' or 'fault' suffer from the same vagueness. But isn't the Learned Hand formula (which requires a comparison of prevention costs and expected accident costs) vague as well? The answer is no. Both concepts (prevention costs and accident costs) can be defined and specified. In some cases it may be difficult to compare both costs, since courts do not have exact figures on their magnitude (though the Learned Hand formula does not require exact figures, just information on what is the highest cost). Yet the fact that in some cases it is difficult to reach conclusions does not mean the doctrine is tautological. With the Learned Hand formula, courts at least know what interests they have to balance.

Describing What Rules Courts Apply Using Different Words Than Used by the Courts Themselves. Danger Hineininterpretierung

Legal scientists have no direct information on what went on in the mind of judges. They have to rely on the written reports. These decisions are written using the current terminology. For instance, it is very difficult to find the word 'misunderstanding' in Belgian cases (see De Geest & De Moor, 1999: 707). How can a scientist then conclude that Belgian courts sanction the least cost avoider of the misunderstanding?

This is a philosophical issue that applies to all branches of science. Biologists don't know what is in the mind of animals. They observe behavior and interpret it. If male sea lions fight with each other just before breeding time, biologists conclude that they fight for 'breeding rights'. Sea lions don't know the word 'breeding right'. They may even not realize why they are fighting. This does not make the biological theory unscientific.

Scientists have a right to describe behavior using other words than the study object uses himself. Words reflect insights, and quite often beings have less insight in their behavior than scientists.

Legal scholars may conclude that their newest doctrine is already applied by courts, even if courts are not aware of it. Courts balance advantages and disadvantages of rules, and may be less specialized than legal scientists in finding the optimal words for these advantages and disadvantages. Even if a court explicitly denounces a doctrine, legal scientists may conclude that this court still implicitly applies it. If someone declares not to smoke, but I see him smoking, I have a right to say that he smokes.

Traditional legal scholarship seems to be misled by too narrow a definition of *de lege lata* and *de lege ferenda*. The traditional viewpoint is that either you describe the existing law (de lege lata) or your make a proposal for a better law (de lege ferenda). Some lawyers erroneously believe that a proposal for a better doctrine is necessarily a statement *de lege ferenda*. A proposal for a better doctrine can also just be a proposal for a better description of current law, and is in that case to be considered as a statement *de lege lata*. Even if the supreme court would reject a doctrine in express words, this does not mean that this doctrine is wrong de lege lata. If some people would openly declare that they have no sexual needs, that would not prove that Freud is wrong either.

For the same reason, legal scholars should not attempt to act as if they have 'discovered' their new doctrine by a closer reading of some terms in the civil code. This would presume that the legislator knows the optimal doctrines and that to read the legislator's words meticulously enough would be sufficient to discover those doctrines. Using this kind of literal/narrow/'black letter' reading of the legislation is acting as if the legislator was a kind of God whose perfect wisdom can be discovered by reading the bible over and over again. Requiring that doctrines be attached to specific words in the law may lead to a suboptimal choice of doctrines. There is no Belgian law that speaks of 'misunderstandings'.

Reinterpreting cases is of course not without danger. It may lead to *hinein-interpretiering*: interpreting in the direction the researcher prefers. But this does not mean that the researcher can conclude whatever he wants: his interpretation should be plausible enough to convince the scientific community.

Building New Doctrines: Normative Philosophy or Value-Neutral Science?

Describing How the Law Influences the Law

As explained in the first section, doctrines can be judged from two viewpoints: the content and the form. As far as the content is concerned, you can either describe the existing legal rules or make a proposal for a better legal rule. The first activity is positive, the second normative. With respect to the form (the aspect we have focused on in this paper), the distinction is slightly more complex. Making new doctrines that attempt at describing existing legal rules, is a positive activity. You only improve the description of legal reality. Designing new doctrines that describe non-existing, ideal legal rules is a normative activity.[14]

A difficult point is that the description of the law influences the law. Legislators and courts read the analysis and apply the new doctrine. If the new doctrine was a new description of the reality, this implies that legislators and courts do the same afterwards, but using more precise terms themselves. Again this is not a change of the law as to its content. But in some cases the content may change as a consequence of the new (descriptive) doctrine. The reason is that better words lead to less errors. If the criterion the courts try to apply is the 'reasonable person', intuitively they will balance precaution costs and expected accident costs, but since this balancing takes place at a more unconscious level, errors will be made. If the European courts would openly switch to the Learned Hand rule, they would still do the same, but more consciously. There is a danger that some legal scholars would consider the errors that were made at the unconscious stage as falsifications of the better doctrine.

The fact that the scientific description of human behavior influences human behavior is a more general problem of science, and not only of social sciences. If I go to Ruanda to study gorillas in their natural environment, tney will probably notice me. The fact that there is a scientist in their territory may influence their behavior.

Are Economically Inspired Doctrines Always Superior

Economically inspired doctrines try to describe legal rules directly in terms of costs. Sometimes the concepts that are used are borrowed directly from economics: courts have to sanction the least cost avoider of misunderstandings, courts have to allow coerced transfers only if transaction costs impede contractual solutions, courts have to balance prevention costs and expected accident costs. In other doctrines the inspiration comes from economics. The rule that "in precontractual negotiations you should not mislead the other party as to his chances and the amount at stake" does not contain more economics than any other rule. But the inspiration came from economics: Wils' started from the idea that the fundamental problem is one of asymmetric information. The same applies to the 18 rules in the misunderstandings doctrine.

Economically inspired doctrines have more chances to be superior, for three major reasons. First, since legal doctrines ultimately serve at saving legal information costs, their merits should be weighed in terms of the saved legal information costs as well. Second, the psychology of creative thinking predicts that interdisciplinary scholars have the highest chance to come up with new legal doctrines. Third, and most importantly, what legislators and courts ultimately do is balance the advantages and disadvantages of rules. A theory that is focused on describing these advantages and disadvantages has a higher chance to provide a good description of the legal reality.

The Design of Optimal Legal Doctrines and the Comparative Law Research Programme

The ultimate purpose of comparative law is to find the best legal rules as to the content and as to the formulation. The way to reach that goal is by studying the technical differences between legal rules from different legal systems. This strategy seems to be based on the very optimistic viewpoint that the optimal doctrine must already exist in at least one state and that it is merely a matter of discovering which one. It is a similar optimism that permeates some alternative medical sciences: for all diseases there is a plant that can cure them, we only have to find that plant.

Though studying the technical differences is a source of inspiration, the activity of designing optimal doctrines requires a different methodology. This paper has argued that there is a need for a separate research programme within comparative law, and that this research programme will have some of its roots in law and economics scholarship.

NOTES

1. According to Posner, the consideration doctrine has an evidentiary function: courts presume that contracts that create unilateral obligations lack consent. In addition it serve to sanction opportunistic renegotiations.

2. Wils' doctrine had a third element: a duty to compensate the benefits of anticipatory performance, like in the American case *Hill v Waxberg* (236 F. 2nd 936, 9th Cir. 1956). Hill gave the impression to Waxberg that the latter would get the construction contract if Waxberg helped to get the project approved and financed. Waxberg spent a lot of time and money by attending meetings with architects, collecting information required by the Federal Housing Authority, etc. After the project had been approved, negotiations started but broke off. Waxberg successfully sued for compensation. De Geest (1994, 142–143) has argued that from a technical point of view it would be better to solve *Hill v Waxberg* by a doctrine on tacit acceptance.

3. Wils (1993) illustrated his rule with some American cases as well.

4. E.g. Vred. Menen, 27 June 1990, *T. Vred.*, 1992, 7.

5. Cass.fr. 7 March 1972, *Bull.Civ.*, 1972, IV, nr. 83.

6. Under American law, quasi contracts form just a subcategory of the law of restitution (for unjust enrichment). The term quasi contracts is generally reserved for money claims for the redress of unjust enrichment (excluding for instance remedies involving specific restitution).

7. Sometimes the fourth criterion is split into (d) there should be no legal ground and (e) there should be no other 'action' available to obtain compensation. See e.g. Kruithof et al., 1994, at p. 619.

8. These four sources of high transaction costs are distinguished by looking at situations from an ex post viewpoint. From an ex ante point of view, a contractual solution is impossible because of the high number of possible partners. More specifically, there are the following categories: (a) accidents (errors); (b) the performance of non-existing obligations, for instance arising from void contracts (errors); (c) emergency situations (bilateral monopoly, lack of time); (d) divided property (bilateral monopoly); (e) many creditors having the same bankrupt debtor (bilateral monopoly, or in a sense this is also a case of divided property, since all creditors are partial owners of the same assets); (f) neighbourhood (bilateral monopoly); (g) licences strongly needed by consumers or by other inventors (bilateral monopoly). See Bouckaert and De Geest (1995).

9. Strangely, Long (1984) presented his theory as an alternative to the law and economics approach. The difference according to Long would be that he used the Pareto criterion instead of the Kaldor-Hicks criterion.

10. Liège, 25 January 1991, *Rev. Rég. Dr.*, 1991, 421.

11. Rb. Gent 3 maart 1980, *Rechtskundig Weekblad*, 1984–1985, 626 (discussed by Kruithof et al., 1994, p. 478–479) in a paragraph entitled 'rechtsverwerking' (transformation of rights).

12. Cass. 20 February 1992, *Rev. Liège*, 1992, 530. Cass. 5 June 1992, *R. Cass.*, 1992, 212.

13. Storme, M. E., 1992, 'Repelsteeltje, de windmolen en de zwaanridder. Of: Het Hof van cassatie en de rechtsverwerking', note under Cass. 5 June 1992, *R. Cass.*, 1992, 212; Storme, M. E., 1990, *De invloed van de goede trouw op de kontraktuele schuldvorderingen*, Brussel, Story-Scientia.

14. Of course, modern economic analysis has developed strategies to turn a normative activity into a positive one. If you agree on a basic norm like efficiency, a statement on whether a legal rule serves that norm becomes an "is" statement. See De Geest (1994, ch. 19).

REFERENCES

Bouckaert, B., & De Geest, G. (1995). Private Takings, Private Taxes and Private Mandatory Services: The Economic Doctrine of Quasi Contracts. *International Review of Law & Economics, 15*, 463–487.

Bouckaert, B., & De Geest, G. (1998). Quasi Contracts. In: P. Newman (Ed.), *The New Palgrave Dictionary of Economics and the Law* Vol. 3 (pp. 199–203). London, Macmillan.

Calabresi, G. (1970). *The Costs of Accidents: A Legal and Economic Analysis*. New Haven, Yale University Press.

Calabresi, G., & Melamed, A. D. (1972). Property Rules, Liability Rules and Inalienability: One View of the Cathedral. *Harvard Law Review, 85*, 1089–1128.

Cooter, R. D., & Ulen, T. S. (1988). *Law and Economics*. Glenview (IL), Scott Foresman.

De Geest, G. (1994). *Economische analyse van het contracten- en quasi-contractenrecht: een onderzoek naar de wetenschappelijke waarde van de rechtseconomie*, Antwerpen, Maklu.

De Geest, G., & De Moor, B. (1999). Misverstanden tussen partijen over wat is afgesproken: aanzet tot een "least cost avoider" doctrine. *Tijdschrift voor Privaatrecht, 36*, 701–777.

De Page, H. (1967). *Traité, III*. Brussels, Bruylant.

Faure, M., & Van den Bergh, R. (1987–1988). Efficiënties van het foutcriterium in het Belgisch aansprakelijkheidsrecht. *Rechtskundig weekblad*, 1105–1119.

Gordon, J. D. III. (1991). Consideration and the Commercial-Gift Dichotomy. *Vanderbilt Law Review, 44*, 283–315.

Kruithof, R. (1991). La théorie de l'apparence dans une nouvelle phase (noot onder Cass 20 juni 1988), *R.C.J.B.*, 76–80.

Kruithof, R., Bocken, H., De Ly, F., & De Temmerman, B. (1994). Overzicht van rechtspraak (1981–1992) Verbintenissen. *Tijdschrift voor Privaatrecht, 31*, 171–721.

Lando, O., & Beale, H. (Eds) (1995). *The Principles of European Contract Law: Part I: Performance, Non-Performance and Remedies*. Dordrecht, Nijhoff.

Long, R. A., Jr. (1984). A theory of hypothetical contract. *Yale Law Journal, 94*, 415–434.

Mattei, U. A., Antoniolli, L., & Rossato, A. (2000). Comparative Law and Economics. In: B. Bouckaert & G. De Geest (Eds), *The Encyclopedia of Law and Economics Volume One: The History and Methodology of Law and Economics* (pp. 505–538). Cheltenham, Edward Elgar.

Paulus, C. (1970). *Zaakwaarneming*. Brussel, Larcier.

Posner, R. A. (1986). *Economic Analysis of Law (3rd ed.)*. Boston, Little Brown.

Van den Bergh, R. (1991). Wat is rechtseconomie. In: E. H. Hondius, J. J. Schippers & J. J. Siegers (Eds), *Rechtseconomie en recht* (pp. 9–49). Zwolle, Tjeenk Willink.

Van Gerven, W. (1973). *Algemeen Deel*. Antwerpen, Standaard.

Van Velthoven, B. C. J., & van Wijck, P. W. (Eds) (1997). *Recht en Efficiëntie*. Deventer, Kluwer.

Wils, W. P. J. (1993). Who Should Bear the Costs of Failed Negotiations? A Functional Inquiry into Precontractual Liability. *Journal des Economistes et des Etudes Humaines, 4*, 93–134.

NEW PROPERTY, NEW WEALTH

Arianna Pretto

INTRODUCTION: FINANCIAL INSTRUMENTS AS WEALTH

Nowadays wealth in our society is largely made up of financial instruments. Company securities in general and shares in particular have emerged in recent years as the most valuable items in people's portfolios. This calls for a revision of the way we conceive the law of property.

Under Italian law financial instruments in their early days were known to lawyers as 'moveable values' (*valori mobiliari*) (Rabitti, 1992: 107, 122–123). The phrase signified anything in which it was possible to invest on the financial market. This evidenced the connection between market and property. On the one hand, part of the reason why financial instruments are so valuable is because they are very easily tradable and their value is thereby accrued. On the other hand, investing means no more than learning to shape one's proprietary assets.

The market certainly influences the taxonomy and the language of property in that it modifies the way financial instruments are understood as property. The market suggests that financial instruments are property in the sense of wealth. This meaning is nearer the social or the layman's sensitivity than the legal one. Socially, it is apparent that financial portfolios are a primary source of wealth. Legally, one would be tempted to understand property in the sense of property rights. In reality, it might be incorrect to assume that rights *in rem*, strictly understood, may be asserted in financial instruments, in that many species of these 'moveable values' are bundles of rights *in personam*, the person of inherence varying considerably. Shares, for instance, consist in personal rights which are

---

Law and Economics in Civil Law Countries, Volume 6, pages 125–140.

ISBN: 0-7623-0712-9

asserted against the company issuing them.[1] Actual rights *in rem* in the company assets can be very rarely asserted and indeed only in some undesired contingencies such as bankruptcy.[2] In the case of shares, for instance, a shareholder will be able to raise a claim to a quota of the assets left after the liquidation of the company. However, leaving aside these marginal *in rem* implications, the market-shaped meaning of property is as 'wealth'. As such, securities can be alienated and purchased just as any other good or form of wealth.

The thesis of this paper is that nowadays the assumption that the key features of property law are those of real property is a distortion. Notwithstanding that the importance of moveable property has increased extraordinarily in the past two centuries, the law relating to things is still characterised by the presence of a number of institutions that were clearly thought out with reference to real property. Under French law, one instance of the tyranny of land in shaping the law of property may be seen in the *droit de suite*. Although its definition as the power to exercise one's real right over a thing in any circumstances, regardless of where the thing is located, is apparently neutral, its application to moveables turns out to be utterly marginal. In Carbonnier's words, 'en matière mobilière, le droit de suite est généralement paralysé par la maxime de l'article 2279 ['la possession vaut titre' ('in the matter of moveables, the rule in art. 2279 ['possession equals title'] generally paralyses the droit de suite') (Carbonnier, 2000: 71–72) It is argued that, at a time when the economic importance of financial instruments is unequalled, this 'land-centric' view of property law is no longer acceptable. The inherent value of these moveables challenges the postulate *res mobilis, res vilis*, calls for lawyers' attention and claims to play a substantial role in re-shaping the meaning of the word 'property' (Carbonnier, 2000: 88).

Financial instruments are personal property in England and moveable things on the continent. Concentrating on securities as wealth is the first step towards locating them within the context of property law and, *a priori*, private law. What may seem an unusual perspective may, in reality, lead to discover the economic content of the legislation that we purport to examine. Max Weber's study of the categories of legal thought contained the kernel of this thought. He declared that he was "especially interested in observing the extent and the nature of the rationality of the law and, quite particularly, of that branch of it which is relevant to economic life, viz., private law" (Rheinstein, 1954: 61). The link between private law and economics was thus implicitly stated.

In other sectors, such as enterprise, it seems more widely accepted that legal tools should serve market needs. Thus, it has recently been suggested that business organisations should be viewed as a product on offer to potential customers, i.e. the business community. The question has been asked whether such products of U.K. law as corporations are of a satisfactory standard to meet the needs of the market. The very emergence of business forms has been explained not only with reference to "deliberate facilitation by legislature", but also to "organic development through evolving business practice". This is tantamount to admitting that the market influences legislation (Milman, 1999: 2–6). However, whilst willing to accept that the market may influence corporate law or serve its needs, private lawyers are still reluctant to acknowledge that the evolution of the law of property may be itself market-shaped. It is certainly a form of path dependence that private lawyers should feel uncomfortable coupling the words 'market' and 'property law'. One reason for this embarrassment may be that what was traditionally considered as the only relevant form of property, namely real property, was never really sold on an open market. The sale of immoveables has been taking place entirely as a retail sale over the centuries, thus first originating and then perpetuating the schism between market and property. Whatever the reason, lawyers are clinging on to a traditional idea of property, within which things are fairly static and present themselves as the *substratum* in which rights *in rem* may be asserted.

This paper argues that this approach to property can no longer be justified in the light of economic reality and attempts to demonstrate that the understanding of the law of property as wealth is influenced by market considerations. Failure to accept this view would entail an unrealistic approach and serious deficiencies in the study of the modern law of property.

METHODOLOGICAL PREMISE

The tenor of this paper is rather legal than economic. A short premise is necessary by way of justification of its contents. It is no doubt in the spirit of this book to refute the argument "that the economist cannot possibly compete on the lawyer's turf because the economist lacks formal initiation into the mysteries of legal thinking" (Posner, 1990: 353). It has been condemned as "just another form of essentialism" to assume either that law is what is done by a person suitably qualified with a law degree and by no one else or that economics is what is done by a person holding a doctorate in economics and by no one else. What follows partakes of that kind of economics that is done in "a less fancy, less polished, less sophisticated, less rigorous, less mathematical" way, but which is nonetheless believed to be capable of enlarging the knowledge of law (Posner, 1990: 369).

One plausible way of approaching a legal topic with empirical economic tools may be to observe to what extent the vocabulary of economics is employed in discussing a legal matter. While we cannot demand that the articulation of legal rules, whether judicial or statutory, must contain such language, we can try and detect its presence as an indicator that the new property is market-shaped. The empirical remark that the terminology of economics is being used to describe new types of 'goods' and that forms of property which are frequently exchanged on the market draw the attention of the legislature is a step towards the convergence of the discipline of law and that of economics, and a necessary premise for interdisciplinary work, which is at the core of this book.

A comparative legal and economic approach has been regarded as almost consequential in this context, since economic transactions have traditionally been studied by economists in a supranational perspective. This is sufficient to detect a deficiency whenever the corresponding legal topic is studied only at a national level.[3] Inevitably, a municipal approach to law will constitute a limitation to a common research programme in law and economics. A comparative approach should work around the obstacle.(see Mattei & Pulitini, 1990).

Most of what follows is an empirical observation of some changes that are taking place in the law of securities and a reflection on the terminology that most suitably describes them. No attempt is made to engage in more 'technical' economic analysis. The law is stated as of the end of June 2000.

REGULATION AND *FINANCIAL INTERMEDIATION*: TWO FEATURES FOR THE NEW WEALTH

The new wealth has two main features. Firstly, it circulates in a very special way, in that the presence of the transferor and transferee is often complemented by a third subject, namely the intermediary. The case of shares illustrates this phenomenon well. Entry on the register of the issuer is the traditional way of acquiring shares and qualifies as what we may call 'direct holding' of investments. However, this system has gradually been replaced by an 'indirect holding' system through one or more custodians of securities, who function as intermediaries between the issuer and the investor-shareholder.

From a strictly technical point of view, two phenomena have accompanied the appearance of indirect holding on the securities market scenario, namely dematerialisation (Reed, 1991) and immobilisation. Pursuant to the former, paper as the tangible evidence of the transfer has disappeared taking individually issued certificates with it, replaced by the mere confirmation from the issuer's agent to the investor that securities of a stated type and amount have been issued to him and placed on an electronic record. According to the latter, tangible securities certificates are deposited with a custodian in a vault, in order to eliminate the need for physical movement of documents in transfers of ownership. The custodian terminates any direct relationship between issuer and investor, so that the investor's entitlement is thereafter against the custodian and no longer against the issuer. When the securities are held and traded internationally across several jurisdictions, the institutional structure of custodianship arrangements is referred to as 'global custody' (J. Benjamin, *The Law of Global Custody*, Butterworths, London, 1996, p. 1). In a global context the client, whether investor or issuer of shares, gives its instructions to a central custodian, who has them carried out through a network of sub-custodians or depositories located in the jurisdictions where the securities are traded (Beaves, 1998: 117–118). Two among the services provided by a global custodian are of particular interest for our analysis: the safe-keeping of securities and their so-called 'settlement', that is the activity of trading them by receiving them in and delivering them out. Custody and trading of securities are often among the services provided by modern intermediaries, who may avail themselves of computerised devices.

Taking a somewhat simplified view, intermediaries may be said to fulfil the role which was traditionally the broker's. They also supply additional services. One of these is to administer the technical information which accompanies the circulation of securities. This information can hardly be obtained and administered by a single investor and it is only thanks to the intervention of an intermediary that this wealth will appear to its purchasers to be easily tradable. We will refer to this phenomenon as 'financial intermediation'.

The second main feature of the new wealth is that it is regulated in great detail. It will be noted that self-regulation, rather than an externally imposed set of provisions, has always been the rule on the stock exchange. It has sometimes been the case that self-regulatory codes can receive the *imprimatur* of legislative recognition. Notwithstanding that transactions on the stock exchange were originally left to self-regulation, awareness of the economic importance of such transactions, among other things, has led the legislature to produce penetrating forms of regulation.

Regulation and intermediation seem to be strictly linked in that the presence of intermediaries is currently the aspect of the market where the need for regulation seems to be most intensely felt. The modern tendency towards regulation can be found in both English and Italian law,[4] although under English law it is not clear how external regulation may combine with the unwritten rules of equity which have traditionally governed fiduciary relationships (Harpum 1997: 150, 168). This is a slippery ground and a potential source of conflict.

Let us first briefly examine the English *Financial Services and Markets Bill,* which, as of June 2000, has received the Royal Assent and should soon become the law in England. It will re-organise regulation in the financial sector.[5]

Regulatory functions are going to be attributed to the *Financial Services Authority* and statutory regulation is soon going to replace self-regulation. Various areas of financial business, such as banking, insurance and investment business, are going to be covered.[6]

Only a limited range of authorised subjects will be able to carry on the investment business. They will need to obtain an authorisation to do so.[7] The legislature is therefore imposing full control on intermediaries (MacNeil, 1999: 725–731). The expertise of the Financial Services Authority will be present in the new legislation to such an extent that worries have been expressed as to the lack of a competitive environment for the creation of rules, which could inhibit innovation in legislative techniques (Lomnicka, 1999: 480, 488–489).

Along the same lines, two years ago Italian law passed the fundamental statute on financial intermediation *(Testo Unico delle disposizioni in materia di intermediazione finanziaria).* Secondary legislation has followed to enact it.[8]

One crucial point about regulation is where to set the balance which makes regulation itself economically efficient. Both the Italian and English legislature have chosen to vest regulatory functions in the financial sector in one authority (in the former case the Commission for the Stock Exchange (Consob), in the latter case the Financial Services Authority), flanked by one or more supervising authorities (in the former case the Central Bank (Banca d'Italia), in the latter the Bank of England jointly with the Treasury). While it can be assumed that concentrating legislative power in one subject can cut the costs of legislation, this interplay of supervision may lend itself, at least in the Italian case, to a confusing proliferation of secondary legislation. The number of Consob decisions meant for the enactment of the statute on financial intermediation (four as of April 2000) is likely to increase, thus often requiring the expertise of professionals for interpretation.

Another difficulty concerns the need to award to a party the sufficient degree of protection, while at the same time avoiding excessive burdens for the other involved parties. The degree to which market institutions should be regulated is a sophisticated issue, which can lead to regulatory regimes differing widely in scope: possible aims may include equity between market participants and the regulation of the conduct of a business medium in order to control its effect on the competitors.[9] The Italian legislature has sought to achieve these aims by imposing a 'bilateral' duty of information: on the one hand, the intermediary must keep the client informed at any time; on the other hand, he must acquire from the investor all the information which will allow the intermediary to look after the client's interests properly. It is therefore implied that the investor must be ready to supply such information. A parallel duty of transparency seems to exist upon the intermediary towards the authorities in charge of maintaining order on the market. It is a reassuring thought that, at least in theory, transparency is proposed as the default status. This should prove an efficient solution, for in its absence the parties would be left to face considerable transaction costs in order to acquire autonomously all the information that the legislature imposes as a direct consequence of the transparency requirement.[10] Furthermore, the trade-off between efficiency and equity seems to fade, since protection of the weak party (generally the small investor and worse cost-avoider) is achieved at a relatively low cost. On a more general level, it is hardly an exaggeration to state that the costs involved by the status quo prior to legislation are often mainly information costs (Mattei, 1997b: 537–540).

From the perspective of property as a category, the definition of whose brand new boundaries claims to be the *leitmotiv* of this paper, the interference of externally imposed regulation with the contractual agreement between intermediary and investor shows that the distinction between private and public law is inadequate as far as the new wealth is concerned. Trying to locate the new property within this traditional partition of law makes as little sense as asking whether financial intermediation is a creation of contract or statute, while it is both.

ANCIENT BREACHES AND MODERN LEGISLATION

A justification of the need for penetrating forms of legislation concerning financial intermediaries comes from English case law, which offers countless instances of what happens when the patrimonial solidity of an intermediary fades away and suggests the necessity for a clear definition of patrimonial requirements.

The consequences that the poor clients of an insolvent broker may face in terms of the recovery of the funds and securities that they had placed in his custody have been known for centuries and are well illustrated in *Taylor v Plumer.*[11] In this case the court had to resort to the relationship between principal and factor[12] to establish that goods held on trust for the original owner, which are in the possession of a factor authorised to dispose of them, will not pass to his assignees in bankruptcy. Not only will the principal be able to recover the misappropriated goods, but also to trace[13] into the proceeds of their sale.[14] The role of modern collective intermediaries cannot be too different from the traditional role of individual ones as regards the need for the investor's protection.

There is a lot more to the link between property and intermediation than the mere mechanism of trading. The *quid pluris* is the fiduciary aspect. When a third party who is supposed to act as an intermediary violates his fiduciary duty the investor is in need of protection, particularly in the event of the intermediary's insolvency. Italian law seeks to protect the investor through art 22 TUF, which contains the principle of double patrimonial separation between the clients' and the intermediary's assets and among the individual clients' own accounts. This principle stretches to cover the event of insolvency.[15] The link between property and *fiducia* is very intense.[16] A fiduciary situation is often born from the entrustment of property to a subject. Custody of financial instruments is an example of this.

Breaches of *fiducia* are just an example of all breaches taking place on the market. Eight decades ago Max Weber was too optimistic in stating that:

> Market behavior is influenced by rational, purposeful pursuit of interests. The partner to a transaction is expected to behave according to rational legality and, quite particularly, to respect the formal inviolability of a promise given. These are the qualities which form the content of market ethics. In this latter respect the market inculcates, indeed, particularly rigorous conceptions. Violations of agreements, even though they may be concluded by mere signs, entirely unrecorded, and devoid of evidence, are almost unheard of in the annals of the stock exchange.[17]

Antoine Loysel in the coûtume de Cambrai was probably more realistic when remarking that 'de tous marchés, on en vuide par intérêt'.[18] The Italian legislature was clearly aware that the same 'interest' governs the infringement of market duties. Awareness that the market ethics are far from idyllic led to the statute on financial intermediation, which chooses to describe the actors of the market in great detail.

THE IDENTITY OF FINANCIAL INTERMEDIARIES

Nowadays it seems inevitable that, in order to become owners of securities *iure proprio*, it is necessary to possess them *iure alieno*, namely through an intermediary. The numerous pathologies affecting market transactions have pushed the legislature to specify in detail the identity of those who may offer services of administration of individual investment portfolios on behalf of a third party *(gestione su base individuale di portafogli di investimento per conto terzi)*. Financial activities are now precluded to individual brokers. Evidently, these are not deemed to be financially sound and are in every respect less solid (Gaggero, 1997: 579, 590) than a corporate intermediary. Decisions delivered five years ago, concerning the liability of *remisiers* and stockbrokers for economic loss due to their inept performance in executing a mandate, appear old-fashioned.[19]

Professional investment services are restricted to banks and investment firms (i.e. the so-called SIM and EU and non-EU investment firms) (art. 18 TUF). Derivatives trading (art. 1 co. 2 f-j: futures, swaps and other contracts) can be carried out, in their own name, by other subjects inscribed in a special list according to banking law provisions (art. 107 T. U. bancario). Further provisions apply to accessory services. Corporations which primarily run collective investment schemes (*società di gestione del risparmio*) can occasionally administer individual portfolios on behalf of third parties. Hence, the broker gradually turns into a dealer who provides multiple services.[20]

Authorisation (art. 19) is not issued by Consob, in agreement with Banca d'Italia, unless the corporate model is adopted. Competence and honoured behaviour are required from the members of the corporation (art. 19 co. 1 letters *f* and *g*). An appropriately prudent dealing (co. 2) must be guaranteed. The conduct of newly created intermediaries must be 'diligent, transparent and correct' (art. 21 TUF). The *ratio* of this provision aims expressly at protecting the clients' interests and the integrity of the markets (*interesse dei clienti e integrità dei mercati*, letter *a*). Information must be acquired by intermediaries from clients and clients must be kept informed about any initiative undertaken (letter *b*). Efficient performance of the services (*c*) and fitness and competence in providing the service are vital. Is Weber's ethics back?

As is well-known, the basic assumption of Economic Analysis of Law is that all people are rational maximisers of their satisfactions in all of their activities which involve choice (Posner, 1990: 353; Rudden, 1985: 93), but the legislature is diffident about the investor's talents: regulation goes so far as to control the potential owner's idiosyncrasies. This owner will often be advised as to the fashion in which to shape his portfolio; his investment choice will not be completely free. The new wealth can be traded at the touch of a keypad but it is far from liberalised. The Italian owner's judgement is complemented by that of the Treasury, the Bank of Italy and the Consob, with whom the regulatory functions are vested and who approve or disapprove of the subjects to whom the wealth is to be entrusted.[21]

In particular, the requirement of transparency, which obliges the intermediary to account for his *gestio* to both the Consob and the client, necessarily complements the high degree of technicality of the new wealth. Is transparency the new market ethics? At the very least, it remedies the information asymmetry which plagues small investors in the evaluation of the quality of financial services. Put another way, securities, as a highly technical form of wealth, make recourse to a competent intermediary almost compelling for the client. Transparency puts a reassuring seal to this relationship.

The client's market choice has been made for him at least as regards the subjects who will deal with his wealth, although he will be able to communicate his desires to the intermediary as to what he would like to see included in his portfolio. Financial instruments have been called 'problematic goods' (Pauletto,

1996: 54) in that their administration implies a double flow of information from client to intermediary, as well as vice-versa. Thus, the intermediary must conform to the degree of risk that the client intends to bear and avoid stepping beyond that level. In this respect, the idiosyncratic preferences that are the main feature of property are respected.[22]

DISINTERMEDIATION AND ECONOMIC AWARENESS

We have so far shown that the recently drafted provisions reflect the economic reality according to which the new wealth seems to need intermediaries to be exchanged. However, most recently, the very same market environment seems to have generated one situation that the law as yet is unable to encompass. We are talking about electronic trading of securities via the Internet. The law on this subject exists in terms of legal scholarship only. Specialised journals, having begun to realise the speed of these property transactions, are not really capable of monitoring their legal profiles. Sometimes regulation is invoked, at other times its failure is foreseen (Tunkel, 1999: 133).

What is sure is that Internet-based mechanisms known as bulletin boards and crossing systems represent a counter-tendency in that they seem to favour disintermediation: supply and demand of securities meet on a website and direct access to commerce is fostered (Cohen, 1999: 299–303). The next challenge for the law will be to answer the question of where intermediaries have gone in such a case. Computerisation exacerbates the difficulties of legal analysis and increases risks of economic loss for investors, who are often far from experts in market transactions.

On the occasion of the Consob Annual Meeting with the Financial Market (10 April 2000), the Consob Chairman Spaventa[23] has stressed the importance of spreading 'financial knowledge and financial culture.' Investors should not rely on legislation for their protection. They should instead achieve their own autonomous understanding of market mechanisms. This understanding is as important as the constant vigilance exercised by Consob. The new wealth needs economically aware investors. It is only on this premise that the ideally greater efficiency fostered by disintermediation can be fully appreciated.

MARKET-SHAPED TERMINOLOGY FOR THE NEW WEALTH

Where the influence of economic considerations on the law becomes apparent is in the use of terminology. One of the most apparent cases of 'market-influenced' legal institutions is the set of rules designed to apply to new market mechanisms for the trading of shares. The language employed in the description of those devices bears strong reminiscences of the terminology of law and economics. One example will suffice.

The access to German capital markets for companies and investors is provided by the Deutsche Börse Group, which is a fully electronic market offering a wide spectrum of services ranging from securities and derivatives trading to clearing. This market is based on an electronic trading platform. Buying and selling orders placed by traders anywhere world-wide are inputted into the order book on the central computer and matched. Transactions are then carried out automatically. Last year a new European clearing house, called Clearstream, originated from the merger between Deutsche Börse Clearing AG, which specialised in securities clearing and settlement, and the international settlement system Cedel International, based in Luxembourg, whose area of expertise was international bond clearing and settlement. Clearstream is endowed with a real-time settlement system and settles all transactions carried out through the electronic platform. Clearstream works as a central depository and custodian for internationally traded securities. The securities forming the clients' portfolio holdings are stored and share certificates are immobilised. Through the central custody facility a large amount of certificates may be transferred by simple book-entry whenever it is required, thus eliminating the need to move paper around. The central custodian holds nearly all securities admitted to official listing on the stock exchange.

The above-mentioned information can be obtained by accessing the website of the Deutsche Börse Group (http://deutsche-boerse.com), whose objective is to become the pre-eminent exchange organisation and to provide access to the most attractive securities and derivatives markets. An ambitious statement of intents welcomes us: 'Our mission is to improve the efficiency of capital markets'. There follows a list of the range of services provided by this fully integrated exchange organisation world-wide, such as trading, clearing, settlement, custody, information and infrastructure services. Emphasis is placed on the low costs that the organisation hopes to achieve, so that both intermediaries, vendors, investors and issuers world-wide would be encouraged to avail themselves of these services.

It is interesting that among the intents of this kind of institutions, which clearly aim at more efficient forms of trade, is to 'initiate and support improvements of the regulatory framework'. It is likely that such regulation will serve market needs or be shaped accordingly.

The terminology of economic analysis of law also crops up in the promise of cost savings for market participants. The so-called mechanism of 'single access' considerably reduces the complexity of trading operations in that it enables customers to pool liquidity, after which all clearing and settlement procedures required in national and international cash market trading can be easily carried out. Fast and cost-effective settlement of exchange-based transactions, securities administration and safe custody are all provided within the same framework. Enhanced efficiency and tangible cost advantages for customers are the economic goals that the system pursues.

CONCLUSION

The features of financial instruments understood as the new store of wealth are strongly dependent on market mechanisms for the trading of these moveables. On the one hand, the high degree of technicality of this new form of property and its extraordinary propensity for circulation explain the need for intermediation in its acquisition and holding (Rudden, 1997: 148). On the other hand, its considerable value and the possibility of great economic loss associated with it justify the massive presence of legislation surrounding it. We have tried to stretch the language of property to encompass this new wealth, which has been perceived as such on the market before being known at law as the subject-matter in which rights can exist.

Any legal system that purports to call itself realistic must acknowledge that securities are primarily wealth and shape its categories according to this perception. The rubric that best lends itself to express this idea is that of property. Hence the taxonomy of property must be able to govern the commercialisation of private law if it wishes to remain dominant. It has been predicted that failure on the part of property law to achieve this goal would lead to rather drastic consequences (Mattei, 1997a): sooner or later the category would suffer from terrible weakness and loss of importance and possibly be doomed to disappear. Hence property law must learn to accept the suggestions coming from the market as to which forms of wealth are worthy of legal attention.

Shortly after the beginning of last century Max Weber illustrated the relation between legal and economic order as follows:

> The empirical validity of a norm as a legal norm affects the interests of an individual in many respects. In particular, it may convey to an individual certain calculable chances of having economic goods available or of acquiring them under certain conditions in the future.[24]

The newly created rules on financial intermediation help investors to assess their chances of obtaining the securities they wish to purchase and draw a picture of the conditions under which such wealth can be acquired. In conclusion, company securities are asking from law the same degree of attention that they have managed to attract from economics. Failure to relate the law of property to new valuable items of wealth entails a loss of importance for this branch of law and an intolerable abstraction from economic reality. Nowadays company securities, and shares among them, certainly qualify as the primary store of wealth. New legal institutions for their trade, such as financial intermediation, may be tackled with the new language of property and must be so dealt with in order to avoid the sclerosis of the traditional taxonomy. Although Portalis condemned the commercialisation of the law and regretted that 'il est des contrées où les idées de la saine morale ont été (. . .) obscurcies et étouffées par un vil esprit de commerce' ('the vulgar spirit of commerce has obscured and suffocated the principles of healthy morals') (Fenet, 1830: 119), we hope to have shown that legal ideas can no longer refuse to face this 'vil esprit'.

NOTES

1. Among which the right to vote in the general meeting, the right to dividends and to return of capital in the event of winding up (Davies, 1997: 300–301).
2. Cf. R. Grantham, *The Doctrinal Basis of the Rights of Company Shareholders,* in 57 "Cambridge Law Journal", 1998, p. 554, pp. 582–583.
3. Cf U. Mattei, 'Economic Analysis and European Legal Scholarship', in *Dealing with Integration. Perspectives from Seminars on European Law*, Iustus Forlag, Uppsala, 1995–6, p. 53, pp. 63–67.
4. The desirability of an expansion of the concepts of control and guidance is debated in G. P. Gilligan, *Regulating the Financial Services Sector*, Kluwer Law International, The Hague-London, 1999.
5. *Financial Services and Markets Bill (FSMB).* The latest version as approved by the House of Lords on 9 May 2000 can be viewed at http://www.parliament.the-stationery-office.co.uk/, though the final text of the statute may actually differ.
6. Clauses 1–16 (regulator), Clauses 17–28 (regulated and prohibited activities).
7. Clauses 29–37.
8. D. Lgs. 24 febbraio 1998 n. 58, hereinafter 'TUF'. The provisions are explained in detail in C. Rabitti Bedogni (Ed.), *Il Testo Unico della Intermediazione Finanziaria. Commentario,* Giuffrè, Milano, 1998; G. Alpa and F. Capriglione (Eds), *Commentario al Testo Unico delle disposizioni in materia di intermediazione finanziaria*, Cedam, Padova, 1998. Statutory instruments for the enactment of such legislation include the *Regolamento di attuazione*, as approved and amended by Consob (delibera n. 11522, 1 luglio 1998; delibere n. 11745, 9 dicembre 1998; n. 12409, 1° marzo 2000; n. 12498, 20 aprile 2000).
9. Prior to the enactment of the Financial Services Act 1986 the White Paper, *Financial Services in the United Kingdom: A New Framework for Investor Protection* (Cmnd, 9432 (1985), para 5.2, explained the preference for self-regulation (i.e. regulation by one's peers) within a statutory framework, as opposed to governmental regulation, as offering 'the best possibility of linking adequate investor protection with a competitive and innovative market'. (See Page 1987: 306).
10. Art. 21, co. 1, lett. a) e b) TUF.
11. (1815) 3 M&S. 562, 105 ER 721, 2 Rose 457, [1814–23] All England Reports 167 (K.B.), discussed in L. D.Smith, *The Stockbroker and the Solicitor-General: The Story behind* Taylor v. Plumer, in 15 "The Journal of Legal History", 1994, pp. 1–22..

12. The profiles of agency of this case are analysed in Graziadei 1995: 123–134.

13. L. D.Smith, *Tracing in* Taylor v. Plumer. *Equity in the Court of King's Bench,* in "Lloyd's Maritime & Commercial Law Quarterly", 1995, pp. 240–68; L. D.Smith, *The Law of Tracing,* Clarendon Press, Oxford, 1997, pp. 67–71; S. Evans, *Rethinking Tracing and the Law of Restitution,* in 115 "The Law Quarterly Review", 1999, pp. 469–470.

14. Cfr. *L'Apostre v. Le Plaistrier* 2 Equity Cases Abridged 113n, 22 ER 96; *Copeman v. Gallant* 1 PWms 314, 24 ER 404; *Whitecomb v. Jacob* 1 Salkeld 160, 91 Er 149; *Ryall v. Rolle* 1 Atk 165, 26 ER 107.

15. Art. 57, co. 4 (more in general, artt. 56–60). Cf also art. 91, co. 2 e 3 T. U. bancario (liquidazione coatta amministrativa) and art. 21, co. 1, lett l) L. 52/96, providing for enactment of directive 93/22 CE. See G. Gugliotta, commento all'art. 21 co. 2 TUF, in C. Rabitti Bedogni, cit. *supra* n. 22.

16. So intense that property has been defined as a meta-language that the courts employ in order to identify a fiduciary situation (see Glover, 1997: .272–273).

17. M. Rheinstein, *Max Weber on Law in Economy and Society,* Harvard University Press, Cambridge, Massachussets, 1954, pp. 193–194.

18. M. Dupin and E. Laboulaye, *Institutions coutumières d'Antoine Loysel,* Paris, 1846, p. 414, cited in B. Rudden and P. Juilhard, *La théorie de la violation efficace,* in 38 "Revue Internationale de Droit Comparé", 1986, pp. 1015–41, p. 1041.

19. Trib. Milano 9 ottobre 1995, in "Banca, Borsa e Titoli di Credito", 1996, p. 563. Also, F. Bochicchio, *Gestione impropria da parte dei promotori finanziari: la regolamentazione delle attività di investimento tra valutazioni di merito e lo statuto degli operatori economici professionali,* in 26 "Giurisprudenza Commerciale", 1999, I, p. 336.

20. P. Iemma, commento agli artt. 18–20 TUF, in C. Rabitti Bedogni, 1998, p. 162.

21. D. M. 2 aprile 1999 'Determinazione, ai sensi dell'art. 106, comma 4, lettera b), del D. Lgs. 1 settembre 1993, n. 385, dei requisiti patrimoniali relativi agli intermediari che svolgono in via esclusiva o prevalente attività di rilascio di garanzie nonché a quelli che operano quali intermediari in cambi senza assunzione di rischi in proprio *(money brokers)'.*

22. Art. 28 commi 2–3 Regolamento di Attuazione (enactment rules of TUF), as modified by Delibera Consob n. 12409/2000. Paragraph 2 provides that intermediaries cannot perform any operation or offer advice or any services of *gestio* without first informing the investor about the nature, risks and implications of these operations, the knowledge of which is essential for the client to make his own investment choices.

23. Consob website, http://www.consob.it/; President Spaventa's original words were as follows: 'La tutela degli investitori dipende [anche] dalla loro capacita' di comprendere autonomamente i meccanismi di funzionamento del mercato [. . .]. Rientra tra i compiti non scritti di un'autorita' come la Consob diffondere cultura finanziaria tra il pubblico, che vuol dire prima di tutto conoscenza degli strumenti e delle regole'.

24. M. Weber, in Rheinstein, 1954, p. 15.

REFERENCES

Alpa G., & Capriglione, F. (Eds) (1998). *Commentario al Testo Unico delle disposizioni in materia di intermediazione finanziaria.* Padova: Cedam.

Beaves, A. W. Global Custody- A Tentative Analysis of Property and Contract. In: Palmer & McKendrick (Eds), *Interests in Goods* (2nd ed.). London.

Bochicchio, F. (1999). Gestione impropria da parte dei promotori finanziari: la regolamentazione delle attività di investimento tra valutazioni di merito e lo statuto degli operatori economici professionali. In: *Giurisprudenza Commerciale, 26,* 1999, I, 336.

Carbonnier, J. (2000). *Droit civil, Tome 3 – Les biens* (19th ed.). Paris: Presses Universitaires de France.

Cohen, P. D. (1999). Securities Trading Via the Internet. In: *Journal of Business Law.*

Davies, P. L. (Ed.) (1997). *Gower's Principles of Company Law* (6th ed.). London.

Evans, S. (1999). Rethinking Tracing and the Law of Restitution. In: *The Law Quarterly Review, 115,* 469–470.

Fenet, P. A. (1830). *Recueil complet des travaux préparatoires du Code civil,* t. 14.

Gaggero, P. (1997). Esclusività ed estensione dell'oggetto sociale delle imprese di investimento. In: *Contratto e impresa/Europa, 2.*

Gilligan, G. P. (1999). *Regulating the Financial Services Sector.* The Hague-London: Kluwer Law International.

Glover, J. (1997). The Identification of Fiduciaries. In: P. Birks (Ed.), *Privacy and Loyalty.* Oxford: Clarendon Press.

Grantham, R. (1998). The Doctrinal Basis of the Rights of Company Shareholders, *Cambridge Law Journal, 57.*

Graziadei, M. (1995). *Diritti nell'interesse altrui: undisclosed agency e trust nell'esperienza giuridica inglese.* Università degli Studi di Trento.

Harpum, C. (1997). Fiduciary Obligations and Fiduciary Powers-Where Are We Going? In: P. Birks, *Privacy and Loyalty.* Oxford: Clarendon Press.

Lomnicka, E. (1999). Financial Services. In: *The Journal of Business Law.*

MacNeil, I. (1999). The Future for Financial Regulation: The Financial Services and Markets Bill. In: *The Modern Law Review, 62,* 725–731.

Mattei, U. (1995). Economic Analysis and European Scholarship. In: *Dealing with Integration. Perspectives from Seminars on European Law* (pp. 63–67). Uppsala: Iustus Forlag, 1995–1996.

Mattei, U. (1997a). Qualche riflessione su struttura proprietaria e mercato. In: *Riv. Crit. Dir. Priv., 15,* pp. 19 ss.

Mattei, U. (1997b). A Transaction Costs Approach to the European Code, *European Review of private Law, 5.*

Mattei, U., & Pulitini, F. (1990). Modelli competitivi, regole giuridiche ed analisi economica. In: *Quadrimestre.*

Milman, D. (1999). Regulation of Business Organisations: Into the Millennium. In: D. Milman (Ed.), *Regulating Enterprise: Law and Business Organisations in the U.K.* Oxford: Hart.

Page, A. C. (1987). Financial Services: the Self-Regulatory Alternative? In: R. Baldwin & C. McCruden (Eds), *Regulation and Public Law.* London: Weidenfeld and Nicholson.

Pauletto, L. (1996). *Società fiduciarie e servizi d'investimento* (2a ed.). Aggiornata, Torino: Giappichelli.

Posner, R. (1990). The Economic Approach to Law. In: *The Problems of Jurisprudence.* Harvard University Press.

Rabitti Bedgoni, C. (Ed.) (1998). *Il Testo Unico della Intermediazione Finanziaria. Commentario.* Milano: Giuffrè.

Rabitti, G. L. (1992). Valore mobiliare ed investment contract. In: *Contratto e impresa, 8,* 122–123.

Reed, C. (1991). *Electronic Finance Law.* Cambridge: Woodhead-Faulner, 111–128.

Rheinstein, M. (1954). *Max Weber on Law in Economy and Society*. Cambridge (Mass.): Harvard University Press.

Rudden B., & Juilhard, P. (1986). La théorie de la violation efficace. In: *Revue Internationale de Droit Comparé*, *38*, pp. 1015–1041.

Rudden, B. (1985). Le juste et l'inefficace pour un non-devoir de renseignements. In: *Revue Trimestrielle de Droit Civil*, pp. 91–103.

Rudden, B. (1997). Things as Thing and Things as Wealth, In: J. H. Harris, *Property Problems. From Genes to Pension Funds*. London: Kluwer Law International.

Smith, L. D. (1994). The Stockbroker and the Solicitor-General: The Story behind Taylor v. Plumer. In: *The Journal of Legal History*, *15*, 1994, 1–22.

Smith, L. D. (1997). *The Law of Tracing*. Oxford: Clarendon Press.

Tunkel, D. (1999). Regulating Sinancial Services on the Internet: What Will the Financial Services and Markets Bill achieve? In: *Butterworths Journal of International Banking and Finance Law*, *14*.

REGULATION: THE PUBLIC INTEREST AND THE PRIVATE INTEREST

Anthony Ogus

INTRODUCTION

The word "regulation" has no exact legal or economic connotations, but I take it here to refer to that area of public law which implements collectivist goals, that is, by which the state seeks to direct or encourage behaviour which (it is assumed) would not occur without such intervention. The aim is to correct perceived deficiencies in the market system (and private law) in meeting public interest goals.

So characterised, regulation covers a huge variety of industrial and non-industrial activities and involves a number of different legal forms. There is nevertheless a useful, if also imperfect, distinction between social regulation and economic regulation. Social regulation, which includes such matters as health and safety, environmental protection and consumer protection, tends to deal with two types of market failure: information asymmetries or deficiencies; and externalities. Economic regulation imposes controls on suppliers in industries with monopolistic tendencies.

Outside France, there has been a significant growth of work by lawyers, economists, political scientists and those straddling these disciplines to analyse

Author's note: This is a much shortened version of a paper originally presented in French at the Nancy workshop. The paper was specifically targeted at a French audience and a full version in English for the present collection does not seem justified.

Law and Economics in Civil Law Countries, Volume 6, pages 141–145.

ISBN: 0-7623-0712-9

and evaluate this form of control. In France, there have been excellent, specialist monographs on (say) public economy law, and the law of the environment, but little which has generalised from them. As a foreigner, I seek in this paper to suggest how fruitful analysis can be undertaken, particularly within a law-and-economics framework.

ECONOMIC THEORIES OF REGULATION

To justify regulatory intervention we should first refer to an area of neo-classical economic analysis often referred to as "public interest theory".

Public Interest Theory

Assuming that the legislator is motivated by social welfare considerations, economic analysis provides us with typical reasons why there should be regulation; and the same analysis can subsequently be used to determine whether a given regulation corrects the failing at least cost.

- **Externalities:** the activity imposes costs on third parties – the price therefore does not correspond to its real social cost.
- **Insufficient information:** a purchaser does not have information sufficient to know whether what is offered meets his preferences

Note that non-economic justifications may also exist. These include

- **Paternalism:** contrary to traditional economic assumptions, the legislature does not consider that the individual is the best judge of his or her own welfare.
- **Distributional justice:** to achieve a "fairer" distribution of resources, the intention is to make transfers from one group in society to another.

Private Interest Theory

This theory seeks to explain how politicians and bureaucrats may be motivated to meet the demands of private interest groups for regulation of a particular form. It stems from a hypothesis that those who make decisions about legislation are no different from other utility-maximising individuals. In the "market for legislation" politicians offer "regulatory benefits" according to the demand for them, the price being electoral support.

FORMS OF REGULATORY INTERVENTION

To illustrate the application of the theories in the selection and critical evaluation of different regulatory forms, I take a situation, such as environmental pollution or the manufacture of dangerous products which, on grounds of externalities or information asymmetry, might justify social regulation.

- **Prohibition** The first regulatory option is simply to ban the polluting activity or dangerous product. Where the social costs of the activity or product exceed its benefits, this may be appropriate, but there will often be cheaper ways of reducing the externality. Private interest theory may explain a prohibition unjustified on public interest grounds: take the case of the prohibition of import of English beef, from which French farmers much benefit.
- **Ex ante approval** To protect consumers, legislation may require that firms, before lawfully engaging in an activity or supplying a product or service, must first obtain a licence from an authorising agency; and for such approval they have to satisfy the agency that certain conditions of quality are, or are capable of being, met. The administrative costs of scrutinising all applications is very high and to these must be added the opportunity costs arising from any delay before the licence is granted. Moreover, significant welfare losses arise if the system is used for the anti-competitive purpose of creating barriers to entry. The benefit from prior scrutiny must therefore be very large to justify, on public interest grounds, these substantial costs. Private interest analysis provides a persuasive explanation of the fact that in many countries prior approval systems are used in situations for which they cannot be justified on public interest grounds. The conditions which applicants must satisfy to obtain a licence raise the costs of entry to the market and licensed suppliers are often able to earn substantial rents.
- **Standards Regimes** The standards technique allows an activity to take place without any ex ante control but the supplier who fails to meet certain standards of quality commits an offence. Standards can be subdivided into three categories, representing different degrees of intervention. A **target standard** prescribes no specific standard for the supplier's processes or output but imposes criminal liability for certain harmful consequences arising from the output. **A performance (or output) standard** requires certain conditions of quality to be met at the point of supply, but leaves the supplier free to choose how to meet those conditions. A **specification (or input) standard** can exist in either a positive or negative form: it compels the supplier to employ certain production methods or materials; or prohibits the use of certain production methods of materials. The most important economic variables in choosing

between these types of standards are the costs of being informed on the technological means of achieving the regulatory goals and the administrative costs of formulating appropriate standards and monitoring compliance. In principle, firms should be given choice as to how to meet the goals, since that encourages innovation in loss abatement techniques. Hence, there is a presumption in favour of less interventionist measures. However, the benefits of such measures might be outweighed by the costs of administering them and/or the costs to firms of acquiring information on loss abatement technology. From a private interest perspective, it will profit some regulated firms to support standards when cast in an appropriate form. For example, a proposed regulatory standard will benefit firms which, on a voluntary basis, already adhere to it: they will gain protection from competition by firms who are able to price their lower quality products or services more cheaply.

- **Mandatory disclosure** Rather than impose standards on suppliers, forcing them to adopt (optimal) loss abatement, legislation may simply require that they disclose to purchasers and others information regarding harms or risks which may arise from the activity or product. If regulation forces suppliers to reveal adequate information as to quality/safety, on the basis of which consumers can exercise choice, market transactions will ensure that preferences are met; and there will be no welfare losses from consumers being deprived of choice. On the other hand the potential application of this technique is limited since not all those affected by the product or activity will receive the information and be able thereby to adapt their behaviour or enter into appropriate transactions. Some forms of information regulation may also discourage innovation and consequently protect firms which adopt traditional manufacturing processes.
- **Fiscal or Administrative Charges** As an alternative to compelling optimal loss abatement by the threat of a sanction (often called "command-and-control" regulation) governments can attempt to achieve the same ends by economic incentives. The most important form of such incentive is a tax or charge: conduct is legally unconstrained but if a firm chooses to act in an undesired way it must make the stipulated payment. An important advantage claimed for taxes is that, provided the agency can make a reasonable estimate of the damage costs, it need have no knowledge of the abatement costs. Once a tax has been set to reflect the damage costs, it is left to individual firms to decide whether it is cheaper to pay the tax or else to abate. Further, the system provides better information for firms on the costs they will incur from the legal intervention: the tax represents a certain sum, whereas what they will have to pay if they contravene a standard depends on such uncertain variables as the enforcement discretion of the agency and the sentencing

discretion of the court. These are powerful arguments but without information on abatement costs, an agency will be unable to predict how much damage will actually result from a given set of prices and thus how effective those prices will be in relation to the efficiency goal.

- **Self-Regulation** The formulation and administration of any regulatory regime can be delegated by government to agencies representing the regulated industry. There are some public interest advantages to such arrangements, including the lowering of information, monitoring and enforcement costs. At the same time, as private interest theory would suggest, the system can be used to protect the profits of suppliers rather than protect consumers. Some of the advantages of self-regulation can nevertheless be retained if public agencies play only a residual role.

CONCLUSIONS

In my paper, I seek to convince my French readers that :

- "Regulation" is a coherent and important legal concept
- A taxonomy of regulatory forms reveals important policy choices
- To analyse and evaluate these forms, much can be achieved by an application of the public interest and private interest theories derived from economics.

PART II

LEGAL–ECONOMIC ANALYSIS OF LEGAL ISSUES IN A EUROPEAN CONTEXT

THE ROLE OF INSTITUTIONS IN THE CONTRACTUAL PROCESS

Benito Arruñada*

INTRODUCTION

Human beings increase their productivity by specializing their resources and exchanging their products with other human beings. The organization of exchange is costly, however, because specialized activities need coordination. Even more importantly, incentives have to be aligned, to avoid individuals from misusing exchange to expropriate each other. With civilization, institutions have evolved to safeguard exchange. This chapter analyzes how these exchanges are organized in an institutional environment. It focuses on the dual effect of this environment: as with any other specialized resource, institutions may be used for expropriation purposes. They enjoy specialization advantages in safeguarding exchange but they also make possible new forms of opportunism, causing new costs of exchange.

THE CONTRACTUAL PROCESS

In all exchanges, contracts have to be completed and enforced. Contractual completion involves ascertaining the efficient terms of the exchange. Enforcement means ensuring that these terms are complied with. Problems arise in contractual completion mostly because of lack of information, whilst the problem of enforcement is related to informational asymmetries between the parties, which makes them prone to opportunistic behavior.

Law and Economics in Civil Law Countries, Volume 6, pages 149–167.

ISBN: 0-7623-0712-9

Information scarcity explains the variety and complexity of mechanisms used to complete contracts, i.e. to accurately define the terms and conditions of the exchange or the commitments between the parties. This definition can occur ex ante or ex post—i.e. before or after the parties become committed to each other. It may be carried out by the parties themselves and/or by various social institutions, in particular the legal/court system, involvement of which to a large extent reduces the seriousness of the information problem.[1]

Four types of contractual completion result. In *explicit contracts*, the parties make express provision for a very limited set of the many possible situations which may arise and the steps to be taken in each of them. The *normative system* (customs, usage and laws—in essence, norms and rules in the terms used by North, 1981) provides the parties with a detailed standard contract, filling in many of the gaps left out of their explicit contract and predetermining the contract when the legislator considers it necessary. Decision-making bodies and rules established by the parties constitute *relational contracts* capable of efficiently solving unforeseen situations. Lastly, the *judicial system* "closes" the contract, providing solutions for all remaining unforeseen situations and developing the standard contract through case law. The accompanying figure summarizes these possibilities, taking into account also the fact that either one or more parties may play a leading role in individual or internal contracting and that institutional contracting may be centralized or decentralized.

Whatever the content of the exchange, the proclivity of individuals to advance their interests requires enforcement to ensure they perform their contractual obligations. Different enforcement mechanisms require different degrees of observability with respect to performance. With *first-party* enforcement it is the individual in breach who will evaluate and sanction his own conduct. Evaluation takes place in relation to his own moral code and the sanction consists of a certain psychological suffering which takes different forms, related to religious conviction and self-esteem. *Second-party* enforcement is based on verification and sanction by the party suffering the consequences of breach, who may break off the relationship with the other party or appropriate some hostage or security. Lastly, *third-party enforcement* requires verification by third parties. It comprises centralized systems, such as arbitrators and judges, and decentralized systems. The latter include the quasi-judicial activity of other participants in the market (breach harming reputation and hindering future contracting) and social mechanisms by which human groups ostracize non-performing members.

These contractual solutions may function as substitutes or complements, both horizontally and vertically, in terms of the previous figure.

In principle, legislation defines facilitating rules under which the intention of the parties overrides the provisions of the legal text, which only prevails in the

		INDIVIDUAL SOLUTIONS (internal to the parties)		INSTITUTIONAL SOLUTIONS (external to the parties)	
		Unilateral	Multilateral	Decentralized	Centralized
CONTRACTUAL COMPLETION	EX ANTE	EXPLICIT CONTRACTING		NORMS AND RULES	
		Contracts drawn up by one of the parties only (standard form contract)	Explicit contracts negotiated by both parties (joint contracts)	Usage and custom	Common Law Codified Law Statutory Law
	EX POST	RELATIONAL CONTRACTING		JUDGEMENT BY THIRD PARTIES	
		Authority (e.g. employment and franchise contracts)	Contractual definition of decision-making rules and bodies	Judgment of the parties' conduct by market participants	Litigation (by judicial judgments)
ENFORCEMENT		INTERNAL SANCTIONS		EXTERNAL SANCTIONS	
		Asymmetric sanctions in exercise of authority	No repetition of transactions; hostages	Loss of reputation in the market or in society (ostracism)	Police (enforcement of judgments)
		PRIVATE SOLUTIONS			PUBLIC SOLUTIONS

absence of relevant private provisions. To this extent, private solutions dominate legal solutions in ex ante completion. This situation is most typical in 19th century codification and also in Anglo-Saxon common law.[2] This priority, however, has been inverted in much subsequent legislation, particularly in that passed during the second half of the 20th century, in which the proportion of mandatory rules is considerable, even within the ambit of commercial transactions. On the other hand, virtually all private ex post completion is subordinated to the judicial system, so that it is generally impossible for the parties to deprive themselves ex ante of the (not always desirable) possibility of appealing against their decisions ex post. For these reasons, rather than complementarity among solutions, there is now interference, with institutional solutions reducing the scope of individual solutions.

With respect to substitutions between ex ante and ex post solutions, these are highly varied. Firstly, in the private field it may be thought that the more the contract is completed ex ante, the less it is necessary to complete it ex post. However, the functioning of ex post decision-making bodies and rules makes it more necessary to devote resources to ex ante completion, at least to provide for the basic elements of such bodies and rules. In the institutional field, there is a particular interaction: to the extent that litigation leads to case law, ex ante completion is developed to a greater extent and can be expected to reduce recourse to litigation.

In summary, parties contract within a sophisticated environment made up of the market, the law, and social and moral constraints. This institutional dimension is not a complement but the main feature of the contractual process and there are substantial substitutions and complementarities between most elements of the contractual process.[3]

The rest of the chapter will set aside moral and social solutions and focus on those mechanisms for which political actions are more important. This abstraction of moral and social mechanisms makes more sense now than at earlier stages of development because, throughout history, institutional solutions have become increasingly specialized. For example, the separation of Church and State required differentiation between moral and legal solutions. The same happened later with the separation of the legislative, judicial and executive powers of the State.

EX ANTE LEGAL COMPLETION

Irrespective of the degree of detail that the parties introduce when contracting, the content and terms of the exchange are further defined by the series of rules and norms in force in the field in which the contracting occurs. When it takes place in an institutional environment of a legal nature, exchanges are carried out in accordance with a very extensive contract, even though the parties themselves only expressly agree on the most basic elements of the exchange. Thanks to this legal support, the parties do not need to define separate sets of contingencies and compensation. All they need to do is adapt the standard contract, of great complexity and scope, which the institutional environment both explicitly (by legislation and case law) and implicitly (by conflict solution mechanisms, including litigation) provides for them. These institutional tools enable most exchanges to be completed effectively. The cost of contracting is thus considerably reduced and the parties use highly detailed contracts without having to write them down or even being aware of them. In other words, the cost of writing contracts defining the content of the exchange is reduced because contracts are written in an institutional framework established by the law and ancillary institutions, not in a direct one-to-one relationship between the parties.

Legal completion can thus be seen as a rationalization mechanism. The rationality of the parties is *bounded* when contracting since the contract is not usually of sufficient scope and the parties are not usually in a position where it is worthwhile devoting the necessary resources to completing it, not even to the extent of defining the content of the exchange in a series of likely contingencies. This limitation relates to the *intellectual* rationality of the parties and is a direct consequence of individual mental activity. By settling for the law, the parties opt to base completion of the contract on rationality of an *evolutionary* type, which has generated the greater and more durable part of the law.[4] The parties can thus contract in ignorance, without knowing details of the content of their rights and obligations, trusting in the efficiency and good sense of their legal definition. (This analysis justifies in efficiency terms the objective of legal security so dear to the law, by stressing the necessity that the law and its consequences must be easy to predict).

Certainly, consideration of law as the outcome of evolutionary rationality and, even more, of the efficient nature of norms and rules must be interpreted in relative and not absolute terms. The reason lies in the systematic survival, at least in the short term, of inefficient norms originating in the application of an intellectually defective rationality or, certainly more frequently, an inefficient collective decision motivated by rent-seeking activities in the legislative field. In short, although intellectual rationality and problems of collective action are important in the genesis of legal rules, their survival in the long term constituting a stable legal *corpus* is, at least in the final instance, governed by a logic of competitive adaptation. To the extent that this occurs, we can rely on this legal corpus being generally efficient.

More precisely, two main sources need to be considered in legal completion: customary law, including judicial precedent, which is more important in the common law tradition, and statutory law, which is more important in the civil law tradition. Both sources are closely connected and differences have probably been exaggerated. First, all statutory law is a mixture in variable proportions of evolutionary and intellectual rationality, with 19th century codified law being mainly the distillation of customary law. Second, codified systems of law also benefit from customary law prospectively—the existence of a code does not eliminate the normative capacity of the courts. In the words of Savigny, "codes are not more than geometric dots—jurisprudence draws the lines". It is not even clear to what extent statutory law is more prone to fall prey of inefficient rent seeking than confrontational litigation. The balance probably hangs on whether the political market or the litigation process is closer to perfect competition.

In addition, particular forms of legal completion may serve other purposes. For instance, codification has been used to prevent judicial opportunism by restricting the discretion of the courts. As far as a judiciary is needed for enforcement purposes, a crucial issue is then to contain opportunistic litigation that expands the functions of the courts in an inefficient way. This allows the parties to be relatively free of the risk of opportunistic litigation, which seems to be more prevalent in common law legal systems, especially when courts are allowed to decide on the basis of equity. Certainly, civil law codes contain seemingly flexible concepts such as "good faith", but their meaning is usually unambiguously defined in informational or intentional terms.

Facilitating and Mandatory Rules

Before discussing the failures of the legislative process, a distinction should be made between the roles of the two main types of legal rule, facilitating and mandatory, since they often respond to very different logic. Firstly, *facilitating* or enabling rules can be modified at the will of the parties when they state as much in the contract. They thus fit fully into the efficient argument, since their purpose is to reduce the cost of contracting, providing the parties with a standardized solution to the most typical or common problems that arise with different types of contract. On the other hand, *mandatory* rules are binding on the parties who cannot modify or exclude them. Their existence can be justified by failings in free contracting, whether such failings lie in the presence of external effects or in the irrationality of the contracting parties.

Although important, the distinction between facilitating and mandatory rules becomes blurred and a question of degree when taking into account the implicit coercive capacity of facilitating rules. When agreeing on terms, in a situation of informational asymmetry between the contracting parties, the latter are not entirely free to depart from the facilitating framework since, when trying to do so, they run the risk of being misinterpreted and endangering their negotiating position and, therefore, the contract itself. A function of the law is to prevent the parties from having to manifest their desire to include a particular clause in the formal contract. Such a manifestation can often generate mistrust in the party receiving the proposal, because it indicates that the person suggesting it has some potentially conflictive characteristics (mistrust, informational advantage and, in particular, little disposition to perform). Likewise, proposing a clause that varies from the provisions of the enabling legal rule could be interpreted as a sign of the problematical contractual characteristics presented by the proposer. In these conditions, the facilitating rule to some extent operates as mandatory in cases in which it is costly for one of the parties to depart from it. In these cases, and to the extent that a substantial proportion of contracting parties are faced with this problem, it can nonetheless be expected that contractual usages which avoid the problem will develop. The matter is thus of some short-term importance during the adaptation period following promulgation of facilitating rules that depart from the customary pattern previously established in the corresponding market.

Excess of Mandatory Rules

Human creations rarely respond completely to a logic of efficiency, and legislation is no exception. Although it is arguable whether the inefficiencies and failings are more or less long-lasting, imperfections in the collective decision-making process which legislation generates convert it into a useful instrument for rent seeking, and it matters little to the beneficiaries that its facilitating purpose is thereby undermined, thus converting it into an obstacle to private contracting, exchanges and productive specialization.[5]

In the field of private law, two general types of defect are possible, which translate into an excess or deficit of legislation. It will be argued here that excesses and deficits tend to affect mandatory and facilitating rules respectively. In both cases, social optimization is sacrificed to individual private interests. In the first case, to those of contracting parties and, in the second, to those of intermediaries.

A large number of mandatory rules that govern private contracting are not the result of a logic of external effects or imperfect rationality. They respond, rather, to a desire to achieve advantages or redistribution of wealth. The most important origin of inefficiencies in the legal system surely occurs when some parties to a pre-existing contract or series of contracts manage to legalize breach of their obligations by passage of a new mandatory rule or Act applied with retrospective effect.

Assume, for example, that the parties to a lease were completely free to agree on any terms as to price and period such as, for example, a fixed rent, long term and freedom for the tenant to terminate the lease. These terms are onerous on the lessor and therefore, when he asks for higher rent as compensation, the lessee may prefer to omit them, agreeing on a variable rent, shorter period and/or payment of compensation if he terminates the lease early. It is understandable, however, that after signing leases of this type, lessees have an interest in seeing an Act passed which freezes rents or introduces a system of minimum periods and will support political intermediaries who achieve this, however much such rules may damage future lessees.

The problem affects not only leases but all types of contract, with examples as varied and bountiful as contracts themselves: debtors will want to make it more difficult for creditors to collect, minority shareholders will have an interest in increasing the rights of minorities in shareholder companies, employees who have contracted work without the right to compensation for dismissal will fight for it to be provided by law, etc. In all these cases, the private and social effects are similar. From the private point of view, there is a transfer of wealth: one of the parties to the contract obtains a benefit at the cost of the other. The most harmful effect, however, is of a collective nature. The parties to new contracts will be obliged to use inefficient terms, their inefficient nature (absent external effects or a failure in individual rationality) being shown by the fact that they were not previously included in contracts. Alternatively, they will devote resources to circumventing laws, all of which reduces the value of contracting to both parties and ends up by wasting possibilities for productive specialization. It is not surprising, therefore, that many dwellings tend to stay empty, the worst risks find it difficult to obtain credit, minority shareholders are dispensed with in new companies and numerous potential employees remain unemployed.

The general consequence of inefficient mandatory rules is to raise contractual costs. This makes specialization impossible or forces parties to use suboptimal arrangements. Most European labor law probably has this effect, forcing firms to disintegrate and contract labor through all kinds of commercial law contracts.[6]

Deficit in Facilitating Legislation

Failings also occur in the legal system as a result of insufficient introduction of laws. The origin of this problem is not rent-seeking by contracting participants but by contractual intermediaries, taken in the broad sense.

The fact that the experts who draw up laws also often provide the services necessary to contract in the context of such laws gives rise to a potential conflict of interest. These services include those aimed at reducing the interpretative rigor of regulatory agencies. There may be a radical asymmetry in the incentives of the experts, depending on whether the rules are of a facilitating or mandatory nature, since both excess of mandatory laws as well as shortfall in facilitating laws could benefit experts and intermediaries. This is because both shortcomings increase demand for their services to the extent that they facilitate ex ante contracting, which is complementary to mandatory laws and substitutive of facilitating laws. An example of this argument is provided by some European corporation laws, which have undergone substantial change with a proliferation of mandatory rules. This mandatory nature has even entered areas in which it is scarcely justified, such as that of private companies. Since this legislation is aimed at "closed" companies, which do not sell securities to the public, even the arguments based on external effects that are occasionally used to justify the application of mandatory rules to "open" companies hold little water. Despite the fact that facilitating laws have simultaneously been expanded, the growth in their extent is far removed from that of mandatory legislation. More importantly, there is even further removal from the evolution of facilitating laws in those jurisdictions that are characterized by a relative lack of mandatory provisions such as, in particular, U.S. company law, especially in the State of Delaware.

Without suggesting a causal relationship, it is worthwhile considering the benefits that this normative imbalance between mandatory and facilitating rules can give rise to. The surplus of mandatory rules tends to increase the demand for legal services to circumvent the letter and even the spirit of the law. Two simple examples are provided by the prohibition on multiple voting shares (in force, for instance, in Spain since the 1950 Companies Act). This can be avoided by having a pyramid of companies, but this requires greater outlay on legal services, not just to create the pyramid but also recurrent maintenance of the companies that make it up. Also in the field of company legislation, rules regarding legal capital maintenance are not only pointless but in many jurisdictions are very costly.[7] The relative lack of facilitating laws generates several less visible, but perhaps equally important, effects which are based on the fact that the parties need to use other solutions to complete their contracts. The demand for legal services will therefore tend to increase as such solutions make greater use of explicit contracts ex ante or litigation ex post.

INSTITUTIONAL ENFORCEMENT AND EX POST COMPLETION

Parties do not contract in a vacuum, but within a legal system which provides them ex ante with standardized provisions. It is also possible for them to have recourse to a third party to settle their conflicts ex post. This third party takes two forms: either decentralized market judgment, whose force lies in the loss of future contractual opportunities, or a judicial system whose power comes from the political monopoly of power.[8] Both the market and judges certainly have inseparable completion and enforcement functions. Market participants who turn against a seller or a judge who issues a judgment firstly define the content of the exchange when there is a dispute between the parties and, secondly, act as ultimate enforcers of the contractual obligations so defined. Depending on the features of each case, the relative importance in their work of the completion function in relation to the enforcement function varies. For example, if a lender sues a recalcitrant debtor, enforcement is probably more important than completion in the judicial task of solving the matter. On the other hand, challenging an agreement to distribute the profits obtained by a company, or a dispute regarding dismissal of an employee or termination of a franchise agreement will probably involve considerably more completion, as in these cases the actual content of the exchange as agreed by the parties is less obvious.

The Courts

Institutional Optimum

A large proportion of contractual disputes can be litigated in the courts.[9] These use two main mechanisms for completing contracts:

First, in order to make up for the lack of explicit agreement between the parties, use is made of the general provisions laid down by legislation, case law and commercial custom through the process of "contractual integration" (Larentz, 1958: 112–121). By virtue of this process, "contracts . . . make it obligatory not only to comply with what is expressly agreed but also with all the consequences which, based on their nature, conform to good faith, usage and the law" (Section 1258 of the Spanish Civil Code, taking it as an example of a typical civil law legal system).[10]

Second, a pattern of judicial decision-making tends to be used to fill in gaps in the contract. This pattern consists of an implicit inquiry as to the hypothetical will of the parties in the case that, under conditions of zero transaction costs, the parties had made express provision ex ante, thus filling ex ante the specific gap that the court has now to fill ex post. As it is likely that the parties had come to an agreement generating efficient incentives, it suffices to discover the efficient solution in order also to ascertain the hypothetical will of the parties. It is especially in this field that economic analysis can help, both in preparing judgments and in interpreting case law.[11]

The fact that the majority of contracts or conflicts never reach the courts does not diminish the role of the judicial system. The mere possibility of judicial intervention prevents breach: if the parties anticipate the outcome of a judicial decision they will tend to come to an agreement or avoid the conflict. In other words, the judicial system carries out an enforcement task, not only explicitly, by implementing its decisions or judgments, but also implicitly, by encouraging voluntary compliance in anticipation of an even more costly judicial decision.

Inefficient Sentencing

In principle, the possibility of having recourse to a judge facilitates contracting: by resolving conflicts, the judge will ex post fill the gaps which the parties have not specified, such that if the judge's independence is guaranteed and he has coercive power (or the judge's function is allocated to someone with such power), the costly ex ante stipulation of terms for the exchange and/or enforcement of its obligations by the parties themselves is less necessary. Nevertheless, the efficiency of judicial decisions can also be affected by the interests of the participants, including those of the judges themselves. When this occurs, the judicial solution may be inefficient and it is possible that the parties could more easily contract without the presence of the judicial system. Nevertheless, this presence is usually inevitable since the parties are frequently not in a position to choose the jurisdiction in which they wish to settle their disputes, and legal systems do not usually respect provisions by the parties eliminating ex ante the possibility of litigating ex post, with the exception of arbitration acts.

On this point it is worthwhile pointing out three specific types of failure in the judicial system. These are associated with: (a) deficient identification of judicial opportunism by the parties; (b) defective consideration of criteria of "material justice"; (c) the presence of a possible bias against quasi-judicial action by the parties.

(1) Judicial and arbitration solutions, by which society or the parties authorize a third party (judge or arbitrator) to resolve conflicts which arise in exchanges, provide a further possibility for non-compliance if the parties are able to manipulate the judge to decide in their favor after incorrectly appreciating the merits of the case. A common example consists of considering the merits of the dispute and, in particular, the balance of compensation between the parties, based solely on the ex post situation, but without taking into account that this is often only the outcome of a random event which could have led to different outcomes in which the net balance of compensation would have been different. The existence of the judge thus motivates the parties to devote resources to both bringing about and preventing this manipulation. In many cases the contracts themselves are structured to avoid this type of opportunism. Judicial systems also tend to incorporate mechanisms aimed at protecting the judge from manipulation and ensuring his independence. Whether they achieve this or not is an empirical matter but some systematic biases are frequently present.

(2) It is often considered that implementing the ideal of material justice by means of judicial decisions comes into conflict with legal certainty and economic efficiency. In reality, the consequences are worse. These closely-related principles of certainty and efficiency are often not only affected, but justice itself is harmed. This often happens because, in order to implement individual solutions

which are considered just, the very objectives of justice at an overall level are damaged. The most common case is perhaps when the solution believed just in an individual case favors the weaker party to a contract and, as a result, weak parties to future contracts suffer from a reduction and worsening of their contractual possibilities and conditions. A case brought by a rich creditor against a poor debtor for non-payment serves as an example. If the judgment in this type of case takes into account the insolvency or poverty of the debtor, it is perhaps resolving an individual problem (at root that of providing the latter with an insurance that he perhaps could or could not, depending on the circumstances, have voluntarily contracted). Nevertheless, to the extent that it prevents the creditor from collecting his debt, it places obstacles in the path of all loan contracts that may be subject to similar judgments in the future. As a result, the judgment also harms potential debtors of a similar type to the beneficiary of the judgment, who are deprived of access to credit or will have to pay additional interest. In this respect, the conduct of the judge is inconsistent, since he is acting unfairly, albeit in a general manner, in relation to the type of party to whom on an individual basis he is attempting to dispense justice. Moreover, this type of judgment motivates judicial opportunism by the parties, who will try and place themselves in a position in which justice will favor them. In this way, what is described as justice can even conceal simple contractual expropriation.

(3) Finally, centralized judicial systems frequently exhibit a certain bias against ex post quasi-judicial activities by the parties, even in cases in which these quasi-judicial activities are the result of an ex ante contractual agreement. The parties' interests lie in allocating judicial functions or rights to the party who has the best information and incentives to carry out this judicial task. Two sets of motivation are thus configured: firstly, with respect to information, the contracting parties who are in a central position compared with other parties will have a comparative advantage in this task since their central position provides them with information as a free by-product of their transactions and enables them to make specialist use of all types of resources in these informative and judicial tasks. Secondly, with regard to incentives, those parties who have a better reputation or who are in a position to provide further guarantees have an advantage. In this respect, the size of the undertaking is usually important since it is often associated with greater reputational capital. This quasi-judicial action of the large undertaking is usually attacked in the strictly judicial field when judges often interpret the subject matter of litigation as deriving from greater bargaining power on the part of the larger party and not from the ex post exercise of judicial functions contractually allocated ex ante. We have found, for example, that car manufacturers are assigned rights

in relation to their dealers to complete the contract, defining obligations, assessing their performance and, as the case may be, penalizing them if they consider that they are in breach of their obligations (Arruñada, Garicano & Vázquez, 2001). This quasi-judicial activity, which is common amongst many franchiser companies in relation to their franchisee networks, is essential to control the proclivity of the latter to exploit other members, enabling them to provide their customers with uniform service quality in disparate locations. This does not mean, however, that size is the only relevant variable in terms of asymmetric allocation of quasi-judicial functions, even though it is the most problematical in terms of judicial treatment. Informational advantages may outweigh an eventual advantage in incentives. This helps in explaining why many retailers carry out these quasi-judicial functions, even in their relations with much larger, and supposedly better motivated, suppliers (Arruñada 2000). Nevertheless, the ex post contractual asymmetry tends to be perceived by some judges as unfair (at least this is their justification, although it may also be thought that their real objective is to monopolize completion and external enforcement activities ex post) and they therefore tend to correct it, thus inefficiently restricting the quasi-judicial powers which the private contract itself allocates to one of the parties.[12] (Ex ante competition can be safely assumed because judicial proceedings rarely refer to lack of competition ex ante).

To the extent that legislation and judges restrict the parties' possibilities for establishing efficient ex post decision-making mechanisms the contracting parties must implement strategies aimed at protecting self-enforcement mechanisms from the possibility of judicial intervention. A large part of ex ante contracting serves this purpose. This is probably the case with the inclusion of burdensome terms in contracts—for example, that repairs shall be to the account of the lessee, using the famous United Shoes case (Masten & Snyder, 1993). Despite the fact that these terms are not normally enforced (in United Shoes the lessor in fact carried out the repairs), their inclusion by assigning to one the parties (the lessor) the right to evaluate and penalize the degree of performance by the other party of his obligations (which allegedly, amongst other variables, included proper use and care of equipment) makes them relatively safe from judicial intervention which the latter party may have an interest in seeking ex post.

The foregoing refers to what is conventionally understood by judicial system. If, on the other hand, we use a broader concept, including market activity aimed at punishing what is perceived as contractual breach, the parties will also generally be unable to avoid judgment of their activities by third parties. For this reason, it is also important to take account of the biases that the market may suffer when judging the activities of its participants, particularly when property rights in relation to reputation are poorly protected against opportunistic attack.

The Judicial Activity of the Market

We have taken "judicial" enforcement to mean all those enforcement activities in which the person assessing the degree of compliance and implementing the possible sanction is one or more third parties other than parties to the contract. In this broad sense, not only the courts but also the activity implicitly carried out by the market can be categorized as judge as a result of the fact that the contracting is almost always observed by other participants in the market, who thus obtain useful information for their future contracts. When making this assessment they in fact act as judges in conflicts which previous contracts have given rise to. This is a decentralized system in the sense that the overall decision, equivalent to a judgment, is the result of a cumulative series of individual decisions taken independently and generally not at the same time by market participants.

When, for example, a dissatisfied customer reveals his dissatisfaction to someone who wants to listen to him, those who listen to him also act as "judge" in the "dispute" thus presented since, after accumulating a variable amount of information, they end up forming an opinion and making a resulting decision. Their "judgments" take the form of comments to other individuals and, in particular, end up turning into purchase decisions, both their own and of third parties. On the one hand, the judgment involves failing to acquire the product in question from the particular supplier and often commenting on the matter in turn, after which the cycle again begins with a new potential buyer. On the other hand, a judgment which acquits the producer also, although often implicitly, involves a judgment against the litigant, whose reputation is thus damaged. In both cases, these gains and losses associated with future transactions represent changes in the value of reputation. The importance of all these reputational assessment processes makes it necessary to stress one of the essential functions of the institution we call the "market", that of acting as judge, rewarding and punishing the conduct of those involved in it.

Contractual Enforcement by Organizations and Markets

In the judicial activity of the market, it is potential contractual partners who in the final instance decide on judgments. Nevertheless, a large proportion of the information used to make a decision is often produced by organizations more or less specialized in this task. It is thus seen how entire sectors of economic activity have the basic function of providing information on the situation and degree of past, current and future performance of contractual obligations.[13] This is the case with specialists, such as auditing firms and those that rate debt securities. Furthermore, this information is constantly produced as a by-product of other activities. The most notable example is perhaps banks who, even though not specialists, carry out a function of this type when they report on the solvency of their customers.

The role of the market in solving contractual problems does not end with this quasi-judicial activity. More generally, when the benefits of productive specialization are sufficiently high, the market itself generates all types of external enforcement mechanisms whose activity, on occasions free of cost to the parties, protects this productive specialization in a more or less direct manner. These external mechanisms tend either to facilitate internal contractual structuring and control processes or in themselves constitute monitoring or bonding instruments. For example, in the relationship between shareholders and the management of a public company with specialized ownership and control, these roles are played respectively by the Stock Exchange, which provides a low exit cost for dissenters and an indicator of management performance, and external competition for corporate control, manifested by public take-over bids and other means for gaining control from outside the company. In other contractual relationships, not only information producers appear, as mentioned, but also intermediaries who specialize in resolving specific problems which arise in third party contracts. This is the case with an essential function of banking activity, which is to reduce the cost of the relationship between savers and investors. And also with expert buyers, who select products and guarantee their quality, from department stores to doctors. Or with specialists in enforcing contractual compliance, such as debt collection agencies. These examples show that in some cases the person monitoring or bonding third party activities is a specialist, generally a firm, which charges for its services. In other cases, it is the market itself, as in the case of the market for corporate control, whose activities protect the relationship between shareholders and managers of *all* companies with specialized ownership and control, not only those directly affected.

Assessment of the Market as Judge

The fact that decision makers are market participants ensures that they have powerful incentives to inform themselves adequately when taking their decisions. For example, the buyer of a car has incentives to be informed and, by means of his purchase decision, correctly "judge" the prior conduct of manufacturers. There are also substantial differences in the type of information which different types of third party responsible for completing or enforcing contracts can handle. It is possible that the market is more competent than the judicial system when *verifying* qualitative information.[14] Firstly, the market is not restricted to the use of a particular type of evidence, as are the courts, particularly in countries with codified law in which the modern judicial apparatus is intended to enforce laws rather than facilitate contracts. Secondly, by acting through cumulative individual decisions, possible personal biases and variables are less pronounced.

These purely informative aspects are not the only relevant ones, however. The production and transmission of reputational information is not free of incentive problems, mainly the supply of false information. As a consequence, reputational assets may be subject to a certain degree of expropriation through "reputational blackmail". Certainly, this type of opportunistic conduct is automatically limited in that economic subjects also have a reputation as informers on the reputation of others and it is not in their interests to lose their reputation as informers. If this were to happen, not only would their threats no longer be credible but they would also find it increasingly difficult to safeguard the quality they receive in their future transactions.[15]

The greatest risk in this area often comes from the misuse or incorrect functioning of institutional mechanisms that increase potential damage without any sort of compensation. This might arise with certain consumer regulations which allow frivolous accusations to be published without any thought for the consequences, and with judicial decisions that on appeal are shown to be inadmissible but do not provide compensation. Here it is of interest to note that, because of their very size, large companies may be at risk from small enemies. This is because they never win their cases even if they are in the right. The guilty party is not able to pay compensation and the innocence of the large company is likely to be placed in doubt by the mass media.

CONCLUSION

The interactions between different contractual solutions have been described, considering that parties contract within an institutional environment with laws, courts and markets. Laws improve individual parties' rationality, courts complete and enforce contracts, and markets motivate contractual performance. Public intervention is decisive in making these institutions more or less effective in their facilitating roles. Several perverse tendencies are present, however. In the legal field, there is a surplus of mandatory rules and, at the same time, a deficit in default rules. Courts' activity is also unduly biased, mainly against the quasi-judicial role of the parties and the market. Finally, market enforcement is based on reputational assets that are exposed to opportunism. The presence of these failings is not surprising. Institutional solutions are also part of the specialization and exchange process. They enjoy the advantages of specialization in safeguarding exchange but they themselves also incur new costs of exchange because the added specialization in laws, courts and reputational resources gives rise to new forms of opportunistic behavior.

NOTES

* Professor of Business Organization, Department of Economics and Business, Universitat Pompeu Fabra. E-mail: benito.arrunada@econ.upf.es. Mail: Trias Fargas, 25. 08005–Barcelona. Comments from Celestino Pardo and Cándido Paz-Ares are gratefully acknowledged. Usual disclaimers apply. Work on this project has been supported by the CICYT, a research agency of the Spanish Government, through grant SEC99–1191.

1. This taxonomy is aimed at coping with the variety of solutions and "types of law" usually employed, sometimes even simultaneously, in most economic exchanges and also the variety of functions of explicit formulation of contract terms, along lines similar to Masten (2000). It therefore varies from other conceptions aimed at establishing a correspondence between modes of organization (markets, hybrids and hierarchies, for example) and modes of contracting (traditional contract law, neo-classic law with exception following the "excuse doctrine", and *forbearance* of law), particularly Williamson (1991). It also varies from the formulations which emphasize the role of the type of applicable law (labor, company) in defining the type of contract and, as a result, of economic organization (e.g. Masten, 2000).

2. I refer to "common law" as case law, law made by judges. It actually constitutes a hybrid in terms of degree of centralization: it has evolved through an accumulation of decisions which are decentralized but taken by judicial bodies.

3. In the analysis of contracts, economic theory and part of current law and economics tend often to exclude the institutional environment to make problems easily tractable, with a substantial loss in relevance. For instance, the literature on incomplete contracts pioneered by Grossman and Hart (1986) tends to consider that enforcement of various dimensions of the exchange is fully guaranteed by a judge who simply implements the letter of contractual agreements with no intervention in other dimensions. A similar criticism can be raised on those approaches which emphasize activities of the parties aimed at developing self-enforcement mechanisms (particularly Klein & Leffler, 1981; Klein, 1992, 1996; and Klein & Murphy, 1988, 1997), which tend to exclude the role of the institutional environment.

4. The contemporaneous version of this concept of law was basically developed by Hayek (mainly 1960 and 1973, and for a review and summary, 1988).

5. On the ambiguity of institutional solutions, see North (1990: 59–60).

6. González, Arruñada and Fernández (1998, 2000) analyzed this issue in construction and Fernández, Arruñada and González (1998, 2000) in trucking.

7. For the case of the USA, Mannig (1990).

8. On the economies of joining political power, arbitration and enforcement, see, for instance, North and Thomas (1971: 788).

9. Similarly, the parties may opt to submit these disputes to an arbitration mechanism, generally led by more or less impartial experts. In both cases, with either judges or

arbitrators, the decision makers are centralized, although arbitration constitutes a hybrid formula: its appearance and survival are governed by market criteria, but it functions in accordance with centralized decision-making patterns. In the field of contractual completion, the private production of contractual forms is also located midway between market and centralized solutions.

10. The role of good faith as a general or default provision varies widely in different legal systems. It is minor in Anglo-Saxon countries—although in some of them, such as Scotland, it had greater importance in the past but is now in decline—and very important in Civil Law countries. It is not by chance that this lesser role of contractual integration corresponds to the empirical fact that contracts tend to be much shorter in Europe than in Anglo-Saxon countries.

11. The hypothesis of efficiency in rules of judicial origin was advanced in the first edition of *Economic Analysis of Law* (1973). Posner (1998: 271–275, 565–653) and Cooter and Ulen (1988: 492–499) contain separate inconsistent introductions regarding the efficiency of Anglo-Saxon common law and introduce the main bibliographic references on the matter. Regarding the efficiency of continental civil or codified legal systems, see *International Review of Law and Economics* 11(3).

12. The promulgation of mandatory rules with retrospective effect is also generally related to asymmetric contracts, whose asymmetry is often used as an argument to justify consideration of free contracting as unfair.

13. Their role could be seen recently in the sudden growth of "infomediaries" who grade the quality of electronic commerce operating through the Internet (Peet, 2000: 319).

14. For an application to the auditing industry, see Arruñada (1999).

15. Some very "organized" markets are careful in managing the production of parties' reputation. For example, the American Information Exchange used very formal evaluation processes to ensure quality ("Information Industries: New Ideas on the Block," *The Economist*, 14 March 1992: 79–80). More recently, auction web sites, such as Ebay, have taken a similar approach to ensure compliance in payments and deliveries.

REFERENCES

Arruñada, B. (1999). *The Economics of Audit Quality*. Boston: Kluwer.

Arruñada, B. (2000). The Quasi-Judicial Role of Large Retailers: An Efficiency Hypothesis of their Relation with Suppliers. *Revue d'Economie Industrielle*, *92*, 277–296.

Arruñada, B., Garicano, L., & Vázquez, L. (2001). Contractual Allocation of Decision Rights and Incentives: The Case of Automobile Distribution. *The Journal of Law, Economics, and Organization*, *17*(1), forthcoming.

Cooter, R. D., & Ulen, T. (1988). *Law and Economics*. New York: Harper Collins.

Fernández, A., Arruñada, B., & González, M. (1998). Contractual and Regulatory Explanations of Quasi-Integration in the Trucking Industry. Universitat Pompeu *Fabra, Economics and Business Working Paper Series*, *292*, June.

Fernández, A., Arruñada, B., & González, M. (2000). Quasi-Integration in Less-than-Truckload Trucking. In: C. Ménard (Ed.), *Institutions, Contracts, Organizations: Perspectives from New Institutional Economics* (pp. 293–312). Cheltenham: Elgar.

González, M., Arruñada, B., & Fernández, A. (1998). Regulation as a Cause of Firm Fragmentation: The Case of the Spanish Construction Industry. *International Review of Law and Economics, 18*(4), 145–191.

González, M., Arruñada, B., & Fernández, A. (2000). Causes of Subcontracting: Evidence from Panel Data on Construction Firms. *Journal of Economic Behavior and Organization, 42*(2), 167–187.

Grossman, S. J., & Hart, O. (1986). The Costs and Benefits of Ownership: A Theory of Lateral and Vertical Integration. *Journal of Political Economy, 94*(4), 691–719.

Hayek, F. A. (1960). *The Constitution of Liberty*. London: Routledge.

Hayek, F. A. (1973–1976). *Law, Legislation, and Liberty: A New Statement of the Liberal Principles of Justice and Political Economy*. London: Routledge.

Hayek, F. A. (1988). *The Fatal Conceit: The Errors of Socialism*. London: Routledge.

Hermalin B. E., & Katz, M. L. (1993). Judicial Modification of Contracts Between Sophisticated Parties: A More Complete View of Incomplete Contracts and Their Breach. *The Journal of Law, Economics, and Organization, 9*(2), 230–255.

Klein, B. (1992). Contracts and Incentives: the Role of Contract Terms in Assuring Performance. In: L. Werin & H. Wijkandere (Eds), *Contract Economics* (pp. 149–172). Cambridge: Blackwell.

Klein, B. (1996). Why Hold-Ups Occur: The Self-Enforcing Range of Contractual Relationships. *Economic Inquiry, 34*(3), 444–463.

Klein, B., & Leffler, K. (1981). The Role of Market Forces in Assuring Contractual Performance. *Journal of Political Economy, 89* (August), 615–641.

Klein, B., & Murphy, K. M. (1988). Vertical Restraints as Contract Enforcement Mechanisms. *Journal of Law and Economics, 31* (October), 265–297.

Klein, B., & Murphy, K. M. (1997). Vertical Integration as a Self-Enforcing Contractual Arrangement. *American Economic Review, 87*(2), 415–420.

Larentz, K. (1958). *Derecho de Obligaciones*. Volume I. Madrid: Editorial Revista de Derecho Privado.

Mannig, B. (1990). *Legal Capital*. Westbury: Foundation Press.

Masten, S. E. (1988). A Legal Basis for the Firm. *Journal of Law, Economics and Organization, 4* (spring).

Masten, S. E. (2000). Contractual Choice. In: B. Bouckaert & G. De Geest (Eds), *Encyclopedia of Law & Economics*. Cheltenham: Elgar.

Masten, S. E., & Snyder, E. A. (1993). United States v. United Shoe Machinery Corporation: On the Merits. *Journal of Law and Economics, 36*, 33–70.

North, D. C. (1981). *Structure and Change in Economic History*. New York: Norton.

North, D. C. (1990). *Institutions, Institutional Change and Economic Performance*. Cambridge: Cambridge University Press.

North, D. C., & Thomas, R. P. (1971). The Rise and Fall of the Manorial System: A Theoretical Model. *Journal of Economic History, 31*(December), 777–803.

Peet, J. (2000). E-Commerce: Shopping Around the Web. *The Economist*, February 26.

Posner, R. A. (1998). *Economic Analysis of Law*. New York: Aspen.

Williamson, O. E. (1991). Comparative Economic Organization. The Analysis of Discrete Structural Alternatives. *Administrative Science Quarterly, 36*, 269–296.

TORT LIABILITY IN FRANCE: AN INTRODUCTORY ECONOMIC ANALYSIS

Michael Faure

1. INTRODUCTION: THE GOAL OF CIVIL LIABILITY

1.1 Compensation or Deterrence?

The French lawyers writing on civil liability are relatively clear about the goal of tort law: although it is recognised that tort law can serve a variety of goals, the purpose which is mostly stressed is the victim compensation argument. It is precisely because victim compensation is considered a primary goal of tort law that many have criticised the liability based on fault, since this could not guarantee victim compensation adequately.[1] This seems to be a different approach than the approach taken in the economic literature, which very much stresses that tort law is a system meant to deter a behaviour which could lead to accidents. Economists therefore often argue that their approach is *ex ante*, whereas the legal approach is rather *ex post*. In the economic approach the basic idea is that the foresight of being held liable *ex post* may give an injurer ex ante an incentive toward careful behaviour. Tort rules are thus seen as instruments to guide the behaviour of potential parties which could be involved in an accident. Economists would obviously argue that they are interested in victim protection as well, but rather in an earlier stage: they would rather stress prevention of accidents; thus more accidents can be avoided and the need of victim compensation *ex post* might disappear.

Law and Economics in Civil Law Countries, Volume 6, pages 169–181.
2001 by Elsevier Science B.V.
ISBN: 0-7623-0712-9

1.2 Art. 1382CC

It can be held that this basic idea that tort law primarily serves deterrence is also incorporated in the traditional article 1382 of the French Civil Code, as it was drafted in 1804. This article holds that the one who causes damage to another is bound to compensate this damage on the condition that it was caused by his fault. Hence, article 1382 of the Code Civil (hereafter CC) does not contain an absolute guarantee of victim compensation. The necessity to compensate the victim depends upon the behaviour of the injurer. Thus it can be argued that article 1382 CC is primarily a rule aiming at the control of the behaviour of the injurer rather than a rule aiming at victim compensation. This is obviously also seen by French scholars such as Tunc who therefore have argued against a tort liability based on fault (see Tunc, 1989: 170–171).

1.3 Empirical Evidence

Obviously the whole idea of economic analysis relies on the assumption that potential parties to an accident will actually behave more careful under the foresight of being held liable. Whether this is a realistic assumption is obviously to a large extent dependent upon empirical proof. The (mostly North-American) studies which have been executed so far indicate that the deterrent effect of tort rules seems to be stronger in cases of e.g. product liability or environmental liability (when deterrence is aimed at enterprises) rather than with e.g. traffic liability (when liability rules aim at "ordinary people") (Dewees, Duff & Trebilcock, 1996: 205–205, 288–290). However, even in case of "ordinary people" there has been some empirical evidence that e.g. an automatic compensation of traffic victims would lead to an increase of the number of accidents,[2] but these results have been under critical attack (see Dewees, Duff & Trebilcock, 1996: 22–26). In addition, it can be argued that if one would deny the deterrent effect of tort rules and one would argue (as many French lawyers do) that victim compensation should be the primary policy goal, there are probably many other instruments, such as insurance, social security and compensation funds which can reach this compensation goal at lower costs and easier than tort law. For that reason Tunc has always argued in favour of alternatives to the tort system to reach victim compensation.

In the remainder of this paper, I will have a brief look at some features of French civil liability from an economic perspective. Within the scope of this paper it is obviously not possible to repeat or even summarise economic analysis on this point. It seems more interesting to relate the outcomes of the economic literature to the approach taken in French civil law.

2. FAULT LIABILITY

2.1 MC = MB

Following the similar works of Calabresi (1970), Landes and Posner (1981) and Shavell (1987) in this domain, it is now accepted that from an economic perspective liability rules should give incentives for a reduction of the total social costs of accidents. Of particular importance in this respect are the costs of prevention and the expected damage. It is held in this economic literature that efficiency can be reached if the potential injurer is required to invest in care up to the point where the marginal costs of preventive measures equal the marginal benefits in reduction of the expected damage. In other words: tort rules should give the potential injurer incentives for careful behaviour, but accidents should not be avoided at all costs. This weighing of marginal costs versus marginal benefits hence leads to a point of optimal care which the injurer should follow.[3] The fault rule can be one of the legal rules giving incentives to the potential injurer to follow the optimal care. The level of optimal care will under a fault rule, however, be determined by the judge and can be developed as a result of case law.

2.2 Learned Hand in France

It is certainly possible to incorporate the economic notions of fault (through weighing marginal costs versus marginal benefits) into article 1382 of the French Civil Code. This would mean that the French judge would examine whether it would have been possible for the injurer to avoid the accident by investing additionally in prevention whereas these additional investments would have substantially reduced the accident risk. Such an explicit weighing of costs and benefits can almost never be seen in French case law based on article 1382 CC. However, the very notion of fault, incorporated in article 1382 CC implies that it is apparently not necessary to avoid all accidents at all costs. The injurer is indeed only bound to compensate the victim when the accident was caused by his fault. Hence, the very notion of article 1382 CC provides room for the cost-benefit weighing as prescribed in the economic model and sometimes the French judge might implicitly have referred to economic criteria (see Van den Bergh, 1988).

However, an explicit comparison of costs of precaution versus the expected damage, as was the case in the well-known American Learned Hand case can not be found in French case law.[4]

In French legal doctrine it is held that a fault constitutes the fact that the injurer did not behave as a reasonable man.[5] At first sight this rather abstract and vague notion has little to do with the cost-benefit weighing of economic analysis. Nevertheless, some elements can be identified in French legal doctrine or case law, which refer somehow to economic notions. In this respect we can e.g. refer to the fact that it is held that the fault notion in French civil law requires that the damage was predictable and avoidable (Malaurie & Aynes, 1998: 56). This predictability could refer to the probability that a certain act could entail a risk of damage. Also, the predictability requirement refers to the notion that liability rules are ex ante instruments to give incentives towards careful behaviour. The predictability requirement of French civil law therefore enters nicely into economic theory.

One should note, however, that some French lawyers try to change the theoretical basis of civil liability by leaving the idea of fault and replacing it by different notions such as the ideas of created risk and guarantee. These ideas, roughly speaking, mean that the one who created a risk is also held to compensate the damage which was caused as a result of this risk.[6] These ideas are obviously too large to fit into the economic model. The risk notion leads to a too large liability, without taking into account the costs of precaution and the expected damage.

2.3 Bonus Pater Familias

There is, however, another notion, which plays an important role in French law, more specifically in the interpretation of the fault notion of article 1382 CC, which is the *bonus pater familias*. The standard refers to the conduct of a normally careful and prudent person, capable of conducting himself with care and diligence. A problem which we did not discuss so far is that the costs of care (and therefore the optimal care) might be different for every individual. Thus it has been argued that if the legal system could, at relatively low costs, distinguish between several types of injurers, it would be efficient to hold them to different standards of care (Diamond, 1974). In French law the appreciation of the care exercised by the bonus pater familias is done "in the abstract" (see Starck, 1996: 272, 295–296). This can be understood. An appreciation "in the concrete" which would take subjective circumstances such as education or intelligence of the injurer into account, is very costly. However, if a classification is possible at relatively low costs, it can also be found in French law. Therefore French law will take into account external circumstances, such as the whether, time of the accident or geographical conditions. The information costs to verify these elements and thus adapt the standard of care are relatively low. The same is true with professional liability. If e.g. a doctor's conduct is examined, the criterion will not be the conduct of a careful and prudent person, but of a normally careful doctor. In those cases a differentiation of the standard of care is again possible at relatively low costs.

So far, we can therefore conclude that the approach taken in French civil liability seems, as far as the interpretation of the fault notion is concerned, to follow the economic theory relatively well.

3. STRICT LIABILITY

We already referred to the fact that in French law there is an undeniable tendency to leave the notion of fault and to move towards strict liability, both through case law and through legislation.[7] This trend follows from the idea that civil liability in France should be used as a system to compensate victims. It has also been argued that especially through the development of liability insurance civil liability has been able to fulfill this compensatory function (see Viney, 1995: 23–25, 60–63).

3.1 Economic Test

Also from an economic point of view there are certainly arguments in favour of strict liability in specific cases. This argument is especially strong in so-called unilateral accident cases; these are cases where only one party (the injurer) can influence the accident risk. In such a case a strict liability rule has the advantage that it will lead to a full internalisation of the accident risk. The injurer will indeed not only take the due care required by case law, but take all possible measures to reduce the accident risk, even if these can not be recognised by the judge. Moreover, strict liability will also induce the injurer to take an efficient activity level, which can not be controlled by a fault rule.[8] From an economic perspective there is, hence, certainly an argument in favour of strict liability in case of unilateral accidents. If the victim can have an influence on the accident risk as well (and the accident is therefore one referred to as "bilateral") it is argued that strict liability might still be preferred if it is held that the injurer's influence on the activity is more important than the victim's influence (Landes & Posner, 1981: 907). The reason that French lawyers plead strongly in favour of strict liability has obviously more to do with the distributional differences between fault and strict liability. Under a perfectly working fault rule a victim will indeed in principle not be compensated, whereas a strict liability rule will in principle (if there is no insolvency risk) lead to victim compensation. That distributional difference is obviously an important reason for French lawyers such as Tunc and Viney to prefer a strict liability rule.

Strict liability regimes can be found in French law both in the Code Civil, as developed through case law, and in specific legislation. Again, it is not possible to discuss all of these cases in detail within the scope of this paper. We will have a brief look at some cases.

3.2 Code Civil

Turning first to the strict liability cases of the Code Civil, we should first discuss the well-known example of article 1384 (1) CC which has created (as interpreted by French case law) a strict liability for damage caused by the objects which one has under his guard. Originally case law held that this only applied to objects which are abnormally dangerous. However, in 1930 the French Cour de Cassation held in the well-known decision Jeand'heur that article 1384 (1) CC contains a general strict liability for all damage caused by an object (see Tunc, 1989: 88). From an economic point of view the strict liability seems too large, since it is not restricted to dangerous objects. Moreover, French case law has even held that the guardian of the defective object can not escape liability by proving that the damage was caused by force majeure. This means that the liability applies even if the potential injurer could not have influenced the accident risk. If one believes, as economic theory does, that liability rules should provide incentives to influence behaviour, this strict liability rule seems far too large.

The same can be argued considering another well-known case of strict liability, being the liability of parents for damage caused by their children, as incorporated in article 1384 (4) CC. Originally this liability was based on a presumption of fault in the guard or in the education. According to section 7 of article 1384 CC it was a rebuttable presumption: parents could still avoid to be held liable if they could prove that they could not be blamed for a lack of surveyance or a bad education. This still fitted into the economic model since it provided parents with an incentive for an adequate surveyance of the kids and for a good education, but avoided on the other hand, a crushing liability even in cases where the parents could not influence the behaviour of the child. This old rule has, however, been modified as a result of the decision "Bertrand" of the French Cour de Cassation on 19 February 1997. On the basis of this decision parents are held liable for damage caused by their children irrespective of any fault in the control or in the education of their children. Such a wide strict liability seems hardly efficient.

In both cases one can notice an important enlargement of liability, which seems questionable on economic grounds. In both cases the enlargement is motivated by victim compensation and very often the insurance argument plays a role as well. The extention of liability is, in other words, not considered problematic since most injurers are covered through liability insurance.

3.3 Special Status

Strict liability cases can also be found in a wide area of special statutes.[9] In that respect French law does not seem to differ very much from tendencies in other West-European legal systems: there is a strict liability for the licensee of a mine (Act of 21 April 1810), for the employer for accidents at work (Act of 9 April 1898), for damage on the ground by aeroplanes (Act of 31 May 1924) and for the licensee of a nuclear power plant (Acts of 12 November 1965 and 30 October 1968). In most of these (and many other) cases it can surely be argued that they enter into the economic arguments for strict liability: most of these cases (think about nuclear accidents) are typical unilateral cases where victims have little or no influence on the accident risk. However, the choice to introduce strict liability in particular cases is definitely not only based on economic criteria. One could e.g. ask why there is a strict liability for nuclear accidents, but not e.g. for the use of explosives or for the chemical industry. The answer is obviously that the choice to introduce strict liability in specific cases is often motivated by political needs (a typical example is the Act of 15 July 1992 concerning the compensation for victims of blood transfusions and aids). The choice of statutory strict liability regimes may to some extent be influenced by special interests (think e.g. of the Act of 27 December 1968, which instituted a compensation fund for victims of damage caused to the crops by wild boars or by game).

There is, however, an important weakness in the statutory strict liability cases, being that in many of these cases (think of the liability for nuclear accidents) there is a financial limit (a so-called cap) on the liability. These financial caps can, more specifically in case of strict liability, lead to serious underdeterrence for the simple reason that the injurer may not be exposed to the full risk of his activity. Moreover, they lead to undercompensation of victims as well. Financial caps are therefore problematic both from an economic and from a victim compensation perspective. That these financial limits on liability e.g. in case of the regulations concerning damage caused by marine oil pollution, cause serious problems, has been shown again recently with the disaster caused by the oil tanker Erika before the coast of Brittany. The fact that tanker owners are (as a result of financial caps) not fully exposed to the accident risk may negatively have affected their incentives to implement appropriate precautionary measures and leads *ex post* obviously to undercompensation of the victims.

In sum, one can notice that the strict liability in France, as developed in case law on the basis of articles from the Code Civil of 1804 seems to go a lot further in many cases than economic analysis predicts. Defended by "victim compensation" strict liabilities are introduced even in cases where the injurer can hardly influence the accident risk. Moreover, the choice to introduce strict liability in special statutes seems not only to have been based on economic criteria; special interest may have played a role in that respect as well. However, on one point economic and legal analysis seem to go hand in hand: if strict liability is introduced, the potential injurer should in principle be fully exposed to the risk. Financial limits on liability may lead both to underdeterrence and to undercompensation.

4. IMPUTABILITY

Under French law the act also has to be imputable to the tortfeasor. This condition, which is also referred to as the blameworthiness requirement, relates to the free will and the capacity of discretion of the tortfeasor (Faure & Van den Bergh, 1987: 100). This blameworthiness requirement is a very basic notion for economic doctrine since it would make no sense to hold someone liable if he could not have influenced the accident risk. Indeed, if the injurer does not act of his free will, liability does not seem to have any influence on the incentives to take care. Thus the imputability requirement has a clear economic rationale: giving incentives for prevention.

In French law the imputability was traditionally considered a condition for fault liability (see Starck 1996: no 396). However, a consequence of the imputability requirement is obviously that there may be accidents for which the tortfeasor is not held liable because the act is not imputable to him. This was felt as unacceptable by French legal doctrine who stresses the importance of victim compensation. Therefore the notion of objective faults, "faults without imputability" was introduced (see Starck, 1996: 56; Viney, 1995: 33). As a result of this doctrine and evolutions in case law the imputability no longer seems to be a condition for liability. This clearly is problematic from an economic point of view.

An example of this evolution can be found if one regards the situation of mental patients. Before 1968 French law generally accepted that mental patients who are in such a state of mind that they can not control their acts can not be held liable. A consequence of that position is obviously that victims who are damaged by a mental patient in such a state of mind receive no compensation. Therefore the legislator completely changed the approach in 1968 by introducing an article 489–2 in the Civil Code, which provides that the one who causes a damage to another even if he was in such a state of mind that he could not control his acts is nevertheless bound to compensate. From an economic perspective, this seems inefficient since such a liability can not contribute to providing incentives for prevention. Again, victim compensation was advanced as the main reason for this legislative change. Viney once more stressed that insurance should be taken out on the behalf of mental patients, so that once more the liability insurance would take over the compensation function of tort law (Viney, 1985).

The only defences which are still accepted (and also only to some extent) in French liability law are force majeure and the contributory negligence of the victim. But e.g. as far as the liability of the guardian for defective objects (1384 (1) CC) is concerned, we should refer to a decision Desmares of the French Cour de Cassation of 21 July 1982, which held that the victim's contributory negligence could not lead to any (even partial) reduction of the liability of the guardian. This decision has, however, been reformed by several decisions of 6 April 1987, which re-introduced the victim's fault as an element to reduce the liability of the guardian.[10]

5. THE ACT BADINTER ON TRAFFIC LIABILITY

5.1 Principles

The tendencies described above in French tort law, towards more victim compensation and an increased reliance on insurance, can probably best be seen in the system of traffic liability as this has been introduced in France by the Act of 5 July 1985, often referred to as the Act Badinter, being the minister of justice who introduced this act. The act provides a relatively simple basic principle, being that all victims of a traffic accident, with the exception of drivers, are compensated for the damage they suffer as a result of an accident. This indemnification is guaranteed by the liability insurer of the motor vehicle, which is involved in the accident. This obligation to indemnify the victim is an almost absolute one: force majeure or the simple fault of the victim can not exclude the obligation to compensate the victim. The victim's right on compensation is only (totally!) excluded if the victim committed an inexcusable fault which was the exclusive cause of the accident.

5.2 Strict Liability

The introduction of a strict liability for traffic accidents as such corresponds with the economic model. One can certainly hold that the influence of the victim on the accident risk is less important than the influence of the car driver. Hence, it seems more important to control the behaviour of the car driver than that of a victim, so that a strict liability rule seems warranted. However, the strict liability under the Act Badinter already applies as soon as the motor vehicle is "involved" in an accident which caused damage to the victim. Concerning this "involvement" (implication) of the motor vehicle, a wide case law has developed, which made clear that it is absolutely not necessary that the motor vehicle itself should have intervened in the accident; the strict liability is applicable even if the motor vehicle played a totally passive role. Hence, case law accepted the strict liability under the Act Badinter in cases where the motor vehicle was parked in a perfectly legal way without hindering the traffic. Hence, since the strict liability applies as soon as the motor vehicle is "involved" this means that there is liability even if the care driver could not influence the accident risk through his behaviour. The Act Badinter is therefore a pure compensation mechanism and no longer a system which aims at providing incentives for prevention. This is also clear from the fact that the car diver is liable even if the accident was caused by force majeure.

5.3 Victim's Fault

Also the way in which the victim's contributory negligence is taken account of in the Act Badinter seems doubtful on economic grounds. "Normal" contributory negligence is not sufficient to reduce the liability of the car driver. The Act Badinter only takes into account the inexcusable fault of the victim which had to be the exclusive cause of the accident. If that is the case, the victim totally looses his right on compensation. Again, the way case law interpretes this condition is very victim friendly.[11] To walk through a red light or to walk in the middle of a crossroad in the middle of the night are according to case law not inexcusable faults. Case law held that the fault of the victim becomes in fact only inexcusable in cases where his behaviour is that serious that it shows the conscience of the victim of the probability of damage and the acceptation of these consequences. This case law, which almost excludes the victim's fault as an element to reduce the liability seems to be contrary to the economic notions. Some empirical studies showed that such an automatic compensation of victims may lead to an increased accident risk (see Landes, 1982: 49). Moreover, it might also negatively affect the incentives of injurers (see White, 1989: 308). Until now there are no clear empirical studies available on the influence of the Act Badinter on traffic safety in France. Only Prof. Tunc held that after ten years of the Act Badinter insurance premiums had not increased

(Tunc, 1996) but that obviously says relatively little on the influence of that act on traffic safety.

6. CONCLUDING REMARKS

In this brief paper we merely wanted to show that economic analysis of tort law can be applied to French liability rules as it can to any other legal system. Of course we could only provide a first introduction to the possibility of applying economic analysis on French tort law, but even then some interesting results appear. If one looks at traditional rules, such as the fault notion, the way that French judges seem to interprete these may largely follow economic theory. Although in French case law there are no Learned Hand like evaluations of the standard of care, weighing costs and benefits, some elements of the fault appreciation, such as the predictability requirement, seem to follow largely economic analysis. Also the interpretation of the bonus pater familias rule, which allows for a differentiation of the standard of care in cases where differences can be established at relatively low costs seems to follow economic logic.

More difficult from an economic point of view are, however, the strict liability regimes. More particularly the way in which case law has interpreted traditional strict liability cases of the Code Civil seem often too extensive. In some cases liability is accepted also when this never could have affected the incentives for care. The same holds for the relaxation of the imputability requirement, whereby even mental patients who can not control their acts are held liable in tort. All of these tendencies which are hardly reconcilable with economic analysis are based on distributive justice notions, such as victim compensation.

One could therefore – pessimistically – conclude that economic analysis does not have that much to teach to French lawyers since economics of tort law is apparently based on deterrence, whereas French legal doctrine is apparently based on victim compensation. However, even if victim compensation is considered as a primary policy goal, which is apparently the case in France, economics remains important. It can e.g. indicate that alternative mechanisms may exist, which could reach the goal of victim compensation at lower costs than tort law. It is more particularly for that reason that the well-known French lawyer André Tunc has for a long time advocated insurance based alternatives to the tort system. But even then the question remains important to know what the influence of those alternative systems might be on the behaviour of potential parties to an accident and thus on safety generally. This of course is generally an empirical question. It would definitely be interesting to examine empirically how the French tort and compensation systems have affected the accident risk. In that respect French tort law may prove to provide a highly interesting playground for law and economics scholars.

NOTES

1. See in this respect the many publications of André Tunc (e.g. Tunc, 1989, nos 170–173).
2. This has been argued by Landes, 1982, p. 253.
3. This has been developed by Brown (1973).
4. See for a summary and economic critique of this Learned Hand rule: Brown 1973; Landes and Posner 1981, p. 885.
5. See e.g. Malaurie and Aynes, 1998, pp. 52–55.
6. See for a summary of those notions: Starck, 1947, 1996, pp. 28–50.
7. For an overview of this tendency see Viney, 1995, pp. 34–94.
8. See for these "classic" arguments in favour of strict liability from an economic perspective: Landes and Posner, 1981, p. 877; Shavell, 1980, pp. 7, 19.
9. For an overview see Starck, 1996, p. 34; Viney, 1995, p. 24.
10. On this evolution see Starck, B., 1996, pp. 262–263.
11. For an overview see Starck, 1996: p. 793.

REFERENCES

Brown, J. P. (1973). Towards an Economic Theory of Liability. *Journal of Legal Studies, 2*, 323–349.

Calabresi, G. (1970). *The Costs of Accidents.* New Haven: Yale University Press.

Dewees, D., Duff, D., & Trebilcock, M. (1996). *Exploring the Domain of Accident Law. Taking the Facts Seriously.* Oxford: Oxford University Press.

Diamond, P. (1974). Single Activity Accidents. *Journal of Legal Studies, 3*, 123.

Faure, M., & Van den Bergh, R. (1987). Negligence, Strict Liability and Regulation of Safety under Belgian law: an Introductory in Economic Analysis. *Geneva Papers on Risk and Insurance, 12.*

Landes, E. (1982). Compensation for Automobile Accident Injuries: is the Tort System Fair? *Journal of Legal Studies, 11.*

Landes, W., & Posner, R. (1981). Positive Economic Theory of Tort Law. *Georgia Law Review, 15*, 924–951.

Malaurie, Ph., & Aynes, L. (1998). *Droit civil, obligations*, 9th edition. Paris: Cujas.

Shavell, S. (1980). Strict Liability versus Negligence. *Journal of Legal Studies.*

Shavell, S. (1987). *Economic Analysis of Accident Law.* Cambridge: Harvard University Press.

Starck, B. (1947). *Essai d'une théorie générale dans la responsabilité civile considérée en sa double fonction de garantie en de peine privée.* Paris.

Starck, B. (1996). *Obligations*, Vol. 1, *Responsabilité délictuelle* (5th ed.), by H. Roland and L. Boyer. Paris: Litec.

Tunc, A. (1989). *La responsabilité civile*, 2e éd. Paris: Economica.

Tunc, A. (1996). The Loi Badinter, Ten Years of Experience. *Maastricht Journal of European and Comparative Law, 3*, 336–339.

Van den Bergh, R. (1988). Le droit civil face à l'analyse économique du droit. *Revue internationale de droit économique*, 249.

Viney, G. (1985). La réparation des dommages causés sous l'empire d'un état d'inconscience: un transfert nécessaire de la responsabilité vers l'assurance. *JCP*, I.3189.

Viney, G. (1995). *Traité de droit civil. Introduction à la responsabilité* (2nd ed.). Paris: *LGDJ*.

White, M. (1989). An Empirical Test of the Comparative and Contributory Negligence Rule in Accident Law. *Rand Journal of Economics*.

ALTERNATIVE DISPUTE RESOLUTION IN THE FRENCH LEGAL SYSTEM: AN EMPIRICAL STUDY

Myriam Doriat-Duban

INTRODUCTION

In France, "Alternative Dispute Resolution" (ADR) groups together transactions[1] conciliations[2] and mediations[3] that is all the forms of out-of-court settlements but also some agreements obtained with the help of the judge. Indeed, according to article 21 of the New Code of Civil Procedure (NCCP), "it is part of the mission of a judge to reconcile the litigants". Moreover, in the majority of settled civil conflicts, the agreement is obtained because the judge has advised the litigants to resort to a conciliator or a mediator.

The French legal system has always sought to favour settlement in civil law conflicts. Until 1958, some judges, called "*juges de paix*" were charged to conciliate litigants and they had to judge only if no amicable issue could have been found. In 1958, these judges are substituted by the *Tribunaux d'instance*[4] (Magistrates Courts) and the *Tribunaux de grande instance*[5] (County Courts) but the agreements are always favoured. For instance, the law of February 8th 1995 institutes two new ADR occurring in the shadow of the judge: juridical mediation and juridical conciliation. More recently, another law has encouraged the development of ADR within the scope of the legal reform taking place in France. Thus, the main aim of the law of December 18th 1998 concerning "access to the law and to the out-of-court settlement of disputes" is to provide

Law and Economics in Civil Law Countries, Volume 6, pages 183–197.

ISBN: 0-7623-0712-9

those concerned with a series of solutions to settle a dispute without having to systematically wait for a court's decision. Indeed, legal authorities want to prevent the recourse to "the all-judicial" to meet this demand. More precisely, according to the Minister of Justice, E. Guigou, "recourse to a negotiated mode of dispute settlement should not only be an alternative to the judgement but also to the trial itself; we must cease confusing access to law with access to justice". The main reason to encourage ADR is the rise of demand for justice. Indeed, between 1975 and 1995, the number of civil conflicts has been multiplied by 2.7 in TGI and has doubled in TI. Currently, the number of new conflicts tends to stagnate, but this recent evolution is not sufficient to reverse definitively the trend observed during the last twenty five years. The consequence is the growth of the delays. Thus, the generally accepted idea in France is one of a slow and congested justice (Coulon (1997)) and ADR appears like one of the solutions to make justice more efficient.

Before verifying this affirmation, a brief review of literature about economic analysis of civil conflicts is made. It constitutes the theoretical framework of our study. Then, the data base with which we have made our empirical study is presented. Afterwards, the settlement rate in the *Tribunaux d'instance* (TI) and in the *Tribunaux de grande instance* (TGI) are calculated. Before concluding, we will estimate duration of conflicts in the French civil courts and we will show that a deadline effect can be observed.

ECONOMIC ANALYSIS OF CIVIL CONFLICT

To ensure that the current reform of the French civil Justice will allow to reach the wished aim but equally to define incentive policies to develop amicable resolution, it is important to wonder individual motivations of the recourse to courts. A microeconomic analysis, inspired by the developments of the economic analysis of judicial conflicts, can help to orient the future policies. The litigants in a conflict are submitted to two informational problems, which can be associated with two distinct but complementary analyses. The first one concerns the uncertainty on the law or on rights; it corresponds to the optimistic approach of the economic analysis of civil conflicts (Landes, 1971; Gould, 1973; Posner, 1973; Shavell, 1982a, b). In this approach, the failure of negotiations is explained by the excessive optimism of one litigant on his probability of victory at trial or on the amount of damages. This excessive optimism can be explained, according to Miceli (1997), by an uncertainty on the law that makes a party to commit errors of estimation on the result of the judgement. In these studies, the agreement depends on the perception of a cooperative surplus corresponding to the economy of costs allowed by the agreement. If only one litigant does not detect this surplus, the conflict is judged. This analysis has been criticized by Cooter (1982) and Cooter, Marks and Mnookin (1982) because it does not take into account the strategic aspects of the conflict, litigants being always supposed to behave faithfully. According to Cooter, negotiations can fail even if the two litigants detect the cooperative surplus, simply because one of the litigants attempts to capture the totality or the major part of the surplus retired of the agreement. On this point, he agrees with Posner (1992) who estimates that negotiations in a conflict constitute a typical example of bilateral monopoly, where each litigant tries to capture the most important share of the surplus generated by the agreement. Absence of consensus on the division of the cooperative surplus causes the failure of negotiations even if the litigants are aware of the advantage to settle. The strategic approach of the economic analysis of civil law conflicts has emerged from this critic (P'ng, 1983; Bebchuk, 1984; Schweizer, 1989; Spier, 1992; Deffains, 1997). These studies are centred on the second informational problem to which litigants are submitted in a conflict: the type of the adversary. Partisans of this second approach, largely majority, consider that litigants try to take advantage of their private information to adopt strategic behaviors. Thus, they attempt to obtain from their opponent a more favorable agreement than that obtained with complete information. The problem of adverse selection of the uninformed litigant prevents to settle because of the risk to conclude an agreement opposite to its interests. Then, the only way to preserve them consists to resort to the judge, supposedly able to suppress asymmetries of information. In this type of studies, each litigant chooses his strategy by comparing the increase of the gain of a more favorable agreement with the rise of the probability of negotiations failure (Cooter & Rubinfeld, 1989). These two types of models are complementary. More precisely, optimistic studies are better adapted to the inexperienced litigants, for the first time in a conflict. The strategic analysis, on the other hand, seems to us more adapted to describe the behavior of litigants who seek to satisfy their interests by using their privileged information. Then private information are used for strategic purposes, the main aim being to obtain the most favorable agreement by misleading the opponent.

These two approaches can be used to find rational explanations to judgements but also to research means to incite to negotiate. Indeed, the main aim of the authors is to preview the effect of many policies on the negotiation. For instance, these models show how a rise of trial costs incite litigants to settle (Cooter & Rubinfeld, 1989); they compare rules of costs allocation (Reinganum & Wilde, 1986; Farmer & Pecorino, 1994; Posner, 1996; Doriat-Duban, 2000) or the role of advocates (Rubinfeld & Scotchmer, 1993; Gravelle & Waterson, 1993; Hay, 1996, 1997; Gilson & Mnookin, 1994, 1995).

So, these studies appear very helpful in the framework of the French civil Law reform. But before seeking new policies to encourage negotiation in civil law conflicts, it is very important to describe the French civil justice. This first step is essential to demonstrate the necessity of researching new issues for civil conflicts in France and, particularly, the necessity to develop ADR. Indeed, it is a question of knowing if delays are effectively excessive in the French civil courts and if ADR must be encouraged because French litigants do not settle enough. For this purpose, settlement rate will be calculated and the duration of conflict resolution will be measured. In addition, a deadline effect, defined by Ma and Manove (1993) as a point in time after which the potential value of an agreement is decreased sharply, will be put in evidence. The concentration of agreements occurring in the final stage of the negotiations appears, in the authors' opinions (Roth, Murnighan & Schoumaker, 1988; Swanson & Mason, 1998), to constitute a reasonably robust result[6] and is likely to characterize numerous bargaining situations in the real world. Spier (1992) has demonstrated that it exists theoretically in civil law conflicts and Fenn and Rickman (1999) have shown empirically its existence in England. Our aim is to demonstrate that this deadline effect is also observed in the French civil courts.

DATA BASE

The aim of the empirical study consists in describing the French civil justice by answering two questions:

(1) What is the settlement rate in the French civil courts (TI and TGI)?
(2) What is the duration of litigation according to the jurisdiction and the mode of regulation?

Data used in this study have been collected by the Statistics Department of the Ministry of Justice. They concern conflicts, ended in 1995, in TI and TGI. Our sample contains 873 773 civil conflicts, whose 57.1% have been solved in TGI and 42.9% in TI.

For each ended conflict, available informations are:

- the competent court: TI or TGI;
- the mode of resolution: jurisdictional (judgement) or non-jurisdictional (radiation, withdrawal, conciliation, mediation, . . .);
- the nature of the conflict: the level 1 corresponds to great areas of the civil law (family law, property law, . . .) and the level 2 corresponds to subcategories (in family law, divorce, parental rights, . . .);

- the duration of resolution, given in months until two years, in trimesters between two and three years, in semesters between three and five years, without distinction of duration between five and ten years, without distinction of duration beyond ten years.

To calculate the settlement rate, it is necessary to identify all the tacit agreements among the non-jurisdictional decisions (withdrawal, radiation, . . .) and to suppress the joinders which are non-jurisdictional decisions but not agreements.

Our study shows a very small number of settled disputes. Indeed, the settlement rate in France, independently of the jurisdiction and of the nature of the conflict, is only 22.9%. On this point France clearly stands apart from the U.S.A. where the majority of cases seem to have a cooperative outcome.[7] If this rate shows that the judgement constitutes the principal issue for French civil conflicts, it has little meaning since it does not take account neither specificities of jurisdictions, nor particularities of litigation.

A sharper analysis shows that the settlement rate appears relatively low both in the TGI and the TI (Table 1). In the TI the settlement rate attains only 24.7% which means that less than one quarter of civil cases are settled out of court. But there exists a heavy disparity between case types. The maximum settlement rate (34.4%) is in the field of company law whereas the minimum rate (19.8%) is to be seen in public person law. A relatively high settlement rate may also be observed in property law (29.7%) and labour law (30.1%). Rates close to the average are also present in family law (24.2%), contract law (23.1%) and liability (25.1%). The high rate of disparity is confirmed by a heavy coefficient of variation indicating that, on average, the settlement rate of any given category of conflict has a difference of 19.4% with the average settlement rate.

Table 1. Settlement Rate in TI and TGI.

	Settlement rate	
	Tribunal d'instance	Tribunal de grande instance
Total	24.7	21.6
Family	24.2	20.7
Business	21.7	28.3
Company	34.4	35.7
Contract	23.1	22.5
Liability	25.1	21.0
Property	29.7	23.4
Labour	30.1	17.4
Public Person	19.8	18.5

Although it is low, the proportion of settlements appears to be greater in the TI than in the TGI where its average value is 21.6%. Similar to the TI, considerable disparities are to be found in the settlement rates observed in the TGI. If the maximum rate is always to be found in company law (35.7%, higher than that of the TI), the minimum is now to be seen in labour law (17.4%). The settlement rate increases strongly however when it comes to business law where it now attains 28.3% (i.e. an increase of 6.6 points). If the settlement rate changes very little for contract law (22.5%) when we look at the TGI, it falls sharply, on the contrary for property law (where it loses over 6 points to arrive at 23.4%). The fall in the settlement rate regarding liability is noteworthy but limited (21%, representing a drop of 4.1 points) and in family law (20.8%, i.e. a fall of 3.4 points). The rate disparity in the TGI is also higher than in the TI as the coefficient of variation is 28.6% in the first case as against 19.4% in the second, indicating that, on average, in the cases brought before the TGI, the settlement rate has difference of over 25% with the average rate.

DEADLINE FOR RESOLUTION OF DISPUTES

Average and median durations have been calculated with centers of range given in months. Average durations rise mechanically because of the very long conflicts (more than 2 years). Median durations permit to correct this bias.

Our study allows us to establish three results in TI (Table 2):

(1) average duration of resolution differs according to **the mode of resolution** since the average duration of resolution is 4.9 months for settled conflicts and 5.3 months for judged disputes.

(2) average duration of resolution differs according to **the nature of the conflict**: for judged conflicts, the average duration of resolution comes from 1.2 months for conflicts in the field of public person to 6.7 months in liability law and the coefficient of variation is 33.9%. Similarly, for settled conflicts, the average duration comes from 2.2 months in the field of public person to 7.6 months in company law and the coefficient of variation is 38%.

(3) average duration of resolution is always greater than **median duration** since this last is 3 months for judgements and 2 months for agreements. That means that the majority of conflicts is solved with a short delay, shorter than the average delay. This difference is explained by very long conflicts which create a bias.

The comparison of these results, established with data given by the Ministry of Justice and which concern the year 1995, and the durations published by the

Table 2. Deadline for Resolution of Disputes in *Tribunaux D'instance.*

Deadline for resolution of disputes in TI

	average duration		median duration	
	judgements	agreements	judgements	agreements
Total	5.3 (5.2)*	4.9	3	2
Family	5.7 (4.9)	6.0	3	2
Business	5.8 (5.7)	7.5	13	4
Company	6.2 (3.2)	7.6	4	5
Contract	5.3 (5.1)	4.5	3	2
Liability	6.7 (6.5)	5.3	4	11
Property	6.0 (6.0)	5.8	3	3
Labour	3.0 (2.8)	2.7	2	1
Public Person	1.2 (5.4)	2.2	0.5	0.5

*Duration calculated by the French Ministry of Justice for the year 1997.

French Ministry of Justice for the year 1997 (between brackets in Table 2) shows that the duration of judged conflicts tends to decrease in TI (especially in company law), except for public person law where it rises. We think that one of the explanations of this trend is the decrease of the number of cases since the number of conflicts in TI was 374,550 in 1995 and was 355,342 in 1997.

Average and median durations in TGI are the following (Table 3):

Table 3. Deadline for resolution of disputes in *Tribunaux de grande instance.*

	average duration		median duration	
	judgements	agreements	judgements	agreements
Total	10 (9.6)*	10.7	7	5
Family	8.5 (8.7)	9.4	6	4
Business	14.5 (16.4)	15.2	11	10
Company	7.9 (9.1)	7.2	5	4
Contract	14.3 (15.5)	14.0	11	8
Liability	16.8 (17.5)	17.0	13	11
Property	14.5 (15.3)	13.8	10	9
Labour	5.2 (5.8)	8.0	2	3
Public Person	5.3 (11.9)	11.3	9	7

*Duration calculated by the French Ministry of Justice for the year 1997.[8]

Our study allows us to establish four results in TGI:

(1) average duration of resolution differs according to **the mode of resolution** since the average duration of resolution is 10 months for settled conflicts and 10.7 months for judged disputes.
(2) average duration of resolution differs according to **the nature of the conflict**: for judged conflicts, the average duration of resolution comes from 5.2 months for conflicts in the field of labour to 16.8 months in liability law; the coefficient of variation is 42.2%. Similarly, for settled conflicts, the average duration comes from 7.2 months in the field of company to 17 months in liability law; the coefficient of variation is 33.4%.
(3) average duration of resolution is always greater than **median duration** since this last is 7 months for judgements and 5 months for agreements.
(4) average and median durations are always shorter in TI than in TGI. The stakes, the complexity of the cases (the representation by a lawyer is obligatory in TGI, not in TI), the nature of the conflicts (TGI is the main competent court for family law), the organization of the court (one judge in TI, three judges in TGI) can explain these differences of duration in conflicts resolution. But we can neither verify nor measure influence of these factors on the duration of conflicts resolution, since it is impossible to realize a hazard model with our data.

If we compare durations in 1995 and durations calculated by the French Ministry of Justice in 1997, we can observe an increase of duration of judgements in all fields of the law despite the decrease of number of cases in this court (499,223 in 1995, 469,894 in 1997). The reasons could be the rise of the stock of conflicts to solve despite the decrease of the flux or a greater complexity of the case, notably in company, contract and property law.

Deadline Effect in the French Civil Courts

"The deadline effect" means that a high percentage of amicable settlements may be observed just prior to the negotiation deadline. Spier (1992) takes on the task of checking on the existence of a deadline effect in the field of legal conflicts, in a context of incomplete information, where the under-informed party submits an offer of settlement. Fournier and Zuehlke (1996), Spurr (1997) and Fenn and Rickman (1999) have proved empirically that this effect exists in the field of liability. Our study permits to generalize the deadline effect to other conflicts in the French legal system.

To know if a deadline effect exists in the French civil courts, we propose to observe the settlements and the judgements peaks for each field of the law (graphs 1 and 2) and to compare modal durations of agreements and judgements in each jurisdictions and for each field of the law (Table 4). If they are simultaneous, we can conclude that a deadline effect exists in the concerned field.[9]

Deadline Effect in TI

The "total" curve, gathering all disputes coming under the TI, shows simultaneous peaks for judgements and agreements. Thus, it confirms the existence of a deadline effect in the TI. This result is confirmed by calculus of modal durations (2 months). The deadline effect is particularly acute in business, contract, labour and public person law since modal durations are the same for judgements and agreements. A deadline effect is also visible but to a lesser extent in family, property and liability law. Nevertheless, the difference between judgements and agreements modal durations is weak (one month) and the fact that the two curves have the same shape would appear to confirm the existence of the deadline effect (graphs 1b, 1f and 1 g). Conversely, the deadline effect is invalidated in company law where no peaks of agreement is observed.

Deadline Effect in TGI

Graphs 2a and Table 4 show the existence of a deadline effect in TGI if no distinction is made according to the field of the law. Indeed, modal duration of judgements and agreements are the same and the two peaks are simultaneous. The deadline effect is certain in family law like in TI. In other fields, the existence of the deadline effect is not as certain as in TI. But the modal duration being separated by only one month and the two curves having the same shape, the deadline effect can be validated. It is the case for business, company, contracts, and labour law. The deadline effect is more difficult to prove in property law because the modal durations differs from 2 months. Nevertheless, agreements and judgements are very numerous at three, four and five months and the numbers of judgements is almost the same at three and four month whereas the number of agreements is almost the same between three and four months. Consequently, a deadline effect can be validated.

In other fields, the deadline effect is invalidated. It is the case in liability law and in public person law. It is not surprising that no deadline effect exists

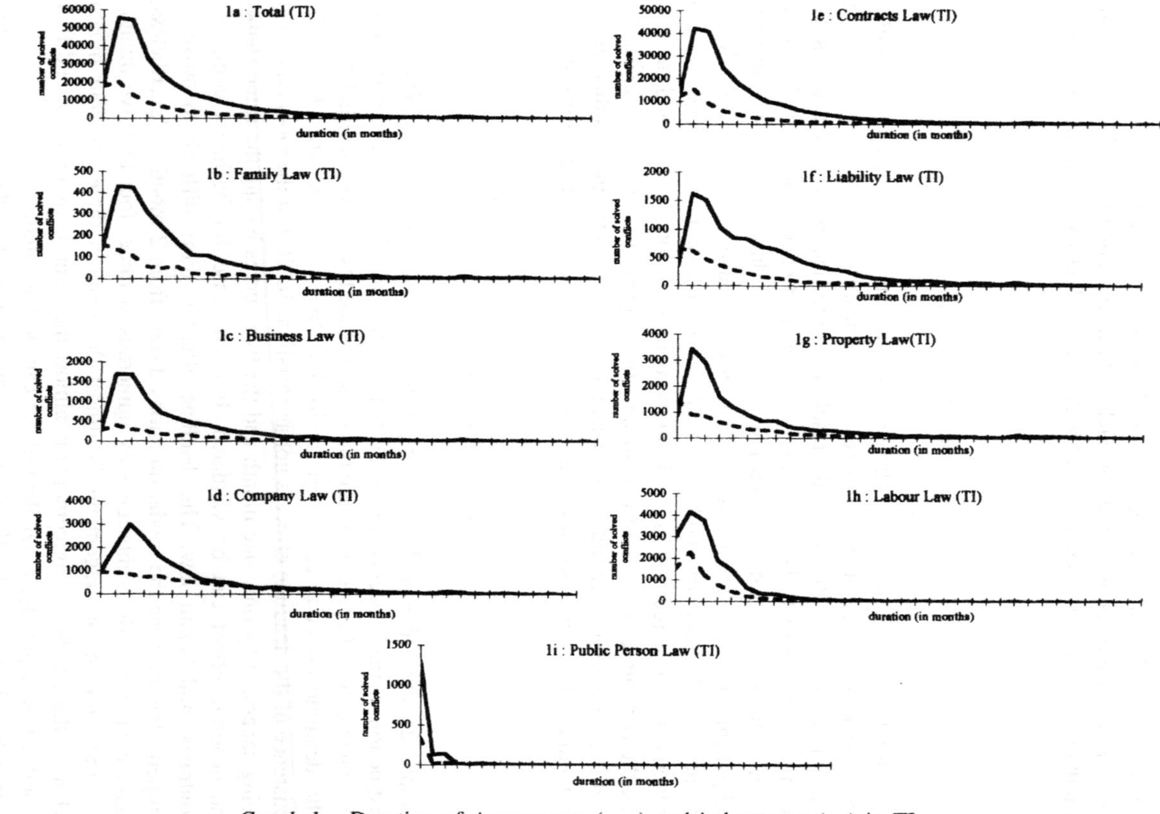

Graph 1. Duration of Agreements (- - -) and judgements (—) in TI.

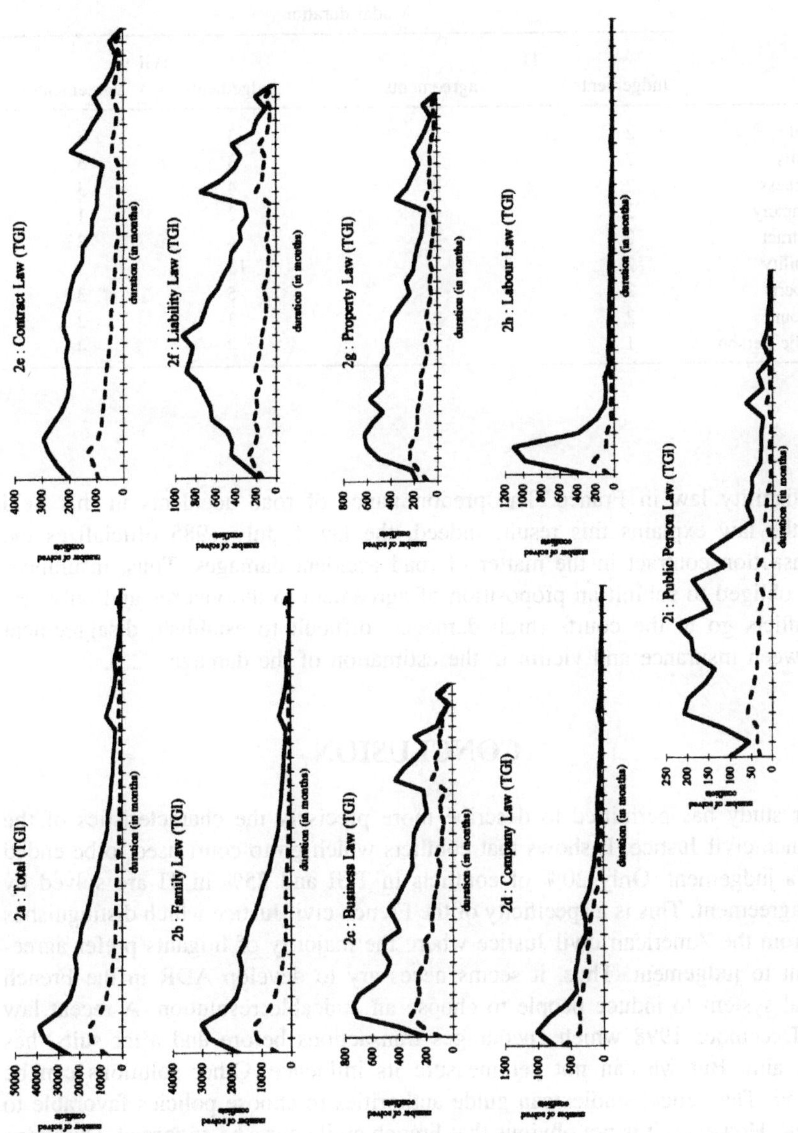

Graph 2. Duration of Agreements (- - -) and judgements (—) in TGI.

Table 4. Modal Duration in TI and TGI.

	Modal duration			
	TI		TGI	
	Judgements	agreements	judgements	agreements
Total	2	2	3	3
Family	2	1	3	3
Business	2	2	4	3
Company	3	1	2	1
Contract	2	2	4	3
Liability	2	1	13	3
Property	2	1	5	3
Labour	2	2	3	2
Public person	1	1	4	4

in liability law in France. The predominance of road accidents in this field of the law explains this result. Indeed, the law 5 July 1985 officializes the transaction contract in the matter of road accident damages. Thus, insurances are obliged to submit an proposition of agreement to the victims and only few conflicts go to the courts (high damages, difficult to establish, disagreement between insurance and victim in the estimation of the damages . . .).

CONCLUSION

Our study has permitted to describe more precisely the characteristics of the French civil Justice. It shows that conflicts which go to court used to be ended by a judgement. Only 20% of conflicts in TGI and 25% in TI are solved by an agreement. This is a specificity of the French civil Justice which distinguishes it from the American civil Justice where the majority of litigants prefer agreement to judgement. Thus, it seems necessary to develop ADR in the French legal system to induce people to choose an amicable resolution. A recent law of December 1998 which encourages transactions before and after suits, has this aim. But we can not yet measure its influence. Other solutions can be found. Theoretical studies can guide authorities to choose policies favorable to ADR. However, it is not obvious that French civil courts be engorged. Durations in TI do not seem excessive. In TGI, the problem appears more serious, notably in contract, liability and property laws. Moreover, data given by the French

Ministry of Justice for 1997 show a rising trend which is more worrying. Neverthless, these durations appear short according to durations of resolution observed in Belgium (Mühl & Vereeck, 1998) or in England (Fenn & Rickman, 1999).

NOTES

1. The transaction is a contract by which the litigants end an existing dispute or avoid a potential dispute (art. 2044 of the Civil Code).

2. Conciliation is an agreement by which the litigants put an end to their dispute, either by transaction or by withdrawal, with the help of a conciliator or of the judge. Conciliation is attempted for civil conflicts judged in the *Tribunaux d'Instance* (Magistrate Courts).

3. The aim of mediation is also to bring people closer together but, unlike to the conciliator, the main goal of the mediator is to offer a solution or, failing this, to encourage the litigants to draw up a plan of agreement by themselves. Mediation is attempted for civil conflicts judged in the *Tribunaux de Grande Instance* (County Courts). French Mediation differs from the American Mediation since the first happens in the shadow of the judge whereas the second takes place out of court.

4. The TI (Magistrates Court), as a special court, takes charge of all financial disputes of less than 30,000 francs (for conflicts included in our study; today, the limit is 50,000 francs). Representation by a lawyer is optional.

5. The TGI covers all civil cases except where a law has given competence to a special court. It deals with cases where the amounts involved are over 30,000 francs (for conflicts included in our study, today, the limit is 50,000 francs). The parties must be represented by a lawyer (article 751 NCCP).

6. This phenomenon is robust, in the sense that the distribution of agreements over time does not respond to changes in the bargaining environment nearly as much as do other features of the outcome of bargaining, such as the terms on which agreement is reached.

7. Numerous American and English authors highlight the small number of cases actually going to court in the USA. Below are a number of examples to underline this phenomenon:

- Priest and Klein [1984] on the basis of various studies state: "it is well known that only a very small fraction of disputes comes to trial"
- Bebchuck [1984] confirms this: "the great majority of legal disputes is not resolved by the courts, but rather through out of court settlements'"
- Miceli [1997]: "the fact that the vast majority of civil cases are settled or dropped just before they go to trial"; his claim is supported by a table showing that the trial rate is below 5% between 1987 and 1993.

8. These durations differ slightly from the durations published in the "Annuaire statistique de la justice" (1999), because we have excluded legal decisions which are not judgements.

9. In a precedent study, we still have sought to test the existence of a deadline effect in the French civil Courts (Doriat-Duban and Deffains [1999]). However, this analysis

was less precise than the study presented in this paper because the shorter durations were expressed in trimesters whereas the durations we use here are given in months. Greater the ranges, less visible the peaks of agreements and judgements. Moreover, decomposition by trimesters can hide some gap between peak of agreements and peak of judgements which can be detected by a decomposition by months.

REFERENCES

Annuaire Statistique de la Justice, édition de 1999. Paris: La Documentation Française.

Bebchuk, L. A. (1984). Litigation and Settlement under Imperfect Information. *Rand Journal of Economics*, *15*, 404–415.

Coulon, J-M. (1996). *Réflexions et Propositions sur la Procédure Civile*. Rapport au Garde des Sceaux. Paris: La Documentation Française.

Cooter, R. (1982). The Cost of Coase. *Journal of Legal Studies*, 1–33.

Cooter, R., Marks, S., & Mnookin, R. (1982). Bargaining in the Shadow of the Law: a Testable Model of Strategic Behavior. *Journal of Legal Studies*, *11*, 225–251.

Cooter R., & Rubinfeld, D. (1989). Economic Analysis of Legal Disputes and their Resolution. *Journal of Economic Literature*, *27*, 1067–1097.

Deffains, B. (1997). L'analyse économique de la résolution des conflits juridiques. *Revue française d'économie*, *12*(3): 57–99.

Doriat, M., & Deffains, B. (1999). The Dynamics of Pretrial Negotiation in France: Is there a Deadline Effect in the French Legal System? *International Review of Law and Economics*.

Doriat-Duban, M. (2000). *L'analyse économique du règlement des conflits: application au droit civil français*. Doctoral Thesis, Université de Nancy 2.

Farmer, A., & Pecorino, P. (1994). Pretrial Negotiations with Asymmetric Information on Risk Preferences. *International Review of Law and Economics*, *14*, 273–281.

Fenn, P., & Rickman, N. (1999). Delay and Settlement in Litigation. *Economic Journal*.

Fournier, G. M., & Zuehlke, T. W. (1989). Litigation and Settlement: an empirical approach. *Review of Economics and Statistics*, *71*, 189–195.

Gilson, R. J., & Mnookin, R. H. (1994). Disputing through Agents: Cooperation and Conflict between Lawyers in Litigation. *Columbia Law Review*, 509–564.

Gilson R. J., & Mnookin, R. H. (1995). Cooperation and Competition in Litigation: can Lawyers dampen Conflict? In: *Barriers to Conflict Resolution* (pp. 184–211). Arrow Kenneth-J.

Gould, J. P. (1973). The Economics of Legal Conflicts. *Journal of Legal Studies*, *2*, 279–300.

Gravelle, H., & Waterson, M. (1993). No Win, no Fee: some Economics of Contingent Legal Fees. *Economic Journal*, *2*, 1205–1220.

Hay, B. (1996). Contingent Fees and Agency Costs. *Journal of Legal Studies*, *25*, 503–533.

Hay, B. (1997). Optimal Contingent Fees in a World of Settlement. *Journal of Legal Studies*, *26*, 259–278.

Landes, W. M. (1971). An Economic Analysis of the Courts. *Journal of Law and Economics*, *14*, 61–107.

Miller, G. P. (1986). An Economic Analysis of Rule 68. *Journal of Legal Studies*, *15*, 93–125.

Muhl, M., & Vereeck, L. (1998). The Economics of Court Delay: a first Assessment of the Situation in Belgium. Communication at the *15th Conference of the European Association of Law and Economics*, pp. 1–33.

Nalebuff, B. (1987). Credible Pretrial Negociation. *Rand Journal of Economics*, *18*(2): 198–210.

P'ng I., P. L (1983). Strategic Behavior in Suit, Settlement and Trial. *The Bell Journal of Economics, 14*, 7–14.

Posner, R. A. (1973). An Economic Approach to Legal Procedure and Judicial Administration. *Journal of Legal Studies, 2*, 399–458.

Posner, R. A. (1992). *Economic Analysis of Law* (4th ed.), (pp. 1–722). Little, Brown and Company.

Posner, R. A. (1996). *Law and Legal Theory in England and America*. Clarendon Law Lectures. Oxford: Clarendon Press.

Priest, G. L., & Klein, B. (1984). The Selection of Disputes for Litigation. *Journal of Legal Studies, 13*, 1–53.

Reinganum, J., & Wilde, L. (1986). Settlement, Litigation, and the Allocation of Litigation Costs. *Rand Journal of Economics, 17*, 557–566.

Roth, A. E., Murnighan, J. K., & Schoumaker, F. (1988). The Deadline Effect in Bargaining: some Experimental Evidence. *American Economic Review, 78*(4), 806–823.

Rubinfeld, D. L., & Scotchmer, S. (1993). Contingent Fees for Attorneys: an Economic Analysis. *Rand Journal of Economics, 24*(3), 343–356.

Schweizer, U. (1989). Litigation and Settlement under two sided incomplete Information. *Review of Economic Studies, 56*, 163–178.

Shavell, S. (1982a). The Social versus the Private Incentives to Bring Suit in a Costly Legal System. *Journal of Legal Studies, 11*, 333–339.

Shavell, S. (1982b). Suit, Settlement and Trial: a Theoretical Analysis under Alternative Methods for the Allocation of Legal Costs. *Journal of Legal Studies, 11*, 55–81.

Spier, K. (1992). The Dynamics of Pretrial Negotiation. *Review of Economic Studies, 59*, 93–108.

Swanson, T., & Mason, R. (1998). Nonbargaining in the Shadow of the Law. *International Review of Law and Economics, 18*, 121–140.

Spurr, S. J. (1997). The Duration of Litigation. *Law and Policy, 10*(2), 285–312.

AN ECONOMIC VIEWPOINT OF CRIMINAL SYSTEMS IN CIVIL LAW COUNTRIES

Nuno Garoupa

INTRODUCTION

The economic analysis of crime and criminal law is now a well-established field within the economic analysis of law. The large body of literature surveyed by Nuno Garoupa (1997) and Mitchell Polinsky and Steven Shavell (2000b) is sufficient proof. This essay is not one more survey of the rational theory of law enforcement. Elsewhere, the reader can find the major contributions of the economic theory to the understanding of criminal behavior and law enforcement. The present article focuses on the fundamentals of the theory, that is to say, the assumptions that support the theory and the criticisms such assumptions have faced.

The second aim of this essay is to address the policy implications for civil law countries of the rational theory of law enforcement from an European perspective. It is of particular importance how the essential differences between common law and civil law countries affect criminal systems.

The next section helps the reader to understand the economic analysis of criminal systems. It briefly exposes the literature and extensively discusses the criticisms to the economic approach. The following section explains how the current theory may be helpful in the analysis of civil law countries. Final remarks are addressed at the end of the chapter.

Law and Economics in Civil Law Countries, Volume 6, pages 199–215.

ISBN: 0-7623-0712-9

ECONOMICS OF CRIME AND LAW ENFORCEMENT

The proposition that crime rates respond to risks and benefits is called the deterrence hypothesis. It is an application of the theory of demand to one of the most important issues in criminal justice. The hypothesis asserts that people respond significantly to the incentives created by the criminal justice system. If so, increasing the resources that society devotes to the arrest, conviction, and punishment of criminals will reduce the amount, and social costs, of crime. As many scholars refer, there is a competing hypothesis that holds that criminals are not deterred by variations in the certainty and severity of punishment. Rather, this hypothesis holds that crime is caused by a complex set of socio-economic and biological factors, and that the appropriate way to reduce the amount of crime and thus lower the costs of crime is to divert resources into channels that attack these root causes of crime.

Although recent public debate has tended to frame these two hypotheses as mutually exclusive, we argue that it is more sensible to view them as complementary in which case the optimal public policy for reducing crime may be a mix of deterrence and policies directed at the root causes.[1]

Suppose that there is a particular crime that we wish to deter, say, fraud. It might be possible to eliminate fraud, or very nearly eliminate it, by having severe punishment imposed with a high probability upon offenders. However, deterring fraud in this way may run into two kinds of difficulties.

First, very harsh penalties may violate the moral and constitutional rights of criminals.[2] The second consideration, which is our direct concern, is cost. Apprehending, prosecuting, and punishing offenders can be expensive. Policy-makers will want to balance these costs against the advantages of reducing crime when making policy decisions. The optimal amount of deterrence does not eliminate crime altogether. The reason for this is that eradicating crime is costly and has a declining social benefit. Policy-makers will also want to allocate their limited resources so as to achieve any given level of deterrence at least cost, that is, they will seek to achieve their goal efficiently.

The economic theory of criminal law enforcement is recent. Gary Becker's seminal paper on law enforcement dates from 1968, and most of the papers surveyed by Nuno Garoupa (1997) and Mitchell Polinsky and Steven Shavell (2000b) have been published in the last fifteen years. Becker posits that criminals are rational utility maximizing decision makers choosing in conditions of risk. The basis of the model is the specification of the potential criminal's preferences. A given offense is committed if and only if:

$$EU = pU(y + b - f) + (1 - p)\, U(y + b) > U(y) \qquad (1)$$

where p is the probability of capture and punishment, U is utility, EU is expected utility, $y + b$ is income if undetected, $y + b - f$ income if punished, y is the certain income, and b is the gain from committing the offense. All monetary gains include psychic components such as fear, excitement, pain which are assumed to be convertible to monetary equivalents.[3]

Gary Becker differentiated the left side of the expression with respect to p and f concluding that the negative partial differentials show that certainty and severity of punishment deter crime. Will the individual accept the gamble? The answer depends upon the individual's attitude to risk, the sizes of b, f, and p, and the utility of the certain income from honesty. Even if the individual is risk-averse he will accept the gamble if its expected value is sufficiently large (p and f are sufficiently low, and the gain in income if undetected is sufficiently high).

William Brown and Morgan Reynolds (1973) take the individual's initial income as the reference point and present a slightly different functional:

$$EU = pU(w-f) + (1-p)\,U(w+b) > U(w) \qquad (2)$$

where p is the probability of capture and punishment, U is utility, EU is expected utility, w is the initial income, b is the criminal gain, and f is the sanction. It is easily seen that both functions are equivalent.

Let me argue here that alternative models of the root causes of crime can be partially reflected in the deterrence models via the specification of the benefits from crime (reflecting difference in employment opportunities, income levels, even biological and psychological variables). In particular, consider an increase in wealth reflecting employment opportunities. Using a second-order approximation in Brown and Reynolds formulation, it can be shown that:

$$\frac{\partial EU}{\partial w} - \frac{\partial U(w)}{\partial w} \approx [(1-p)b - pf]\frac{\partial^2 U(w)}{\partial w^2} + [(1-p)\,b^2 - pf^2]/2\,\frac{\partial^3 U(w)}{\partial w^3} \qquad (3)$$

The effect of employment opportunities and income levels on crime depends crucially on risk preferences (second derivative) and how these preferences vary with wealth (third derivative).

Having specified individuals' choice, we proceed to discuss optimal enforcement. Maximization of social welfare comes out as the natural objective of public policy. The specification of the government's objective function is of some controversy, in particular the inclusion of gains from committing offenses. Nevertheless, a fundamental result is implied by any cost-benefit analysis: a monetary sanction (f) should be maximal because it is a costless transfer whereas detection is costly.

Gary Becker's high-fine-low-probability result is a seminal contribution to modern understanding of crime.[4] Recent papers have been stimulated by Becker's stark result to investigate the circumstances in which a maximal sanction may be non-optimal. These papers extend Becker's seminal model to a variety of aspects of criminal law and law enforcement.

The application of economic analysis to criminal law is based on the proposition that economic efficiency is useful for examining and designing rules and institutions. Economic efficiency, in particular social welfare maximization, is controversial. Richard Posner (1998) refers the use of efficiency as a concept of justice as one of the main criticisms faced by the economic approach to law. Nonetheless, alternative concepts have been considered in the context of the optimal law enforcement literature. Isaac Ehrlich (1981, 1982) in the context of criminal law poses: justice as equality under the law,[5] justice as avoidance of legal error, and justice as retribution and incapacitation. All these alternative concepts seem to suggest a less-than-maximal fine.[6]

Applying economic efficiency is useful in two different roles. First, there is a positive role by explaining the actual behavior of individuals and the structure of legal norms. The second role refers to a normative analysis by suggesting how rules and institutions could be improved. Although the positive and normative role of optimal law enforcement theory can have common features, we distinguish both for the purpose of this essay.

The criticism of the positive analysis of the literature of law enforcement has been devoted to the modeling of criminal behavior using the utility theoretic framework. The normative role has been at the center of the debate in the context of policy design.

MODELING CRIMINAL BEHAVIOR: THE POSITIVE DIMENSION

On the modeling of criminal behavior, the theory faces the usual criticism of the expected utility framework and the usefulness of the assumption of economic rationality. It assumes that the deterrence hypothesis (basically no more than an application of the theory of demand) is a reasonable explanation for some crimes: people respond significantly to the deterring incentives created by the criminal justice system.

As we have argued, we do recognize that this approach ignores other factors that are important when criminal behavior is analyzed, that is, the economic theory assumes these other factors to be exogenous to the model. However, it is our opinion that it still gives some insight regarding how rational individuals behave when confronted with choices that involve criminal acts (in particular, property crimes, regulatory enforcement, tax compliance, traffic rules).

Four themes have been the focus of the criticism:

1. Individuals Have Preferences About Each Possible State of the World

Such preferences are preconditions to the realization of the individual's aims. Some scholars argue that this is highly unlikely: individuals become criminals because of contacts with criminal patterns and isolation from anti-criminal patterns. Therefore, such preferences are constrained by each individual's information set. The information set is shaped by the contact with the criminal world. Some individuals have regard for the law or conventional norms, and others simply do not have it.

This view is not incompatible with the law enforcement theory. In this theory, the gain from committing a harmful act is postulated as an exogenous variable. Different individuals have different gains as they have different contacts with criminal patterns. Individuals with high regard for norms do not commit a crime because their gain is too small (eventually negative); individuals with no regard for norms commit a crime because their gain is too high. By varying the probability and severity of punishment, some individuals change their behavior at the margin. Even if only a small fraction of the population responds to changes on probability and severity of punishment, that is all that matters at the margin.

2. Individuals Maximize Their Utility

A rational individual takes actions in order to realize his objectives to the greatest extent. However, it has been argued that most criminals are not rational individuals. They do not compare marginal benefits with marginal costs but rather answer to sociological norms that have been internalized during their lifetime.

The assumption that criminals are expected utility maximizing decision makers has been particularly criticized. The first argument proposed by such criticism is that empirical contradictions between expected utility predictions and actual decisions have been found. There are already some empirical findings on criminals' behavior which are not consistent with expected utility theory (Feeney, 1986; Block & Gerety, 1995; Eide, 1995, 1998). These recent findings tend to stress that expected utility theory is not a good predictor in experimental situations. However, that does not imply that the alternative theories perform better (Harless & Camerer, 1994; Hey & Orme, 1994).

A second argument is that there is a task complexity: decisions are made in a decomposed fashion using relative comparisons. Potential criminals may find optimization impossible or unduly costly. They may solve a simpler, approximate optimization problem such that the objective function differs from the classic expected utility functional. It has been observed that, while economists assume that criminals are rational, most psychologists and criminologists prefer to accept that criminals are, at most, 'limited' rational. 'Limited' rationality is a weaker version of rationality by which criminals are sensitive to risk and payoffs but do not combine this information optimally (Claster, 1967; Carroll, 1978). More recently, some scholars have have stressed that criminals use highly flexible, contingent heuristics, and the decision to commit a crime depends upon a number of tasks and problem characteristics such as the manner in which information is presented (Johnson & Payne, 1986). However, such evidence is controversial. Criminals seem to have "criminal expertise": they are experts at controlling or minimizing risks (Payne, 1973; Carroll & Weaver, 1986).

A third argument is that people manipulate beliefs: individuals have not only preferences over states of the world, but also over their beliefs of those states. Cognitive assessment of gains and losses relatively to a reference point may imply that the objective function is no longer the expected utility functional.

It is true that the current economic theory of crime and punishment only very recently has started to respond to these criticisms. It seems to me that as long as preferences satisfy first-order stochastic dominance (that is, individuals prefer more to less income), the qualitative results of Becker's theory hold. Hence a more promising approach is the one proposed by Christine Jolls, Cass Sunstein and Richard Thaler (1998) and Alon Harel and Uzi Segal (1999): the behavioral approach to law and economics. Their project is an ambitious one because it blends rational theory with a psychological twist enriching the economic model.

3. *Individuals Respond to Changes in Policy Instruments*

The critics argue that individuals may respond to the perceived changes. However, in most cases, there is a clear discrepancy between actual and perceived values. Therefore the impact of changes in policy instruments is rather small.

My response is that eventually there is a mapping from the actual to the perceived values. Models incorporating such mapping have been developed in the literature.[8] Moreover, the economic theory of imperfect information is now sufficiently powerful and sophisticated. It is true that more research on refining the theory of law enforcement with the sophisticated tools of the theory of imperfect information is needed.

A particular problem seems to be what has been called the "tipping level" (Chamelin, 1991). Criminologists argue that the relationship between the crime and clearance rates is not statistically valid until the arrest probability attains some minimal level (the so-called 'tipping level'). Within the economic approach, we can describe the 'tipping level' as a particular mapping from the actual to the perceived value of the probability such that for a probability smaller than the 'tipping level', the perceived value of the probability is zero. We can then apply some of the results developed in the literature of optimal law enforcement when individuals are not able to observe accurately the probability of punishment.

4. *Empirical Evidence*

The successfulness of the theory as a positive valid analysis depends crucially on the empirical adherence. Measuring deterrence (more precisely, to distinguish it from incapacitation) is difficult. In particular, the empirical analysis of criminal deterrence suffers from two important fallacies: 'the tiger prevention' and 'the warden's survey'. The 'tiger prevention' fallacy is based on the fact that deterrence is an inherently unobservable phenomenon; the absence of the prevented occurrence does not establish a deterrent effect. On the other hand, 'the warden's survey' problem is caused by the fact that most deterrence studies are based on those who were not deterred (Brown, Esbensen & Geis, 1996).

The existing empirical literature seems to have findings in both (positive and negative adherence) directions. Still, the rational approach to criminal activities has a significant predictive power. Most studies corroborate the hypothesis that the probability of punishment, and to a lesser degree also the severity of punishment, has a deterrent effect on crime (Ehrlich, 1996; Eide, 1998).

The term "criminometric studies" has been proposed to characterize the empirical research of criminal behavior (Eide, 1998). The bulk of empirical studies consists of cross section analysis based on macro data. Time series and panel data analysis based on micro surveys are less numerous. The probability and severity of punishment (fines, length of sentence, or time served) are found to have a negative effect on crime. The magnitude of the negative sign is a matter of controversy depending on the estimation method and the data used. Most time series studies give additional support to the hypothesis that the probability of punishment has a preventive effect on crime. The results concerning the severity of punishment are somewhat less conclusive: in some studies is not statistically different from zero.

ON POLICY DESIGN: THE NORMATIVE DIMENSION

There has been criticism of the policy consequences of the Becker's type of models at three levels:

1. Moral Costs and Social Norms

It has been argued that there are incalculable benefits and costs that are not included in the social planner's problem. Alexander Field (1991) argues that the economic considerations on criminal law are not interesting because most of the literature ignores moral or ethical education.[9]

The sociological view of crime proposes a cultural deviance perspective. In other words, criminal sociology looks for an explanation for crime within a set of social norms. Eric Posner (1996, 1998) adds to the current theory of optimal law enforcement precisely on the role of deviant norms. That work develops on the interaction between deterrence and social norms, in particular, when the community chooses punishment as a signal of rejection of a certain type of behavior rather than a deterrence mechanism. Reputation or extra-legal sanctions are useful because they are cheaper than legal sanctions and can be quite effective (Kahan, 1997, 1998).

2. Simplistic View

It has been suggested that the models have a simplistic view of the actual process of law enforcement. As a consequence of the complexity of the actual process, law enforcement cannot be a set of policy rules but is a rather discretionary set of responses to negotiation and compromise.

My view is that this problem is common to many areas in economics, and to almost all fields of science. The controversy around the methodology of economics of the law is surprising because it is no different from the methodology of economics in general (De Geest, 1996). A model is intended as a simplified analogue of the real world: its deductive structure helps one to explore the consequences of alternative assumptions (Townsend, 1988).

Notwithstanding, this is an area of research needing more development, particularly the interaction of the different institutions involved in the law enforcement process. A very useful framework is the bargaining theory (Graetz, Reinganum & Wilde, 1986; Bowles & Garoupa, 1997). Some literature has been focused on the public versus private law enforcement and the behavior of agencies involved in the process. Both positive and normative implications have been derived showing that the economic theory can accommodate the shortcomings of approaching the complexity of the law enforcement process with a tractable model.[10]

A related point is if maximization of social welfare is the natural objective function of public policy. Louis Kaplow and Steven Shavell (1999) and Mitchell Polinsky and Steven Shavell (2000b) have insisted that within welfare economics, social welfare should be the normative criteria. Moreover, it is the only objective function that respects the Pareto criteria.

It has been suggested that social welfare maximization is not the adequate criteria because it overlooks fairness and does not contemplate the possibility that policy makers are not benevolent, but rather pursue their own agenda. Potential offenders, victims and enforcers are rational agents maximizing their selfish payoff. David Friedman (1999) argues that so should politicians. Social welfare is not the natural payoff of politicians. Here the rational theory of law enforcement could find in the Public Choice movement the needed help to address this problem. In particular, when the evidence seems to be that people reject optimal deterrence (Sunstein, Schkade & Kahneman, 2000). A possibility is that people do care about the fairness of punishment, and so the objective function of a policy maker must consider the issue of fairness. As Mitchell Polinsky and Steven Shavell (2000a) discuss, fairness should be included in social welfare because individuals care about it, and not because the policy maker decides to add it. Optimal deterrence (in the classical sense) is rejected because individuals reject it, and not because the policy maker rejects it.

3. Conservative bias

Many sociologists have suggested that the current economic theory of criminal law prescribes politically conservative policies (Malloy, 1990). The perception of a conservative bias derives from the observation that the current economic theory seems to be more of economics of enforcement than economics of crime (Panther, 1995).[11]

The economic theory of crime and criminal law has been above all a theory of deterrence and criminal prevention. If pursuing criminal deterrence is a conservative policy then the economic theory cannot escape such label. What seems to me of some surprise is, in the context of crime, reducing the conservative versus liberal dichotomy to enforcing or not ex ante criminal prevention.[12]

A related point is the economic theory of criminal incapacitation (eliminating opportunity for crime ex post), rehabilitation (eliminating criminal motivation) and retribution. As pointed out by Mitchell Polinsky and Steven Shavell (2000b) this is still a poor area in terms of output research but with a growing empirical literature.

WHY EUROPE IS DIFFERENT FROM THE U.S.

Using the optimal law enforcement theory for policy-making in Europe poses a serious challenge. Institutional design within the European context is different from the North-American reality, starting with the observation that the United States, as the United Kingdom, belong to the so-called common law countries whereas (continental) Europe is part of the so-called civil law countries. Richard Posner (1997) argues that many of the alleged differences are more apparent than real. And even if important, these differences should not deter the growing use of law and economics.

My view is that the optimal law enforcement theory is weak with respect to institutional aspects as I have discussed before. Thus, the use of the above model to prescribe policies is somehow limited. That is not to say we should not use. It just emphasizes the fact that most of the analysis is normative and in that sense ignores positive institutional details. Even so, we can of course use the model to make some comments about stylized facts of criminal systems in civil law countries.

One of the characteristics of civil law is that uncertainty, complexity and asymmetry of information is supposed to be reduced as compared to common law. That characteristic results from the codification of law, the limitations of jurisprudence, and centralization of the judicial system in opposition to a common law system characterized by a collection of disparate doctrines largely judge-made in a decentralized fashion.

The effect of less uncertainty, less complexity and less asymmetry of information on law enforcement is not clear. For example, Alon Harel and Uzi Segal (1999) argue that uncertainty and complexity increase deterrence allowing the government to save on enforcement costs.[13]

However, Lucian Bebchuk and Louis Kaplow (1992) argue that uncertainty could lead the government to reduce the sanction and increase the likelihood of detection (that is, enforcement costs) if the social cost of mistakes increases more with the sanction than with the probability of detection.

More complexity and more asymmetry of information also induce individuals to spend more resources on acquiring information. Thus, less complexity means less waste. However, the expenditure in acquiring information is part of the sanction of engaging in a criminal career, thus increasing deterrence. Complexity is often discussed as an evil to be minimized. In a related paper, Louis Kaplow (1995) shows there is an optimal level of complexity.

A second important characteristic of civil law countries is that legislators are relatively more important than judges in determining the criminal system. Our model poses social welfare as the natural objective function of policy makers.

As argued by David Friedman (1999), social welfare is not the natural payoff of politicians, legislators or judges. That observation raises two natural questions: (a) What are the payoffs of legislators and judges? and (b) Is enforcement different when these two groups have different weights in the decision making?

The general view in law and economics seems to be that when judges are the producers of the substantive law the rules of law will tend to be consistent with efficiency. Nevertheless, a judge as any individual seeks to maximize his or her payoff. Since salaries are usually insulated from deciding a case, reputation and prestige seem to be an important payoff. Judges may apply criminal sanctions according to their perception of its effects on their prestige. Moreover, judges may want to impose their policy preferences on society. These judges may want to impose lower or higher sanctions than the legislature. Conflicts between the Supreme Court and the legislature (and the executive) are likely if judges' preferences differ much from those of politicians.

In the United States, sentencing guidelines have become increasingly popular. Judges must apply statutes in accordance with the terms of the original decision in the enacting legislature. Sentencing guidelines essentially impose a lower bound on sanctions and curtail plea bargaining because of a perception of judges' preferences for reduced sentences. As long as judges decide on questions of statutory interpretation, the independence of the judiciary is assured even though these statutes do limit the decision of judges and could makes jurisprudence less important. However, note that Richard Posner (1998, Chapter 19) argues that conflicts are not likely because neither judges nor legislators like to have their decisions disputed or nullified. Thus, both groups will make an effort to compromise.

Sentencing guidelines and civil law pose a problem if we believe that the legislator is not concerned with efficiency and is easily captured by interest groups. The economic theory of legislation takes a public choice view of institutions. On one hand, interest groups will try to capture the legislature in order to enact a law that favors them. On the other hand, relying on the electoral process for the selection of legislators, the enacted legislation corresponds to the preferences of the median voter. The role of interest groups is limited in the court system, because it is procedurally more difficult and more expensive to affect legislation by capturing judges. By acting through elected officials, interest groups can try to influence judicial appointments. But once the judge takes office, unless by means of corruption, he or she is substantially free from pressure. Thus, interest groups will specialize on capturing politicians and legislators.

An important difference between the role of legislators and the role of judges in affecting sentencing is the fact that the first act ex ante whereas the latter act ex post. Legislators define general rules and guidelines obeying a political orientation. Judges interpret and apply the law to the particular case they rule. Thus, the decisions of legislature are perceived to be applied to all individuals. When committing an offense, individuals know (or can acquire information about) criminal legislation and statutes. Sentencing however is the outcome of court procedures and judicial decisions.[14] Individuals can eventually have a prediction about judges' decisions (eventually taking into account judicial behavior in respect to other cases), but there is more uncertainty. The ability of judges to interpret and overturn criminal legislation becames important in shaping perceptions.

Within this rationale, we would expect civil law countries to have less efficient enforcement policies. Within our theory, we would expect civil law countries to have lower sentences and less frequent use of imprisonment sentences. However, it is well known that in Europe there is greater reliance on monetary fines as the sanction for traditional crimes than in the United States (Morgan & Bowles, 1981). The introduction of sentencing guidelines in the United States and in the United Kingdom has been caused by the perception that sanctions were too low. Part of this apparent contradiction can be explained by considering other relevant variables such as wealth, unemployment, heterogeneity of criminal population, cost of prison system in per-capita terms. Another argument is the disparity of extra-legal sanctions and social norms.

With respect to crime and criminals, social norms are quite different in the United States and in Europe. The use of capital punishment in several North-American states and its repulse in Europe can be partly explained by different social norms. Norms are endogenous to the system in the sense that they result from the historical evolution of a given society and from the interaction between law and social behavior.

The legal system in (continental) Europe differs from common law countries as a result of a distinct political and social historical context. Thus, distinct norms emerge in different societies, depending on the characteristics of the group, the ability to innovate, and the process of internalization. Part of the codification results from the fact that the rulers of Europe (in particular, the distinct French, German, Spanish and Italian principalities and kingdoms) felt the need to harmonize law given distinct norms and traditions. It is easier to influence and innovate legal norms (that is, the legislature) than social norms. In order to understand different norms concerning criminal behavior (including capital punishment), we must attend not only at the relative influence of different philosophical movements but also the fact that it is easier to innovate in Europe than in the United States.

One important (empirically open) question is how different judges' preferences concerning criminal sanctions are in the United States from Europe. Judges are influenced by social norms as much as any individual in a given society. If we have different social norms, we should have different judicial preferences. However, I would expect these differences to be much less significant than those of legislators' preferences. Thus the convergence between civil law in Europe and sentencing guidelines and criminal statutes in the United States and in the United Kingdom in controlling judges.

A third important characteristic relates to the administration of law enforcement, in particular prosecutors and enforcers. The first aspect to analyze is the use of private enforcement in common law and in civil law countries. With few exceptions, there is a public monopoly of criminal law enforcement. However, the history of English criminal law and its administration is substantially different from that of (continental) Europe. England has a tradition of private enforcement whereas civil law jurisdictions have a tradition of public enforcement. In principle, private enforcement can be more efficient than public enforcement. Optimal enforcement can be optimally delegated by taxes (if there is overenforcement) or subsidies (if there is underenforcement). However, the replacement of private by public enforcement in England (and thus in common law jurisdictions) and the little impact of the privatization theories seems to indicate that voters and legislators in both types of jurisdictions have identical views on this matter.[15]

An enforcement agency's decision as to where to concentrate its resources is relevant because of the monopoly position they usually have in determining the likelihood of detection and punishment of offenders. Public enforcers are part of the political process. Political considerations may affect the amount of resources devoted to each case. In the United States, agencies have been criticized for devoting disproportionate resources to trivial cases. In Europe, police bureaucracies have been criticized for being inoperative and usually large old-fashioned bureaucracies.

Public enforcer agencies locally run (eventually subject to direct elections) are usually more affected by public opinion (eventually the median voter) than centralized bureaucracies (appointed by the government). Thus, the allocation of resources in the first type of agencies obeys local political considerations. The allocation of resources in the second type of agencies is usually determined by general political considerations and by the bureaucracy's preferences (in particular, when accountability is weak). Whereas local enforcers may spend too much on trivial cases because of local political considerations, national bureaucracies are usually less flexible and more inefficient.

CONCLUSION

Even though highly criticized and suffering from the usual methodology problems common to many areas in economics, the theory of law enforcement and the economics of criminal law constitutes a body of literature which has contributed to the understanding of crime, its deterrence, and prevention. Even if economics has a limited role to play in the study of crime, it is still a crucial role.

We have identified crucial themes for a research agenda on the rational theory of law enforcement. From the positive side, the development of a behavioral approach to crime and the blend of the theory of law enforcement with the modern work on imperfect information should permit addressing some of questions raised concerning criminal decision-making and perceptions of policy instruments. At the normative side, the sophistication of the institutional law enforcement model within boundaries of tractability will respond to the criticism of modeling oversimplification.

My view is that the optimal law enforcement theory is weak with respect to institutional aspects. Thus, the development of a more institutionally oriented model to prescribe policies will be very useful. I have identified three areas needing further research in the context of civil law countries: (a) the role of judges versus the role of legislators in policy making, (b) the optimal control of sentencing by means of civil code or guidelines, and (c) the emergence of distinct social norms and extra-legal sanctions.

NOTES

1. An integrating perspective has been emphasized by other scholars (Carr-Hill & Stern, 1979; Akers, 1990).

2. Richard Posner (1997) further discusses the distinction between negative and positive liberties. Expanding the rights of criminal defendants conflicts with the protection of property rights.

3. The inclusion of psychic components has been discussed in the literature (Block & Lind, 1975a, 1975b; Baldry, 1980).

4. Several criminologists have pointed out that Gary Becker's contribution to criminal studies was basically to introduce mathematical analysis in the classical studies of Beccaria (On Crime and Punishment, 1764) and Bentham (Principles of Penal Law, 1843) (Gottfredson & Hirschi, 1990). Becker however goes further and derives policy implications from a rational theory of criminal behavior.

5. The term equality under the law refers to ex ante or anticipated equality (equal chances for all offenders to be detected and convicted), and ex post or realized equality (equal distribution of losses from crime among potential victims, and an equal distribution of consequences of law enforcement among offenders committing equal crimes).

6. More recently, it has been developed a game theoretic analysis of crime control where potential offenders consider their perceptions on social fairness when making their decision. It is shown that increasing the legal system fairness increases criminal deterrence (Bueno de Mesquita & Cohen, 1995).

7. It has been argued that the empirical evidence against expected utility is disputable because a systematic theory of errors consistent with requirements of rational action can explain the empirically observed deviations (Bueno de Mesquita & Cohen, 1995). This is a fundamental point since some authors seem to assume that because expected utility theory is a bad predictor, alternative theories necessarily fit better (Ellickson, 1989).

8. See Lucian Bebchuk and Louis Kaplow (1992) and Nuno Garoupa (1999).

9. Moral cost is an example of an incalculable cost that does not allow for a precise definition of harmfulness (Gibbons, 1982).

10. See Richard Posner (1998, Chapter 22).

11. Richard Posner (1998, Chapter 21) uses the economic rationale for the right to counsel, the economic approach to the standard proof in criminal cases or the use of bail as examples to show that the theory can support politically liberal policies.

12. Should we then argue that the British Home Office policy under Jack Straw is essentially as conservative as previous administrations?

13. Assuming individuals do not like uncertainty.

14. Common law systems make more use of juries than civil law countries. There is a trade-off in designing an optimal jury system. Enlarging the jury reduces error costs and reduces the risk of extreme outcomes. There are of course higher transaction costs, including the probability of a hung jury and hence a retrial.

15. An important aspect of public enforcers in Europe is the fact they have been associated with authoritarian political regimes. Part of the history of these institutions goes back to royal centralization and absolutism. This could explain why there is a perception in Europe that these institutions have less monitoring and accountability than in the United States.

REFERENCES

Akers, R. L. (1990). Rational Choice, Deterrence and Social Learning Theory: The Path Not Taken. *Journal of Criminal Law and Criminology*, *81*, 653–676.

Baldry, J. C. (1980). Crime Punishable by Imprisonment: A Note. *Journal of Legal Studies*, *9*, 617–619.

Bebchuk, L. A., & Kaplow, L. (1992). Optimal Sanctions When Individuals Are Imperfectly Informed About The Probability of Apprehension. *Journal of Legal Studies*, *21*, 365–370.

Becker, G. S. (1968). Crime and Punishment: An Economic Approach. *Journal of Political Economy*, *76*, 169–217.

Block, M. K., & Lind, R. C. (1975a). Crime and Punishment Reconsidered. *Journal of Legal Studies*, *4*, 241–247.

Block, M. K., & Lind, R. C. (1975b). An Economic Analysis of Crime Punishable by Imprisonment. *Journal of Legal Studies*, *4*, 479–492.

Block, M. K., & Gerety, V. E. (1995). Some Experimental Evidence on Differences Between Student and Prisoner Reactions to Monetary Penalties and Risk. *Journal of Legal Studies*, *24*, 123–138.

Bowles, R., & Garoupa, N. (1997). Casual Police Corruption and The Economics of Crime. *International Review of Law and Economics, 17*, 75–87.

Brown, S. E., Esbensen, F. A., & Geis, G. (1996). *Criminology: Explaining Crime and its Context*, (2nd ed.). Cincinnati, Ohio: Anderson Publishing Co.

Brown, W. W., & Reynolds, M. O. (1973). Crime and Punishment: Risk Implications. *Journal of Economic Theory, 6*, 508–514.

Bueno de Mesquita, B., & Cohen, L. E. (1995). Self-interest, Equity, and Crime Control: A Game-Theoretic Analysis of Criminal Decision Making. *Criminology, 33*, 483–518.

Carr-Hill, R. A., & Stern, H. H. (1979), *Crime, the Police and Criminal Statistics*. London: Academic Press.

Carroll, J. S. (1978). A Psychological Approach to Deterrence: The Evaluation of Criminal Opportunities. *Journal of Personality and Social Psychology, 36*, 1512–1520.

Carroll, J. S., & Weaver, F. (1986). Shoplifters' Perceptions of Crime Opportunities: A Process-tracing Study. In: D. B. Cornish & R. V. Clarke (Eds), *The Reasoning Criminal: Rational Choice Perspectives on Offending*. Springer-Verlang.

Chamelin, M. B. (1991). A Longitudinal Analysis of The Arrest-Crime Relationship: A Further Examination of The Tipping Effect. *Justice Quarterly, 8*, 187–199.

Claster, D. S. (1967). Comparison of Risk Perceptions Between Delinquents and Nondelinquents. *Journal of Criminal Law, Criminology, and Police Science, 58*, 80–86.

De Geest, G. (1996). The Debate on the Scientific Status of Law and Economics. *European Economic Review, 40*, 999–1006.

Ehrlich, I. (1981). On The Usefulness of Controlling Individuals: An Economic Analysis of Rehabilitation, Incapacitation, and Deterrence. *American Economic Review, 71*, 307–322.

Ehrlich, I. (1982). The Optimum Enforcement of Laws and The Concept of Justice: A Positive Analysis. *International Review of Law and Economics, 2*, 3–27.

Ehrlich, I. (1996). Crime, Punishment, and The Market For Offenses. *Journal of Economic Perspectives*, 10, 43–67.

Eide, E. (1995). RDEU Models of Crime. Working Paper C1, University of Oslo.

Eide, E. (1998). Economics of Criminal Behavior (Including Compliance). In: B. Bouckaert & G. De Geest (Eds), *Encyclopedia of Law and Economics*. Cheltenham: Edward Elgar.

Ellickson, R. C. (1989). Bringing Culture and Human Frailty to Rational Actors: A Critique of Classical Law and Economics. *Chicago-Kent Law Review, 65*, 23–55.

Feeney, F. (1986). Robbers as Decision-Makers. In: D. B. Cornish & R. V. Clarke (Eds), *The Reasoning Criminal: Rational Choice Perspectives on Offending*. Springer-Verlag.

Field, A. J. (1991). Do Legal Systems Matter? *Explorations in Economic History, 28*, 1–35.

Friedman, D. D. (1999). Why Not Hang Them All: The Virtues of Inefficient Punishment. *Journal of Political Economy, 107* (Supplement), S259–S269.

Garoupa, N. (1997). The Theory of Optimal Law Enforcement. *Journal of Economic Surveys, 11*, 267–295.

Garoupa, N. (1999). Optimal Law Enforcement with Dissemination of Information. *European Journal of Law and Economics, 7*, 103–116.

Gibbons, T. (1982). The Utility of Economic Analysis of Crime. *International Review of Law and Economics*, 2, 173–191.

Gottfredson, M. R., & Hirschi, T. (1990). *A General Theory of Crime*. Stanford: Stanford University Press.

Graetz, M. J., Reinganum, J., & Wilde, L. L. (1986). The Tax Compliance Game: Toward An Interactive Theory of Law Enforcement. *Journal of Law, Economics and Organization, 2*, 1–32.

Harel, A., & Segal, U. (1999). Criminal Law and Behavioral Law and Economics: Observations on The Neglected Role of Uncertainty in Deterring Crime. *American Law and Economics Review*, *1*, 276–312.

Harless, D. W., & Camerer, C. F. (1994). The Predictive Utility of Generalized Expected Utility Theories. *Econometrica*, *62*, 1251–1289.

Hey, J. D., & Orme, C. (1994). Investigating Generalizations of Expected Utility Theory Using Experimental Data. *Econometrica*, *62*, 1291–1326.

Johnson, E., & Payne, J. (1986). The decision to Commit A Crime: An Information Processing Analysis. In: D. B. Cornish & R. V. Clarke (Eds), *The Reasoning Criminal: Rational Choice Perspectives on Offending*. Springer-Verlag.

Jolls, C., Sunstein, C., & Thaler, R. (1998). A Behavioral Approach to Law and Economics. *Stanford Law Review*, *50*, 1471–1550.

Kahan, D. H. (1997). Social Influence, Social Meaning, and Deterrence. *Virginia Law Review*, *83*, 349–395.

Kahan, D. H. (1998). Social Meaning and The Economic Analysis of Crime. *Journal of Legal Studies*, *27*, 609–622.

Kaplow, L. (1995). A Model of The Optimal Complexity of Rules. *Journal of Law, Economics and Organization*, *11*, 150–163.

Kaplow, L., & Shavell, S. (1999). Any Non-individualistic Social Welfare Function Violates The Pareto Principle. *NBER Working-Paper* 7051.

Malloy, R. P. (1990). Is Law and Economics Moral? – Humanistic Economics and a Classical Liberal Critique of Posner's Economic Analysis. *Valparaiso University Law Review*, *24*, 147–161.

Morgan, R., & Bowles, R. (1981). Fines: The Case for Review. *Criminal Law Review*, 203–214.

Panther, S. M. (1995). The Economics of Crime and Criminal Law: An Antithesis to Sociological Theories? *European Journal of Law and Economics*, *2*, 365–378.

Payne, J. W. (1973). Alternative Approaches to Decision-Making Under Risk: Moments Versus Risk Dimensions. *Psychological Bulletin*, *80*, 439–453.

Polinsky, A. M., & Shavell, S. (2000a). The Fairness of Sanctions: Some Implications for Optimal Enforcement Policy. *American Law and Economics Review*, *2*, 223–237.

Polinsky, A. M., & Shavell, S. (2000b). The Economic Theory of Public Enforcement of Law. *Journal of Economic Literature*, *38*, 45–76.

Posner, E. (1996). Law, Economics and Inefficient Norms. *University of Pennsylvania Law Review*, *144*, 1697–1754.

Posner, E. (1998). Symbols, Signal, and Social Norms in Politics and The Law. *Journal of Legal Studies*, *27*, 765–798.

Posner, R. A. (1997). The Future of The Law and Economics Movement in Europe. *International Review of Law and Economics*, *17*, 3–14.

Posner, R. A. (1998), *Economic Analysis of Law*, 5th edition. New York: Aspen Law & Business.

Sunstein, C. R., Schkade, D., & Kahneman, D. (2000). Do People Want Optimal Deterrence? *Journal of Legal Studies*, *29*, 237–298.

Townsend, R. M. (1988). Models As Economies. *Economic Journal*, *98* (Supplement), 1–24s.

INDEPENDENCE AND JUDICIAL DISCRETION IN A DUALIST REGIME: THE CASE OF FRENCH ADMINISTRATIVE JUDICIARY

Sophie Harnay and Alain Marciano

INTRODUCTION

The idea that European Law and Economics should draw on the arguments of the American founding fathers of the discipline has been accepted. Accordingly, the major developments in the field relate to the application of economic tools to private law issues. On the other side, however, some prominent authors (for instance Rose-Ackerman, 1994) have insisted on the necessity to pay more attention to public, constitutional or administrative, law. Our focus in this chapter will be on administrative law, a field that has largely been neglected (with some exceptions, as Cooter, forthcoming; Backhaus, 1999; Harnay, 1999; Josselin & Marciano, 1997, 1999). These are crucial rules for they delineate the set of governmental feasible actions, thus influence public policy outcomes and thereby also structure private activities. As noted by Backhaus, "the grouping [of administrative law] together with regulation in the Journal of Economic Literature classification reflects a very specific view of the field which is not shared on the European continent" (1999). For sure, Public Choice theories are an obvious starting point in the direction of an economic theory of administrative law (see on this point, van den Bergh, 1996) for and when questions

Law and Economics in Civil Law Countries, Volume 6, pages 217–229.

ISBN: 0-7623-0712-9

such as "why the law was passed, how the law was passed, or why it has not been repealed" (Tollison, 1988: 339) are addressed. But, the analysis is mainly restricted to the understanding of the judicial branch of the state. As Mercuro and Medema write, Public Choice theory "constitutes an approach to Law and Economics that focuses predominantly on the creation and implementation of law throughout the political process" (Mercuro & Medema, 1997: 84). Administrative law and economics has, nevertheless, to go one step further. Economic tools have to be used in order to investigate the mechanisms of provision of administrative law itself. This is the perspective this paper adopts.

Broadly defined, legal regimes divide in two categories, monist and dualist systems (Josselin & Marciano, 1995), with their related conceptions of administrative law. On the one side, common law countries are based on monist systems. It is then considered that no necessity implies to distinguish private from public litigation; thus, there are no separate administrative tribunals but merely "regular courts". Administrative law is designed with the purpose to limit the powers of government in order to protect the citizen. On the other side, the legal system of civil law countries is dualist in that it clearly defines the domain of public affairs; the State has to be judged and controlled in a separate way. In these systems, administrative law is directed towards the functioning of the administration. The administrative judiciary controls the administration, on behalf of political decision makers. We then propose to analyze administrative law in a civil law, therefore dualist, country. More precisely, we restrict our attention to the analysis of the French system of administrative justice.

The French legal system clearly is characterized by its duality of jurisdiction. Administrative judges belong to the administration. As Michel Debré a former Prime Minister once said, "administrative judiciary does not exist, there is only an administrative staff in charge of judging" (quoted in Lochak, 1994). Thus, even if they enjoy tenure and fixed salaries, administrative judges nevertheless are still a part of a bureaucratic hierarchy. At least as far as it concerns their appointment and to some extent the monitoring mechanism (Lochak, 1994; Chapus, 1998), judges remain structurally dependent from political decision makers. However, at the same time, very few interventions limit the real independence of French administrative judges. Therefore, one can conclude that "the legislature and the executive allow a certain degree of judicial independence that exceeds the structural provisions" (Salzberger, 1993: 353). It is important to note that Salzberger's statement has been raised in analysis of monist legal regimes. Thus France is not only a typical example of a civil law country. Just like in a common law country, the French system of administrative justice provides an illustration of why a government might choose to leave its judges free of any control, just like in a common law country. In other words, the paper also addresses the more general issue of judicial independence. Raised in the context of administrative justice, the question is all the more important that it suggests the possible independence of agents granted with the right to control the state.

The purpose of this paper is to explain how a dualist system deals with the paradoxical co-existence of (structural) dependence and (substantial) independence. A simple model is sketched and historical evidences are proposed to illustrate our theoretical argumentation. Furthermore, even if the same kind of difficulties affect monist as well as dualist systems, one can anticipate that different institutional settings lead to different solutions. We then compare our approach to the standard law and economics literature on judicial independence to show what these differences are. It appears that dualist independence does not receive the same meaning as monist independence; it rather looks like discretionary power.

A MODEL OF JUDICIAL INDEPENDENCE

Dependence, Independence and Stability of Judicial Choices

The theoretical background is provided by a model developed by Shepsle and Weingast (1981), Marks (1988), Gely and Spiller (1990), Ferejohn and Weingast (1992), Cooter and Drexl (1994) and Harnay and Vigouroux (2000). The argumentation presented in these papers is particularly well suited for analyzing the specificity of the French system of administrative justice. We adapt the model as follows. A principal, namely the government, delegates to several agents, the judges, the right to control the actions of the administration. The preferences of each player i on Γ, the one-dimensional set of possible solutions, are represented by a function U_i, $U_i = U_i(j)$. Preferences are assumed to be single-peaked. Let j be the decision of the i-player, $j \in \Gamma$. His set of non-strictly preferred points can be written $\Pi_i^{ns}(j) = \{j' | U_i(j') \geq U_i(j), j' \neq j, j' \in \Gamma$.

The following assumptions about the respective behaviors of the political principal and the administrative judge are made. The principal retains "formal" authority (Aghion & Tirole, 1997). He is therefore able to overrule his agents. Let us remind that the objective the principal assigns to the judge is to control the administration. Therefore, his goal is simply to determine the decision he wants the judge to make and to induce him to decide accordingly through the design of a monitoring mechanism. The principal may not have full information about the agent's costs and actions. However, he neglects possible or actual imperfections in information. This assumption describes the structural dependence characteristic of administrative justice in France. In other words, the system of administrative justice in France raises problems of monitoring in a full information environment.

The mechanism designed by the principal must take into account two constraints involving the agent. Firstly, the principal must provide his agent with his reservation level of utility. Each point of the set of non-strictly preferred point of the agent is supposed to yield him a level of utility at least equal to his reservation level. This constraint is assumed to be satisfied. Secondly, the judge must be induced to choose the best point for the principal. In this respect, the principal must keep in mind that the judge derives negative utility from the reversal of his decisions. Therefore, he trades off stability against his private preferences. In other words, he may choose a point that is not his preferred one. Thus, if D* and D respectively denote the choice he actually makes, both D* and D belong to P but D* and D may differ. The judge chooses a point as close as possible to his preferred point, under the constraint of political feasibility. Monitoring mechanisms (possible reversal and the related sanctions) are thus supposed to influence his decision.

It clearly appears that the principal obtains either directly or indirectly his most preferred decision. Directly, because he decides or he is able to use monitoring mechanisms; The agent is then dependent. Indirectly, when he refrains from using or cannot use his formal authority; The agent is then independent and he engages in a self-restraint strategy, whose purpose is to discourage political control. Independence is defined as the absence of political monitoring, and results from a political agreement made by the decision makers make not to use their capacity to control the judicial product. The principal's trade-off between dependence and independence is influenced not only by the content of decisions made by the agent in either one or the other configuration, but also by the effective possibility of monitoring these decisions. The first situation occurs when there is only one principal, regardless of the number of agents. Following Varian (1992: Chapter 25), we label this case the monopoly case. The second situation results from competition between principals.

A Monopolist Principal

The situation in which a principal delegates to one agent the right to control the administration is trivial. Indeed, there is no interest for one principal in organizing the independence of a single agent. Indeed, the principal retains formal authority. Thus, no institutional mechanism exists that would prevent him from replacing the judicial decision with his preferred point. In other words, the principal is always able to impose his own choice, through the exercise of sanctions (dismissal, pecuniary sanctions, . . .). Since he cannot supply his skills or services to an alternative demander, the agent must comply with the choices of the principal. The only shirking opportunity for him to produce an outcome consistent with his own preferences would stem from informational asymmetries. The assumption of complete information rules out such a situation. Therefore, the agent is never certain to ensure stability to his decision.

Competition between several agents may bring about different effects, according to whether it takes place between two agents of identical type (dependent) or between two agents of different types (dependent and independent). Three situations are possible. Firstly, as demonstrated by the agency theory, competition between two dependent agents improves the situation of the principal, provided that the latter can prevent agents from colluding against his interest (Holmstrom, 1982; Ma, Moore & Turnbull, 1988; Varian, 1990; Sappington, 1991). Indeed, the comparison of the relative performances of the agents reduces informational asymmetries between the principal and his agents. Thus, because of the higher efficiency of monitoring, the principal is able to obtain judicial decisions in accordance with his preferences. The consequences are twofold: not only the principal has no incentive to grant his agents with independence but also the agents are never able to secure the stability of their decisions. Secondly, when competition takes place between two independent agents, both of them are induced to choose a point as close as possible to the most preferred choice of the principal. This follows the logic of Hotelling's model. As a result, independence might be lowered as well as instability could be increased. Thirdly, when he faces a dependent and an independent agent, the principal compares two decisions. We may expect that the decision made by the dependent agent will be closer to the principal's most preferred choice than the decision of the independent agent. The main explanation is that it is possible for the principal to monitor – and then to possibly overrule – the dependent agent, while it is not possible to overturn the choices made by the independent agent. Independence is thus threatened by the existence of the dependent agent, whenever the decision of the independent agent conflicts with the principal's preferences. Then, either the principal attempts to recover authority on the independent agent or he can kick the independent agent out. What is important to note is that the less costly of these two situations is the second one. Indeed, once a principal has granted independence to an agent, it is quite hard to move back. The related consequence is that the stability of the decisions made by the remaining agent is not guaranteed.

Competition Between Principals

Therefore, when there is only one principal, the stability of the agent's decisions is difficult to achieve and independence is rarely sustainable. When a second principal enters the game, independence arises from the competition between the two principals and decisions are characterized by a greater stability than in the previous situations.

Let us assume the existence of two principals, the executive and the legislators whose preferred solutions are respectively denoted P1 and P2. We further suppose that P1 differs from P2. Each principal intends to achieve a judicial decision in accordance with his preferences. At the same time, judicial independence means that none of the two principals monitors the agent. As a consequence, independence can exist as long as the stability condition is satisfied, that is when the set of solutions simultaneously preferred by both principals is empty: $D \in P_{P_1}^{ns}(D) \cap P_{P_2}^{ns}(D)$ and $P_{P_1ns}(D) \cap P_{P_2ns}(D) = \varnothing$. D is then a structure-induced equilibrium (SIE).

Graphically, the set of structure-induced equilibria is located on the segment $[P_1\, P_2]$:

- When D is located within the interval $[P_1 P_2]$, the decision is stable. No political response is possible from the principals. Since any move in a direction or the other, towards P_1 or P_2, would obviously harm either one principal or the other, any political intervention favoring one principal would be disfavored by the other. Since no Pareto improvement is possible, the principals' capacity to react is neutralized. As they cannot agree on an alternative solution commonly preferred to the judicial decision, political decision makers cannot but recognize the agent's independence. From the standpoint of the agent, the interval $[P_1 P_2]$ represents the set of politically viable decisions.
- When D does not belong to the set of equilibrium compromises, it does no longer represent a stable outcome. Pareto improvements are possible. The

principals' response consists in overturning the judicial decision, so as to shift it back within [P_1P_2]. The new choice now closer to the preferences of both principals, results from a political agreement on dependence.

Such an institutional design enables the agent to engage in a strategic behavior. When his preferred point is located within the interval [P_1P_2], he can make a choice perfectly in accordance with his own preferences without provoking any political response. When his preferred point is located outside [P_1P_2], he chooses either P_1 or P_2, depending on which one is closer to D*. P_1 and P_2 represents then a second-best solution that will remain unchallenged. The agent anticipates possible bargaining between the principals. He thus strategically locates his decision within [P_1P_2], in order to avoid a reversal of his decision. Therefore, the final outcome made by administrative courts does not actually result from effective but simply from potential monitoring. Anticipating a political response, the agent chooses a SIE in the first place. In other words, judicial choices are affected by the institutional setting. A "feedback effect" promotes stability of choices and thereby indirectly secures judicial independence.

THE EVOLUTION OF THE FRENCH SYSTEM OF ADMINISTRATIVE JUSTICE

The Monopolisation of Principalship

Even if a major rupture profoundly altered the nature of the French institutions, the organization of the administrative justice system displays a striking continuity (Josselin & Marciano, 1999), since its origins until the end of the nineteenth century. The French Revolution accentuated, without modifying it, a situation dating back to the thirteenth century. The more noticeable characteristic is that the principal remained in the position of a monopolist during more than six hundred centuries. Furthermore, the monopolist principal retained formal authority as was repeatedly stated by lawyers and legal counselors. The King was then usually described as the source and fountain of justice. There is nothing surprising if one talks about a system of *justice retenue* – an expression that clearly points out the King as the ultimate enforcer (see for instance Montesquieu, 1979, XXVIII, 27: 260).

The system of administrative justice has its roots in the decision to split the *Curia Regis* or Royal Court in a King's Council and a Parliament. Both of them were agents of the King and were supposed to assist the King in rendering justice. However, a decisive difference separated the two structures. The King's

Council, which was progressively to evolve in the Council of State, was a dependent agent. It was strictly monitored by the principal; for instance, the King used to follow the Court during its travels and participated in its deliberations. The dependence is perfectly illustrated by Louis XV, saying that the "Council is neither a political body, nor a tribunal distinct from me; I myself act through it" (our translation from a quotation reported in Royer 1996: 99). On the contrary, the Parliament was independent since the King rapidly renounced to any form of control on its actions. The reason is straightforward: the possible control of one agent made useless the control of the second one. Of course, as time went by, the Parliament gained more and more independence and its domain of action also increased. A second but direct consequence was unavoidable: the control exerted on the actions of the King increased.

Obviously, it took a rather long time for the principal, one should say the different and successive principals, to react. Nevertheless, the different laws, from the Edict of Saint-Germain (1641) to the famous laws of 1790 (16–24 August then 6 and 7–11 September), and decrees, 19 October 1656 and 8 July 1661, were designed to exclude the independent agent from the agency relationship. The Council of State was created by Napoleon in 1800 as a dependent agent. Of course, a usual interpretation is that the duality of jurisdiction results from the use by the principal of his formal authority and his will to deny any capacity for the Parliament to judge his actions. We suggest that the important point is that the reaction of the principal was made possible because of the presence of the dependent agent. The independent agent did not survive to the opportunity for the principal to rely on a dependent agent.

Competition Between Principals

The situation lasted until the modification of the Council of State. During the nineteenth century, the ministers also played the role of a first administrative judge. Undoubtedly, the government was in the unchallenged position of a monopolist principal. We have shown in the previous section that competition between principals secured independence. In this perspective, it is of interest to note that competition created the condition for independence. The role of the Parliament must be emphasized as a major determinant of the evolution in the system of administrative justice. The change has been initiated by the Parliament and results from a legal process. In this respect, many debates show how active the elected assembly has been. The increasing role of the Parliament results from the progressive democratization of the French institutions. The source of justice moves, at least partly, from the executive to the citizens and their representants, the legislators. The evolution results in its turn in a modification in principalship. More precisely, two principals – the government and the Parliament – now control the administration. The 1872 law thus acknowledges the shift in sovereign power. The process is completed in 1889 when the Cadot decision increases the professionalisation of the administrative justice. The designations of the members of the Council of State are no longer a prerogative of one or the other of the two principals.

Once granted, independence was not to be seriously threatened. It is beyond our scope to provide an exhaustive inventory of the different rulings illustrating the independence of administrative judges. Many cases show that judges do not hesitate to condemn the administration and that the decisions are accepted by the two principals. These decisions can be interpreted as being in the zone in which independent behaviors are consistent with the goals of the two principals. On the other side, as said previously, if it is correct that judges anticipate sanctions and decide accordingly, one should find very few illustrations of choices made outside the zone of stability. Indeed, one of these very rare situations consists in the decision made in Canal (1962). The Council of State invalidated a decision issued by one of the principals, namely the President of the French Republic, concerning the creation of a special court of justice. But the decision of the Council of State was in its turn invalidated through a joint decision of the two principals. We are typically outside the most preferred choices of the two principals, in the zone where the independence of the agent is not respected.

JUDICIAL INDEPENDENCE VERSUS JUDICIAL DISCRETION

The standard *law and economics* literature demonstrates, both theoretically and empirically that political decision makers benefit from and, therefore, have a vested interest in securing judicial independence (Landes & Posner, 1975). Indeed, they are unwilling to see their choices overturned but no legal mechanism exists that would prevent a legislature to overrule or merely amend the decisions made by a past legislature. On the other side, judges ideally enforce law with respect to the preferences of the enacting legislature, without paying any attention to reward mechanisms. As a result, an independent judiciary substitutes for long-term binding contracts, and increases stability of the agreements made on the political market. A related consequence is that it facilitates the practice of interest groups. Quite paradoxically, the interests of the judges, either as a member of a pressure group or individually, are not explicitly taken into account. The judiciary passively enforces political choices. Independence is not viewed as a goal but only as a consequence of the *goodwill*, or more probably of the self-interest, of politicians who agree not to substitute a political choice for a judicial one. Most subsequent literature relies more closely on incentives for politicians to contribute to independence (see for instance Boudreaux & Pritchard, 1994; Ramseyer, 1994; Ramseyer & Rasmusen, 1997) as well as for judges to enforce political agreements (Anderson, Shughart & Tollison, 1989; Cohen, 1992; Salzberger & Fenn, 1999). Nevertheless, the conception of judicial independence lying at the core of these developments basically remains the same as the one adopted by Landes and Posner.

The literature we are referring to in this paper has rarely been used in order to investigate independence. The underlying concept is rather judicial discretion than independence as such. Though producing similar, although not identical effects, discretionary power differs from independence. In particular, the concept of discretion may be more relevant to understand the behaviors of the administrative judges than the notion of independence.

Firstly, judicial discretion has a less absolute or general meaning than independence. An independent agent is able to make his own choice outside of any type of pressure. More precisely, independence restricts to the absence of political control – for instance, Landes and Posner define an independent judiciary "as one that does not make decisions on the basis of the sorts of political factors" (Landes & Posner, 1975: 875 n. 1). In our approach, we emphasize on the relativity of discretionary power. The freedom of an agent benefiting from discretionary power is limited by the most preferred points of the two principals. If administrative judges locate their decisions within this interval of feasible outcomes, they choose according to their own preferences and avoid political 'censure'. Although the principals retain formal authority, they are incapable to use monitoring instruments within this area, at least as long as they cannot agree on a commonly preferred point. Conversely, judicial discretion does not exist when choices fall outside the interval $[P_1, P_2]$. The importance of these limits is to remind us the unavoidable influence of political pressure on judicial decisions. Of course, independence does not rule out the possibility to take into account such situations. But political encroachments on judicial independence contradict the very existence of independence. *Dependent independence*, or the co-existence of dependence and independence, is then analyzed as a paradoxical mix between structural and substantive independence. With a reference to discretionary power, political infringements are simply interpreted as the political response to non-SIE decisions. There is no longer a paradox.

Secondly, judicial discretion applies in a wider range of circumstances than independence. Indeed, independence is justified mainly in an incomplete information environment, when judges benefit from informational asymmetries or principals suffer from the imperfection of incentive mechanisms. Judicial discretion is less strict a concept. Judges are able to impose their choices, whatever the completeness of the set of information is, once again as long as this choice belongs to the right interval. Indeed, the discretionary power does not result from a lack of information but from conflicts between the principals. Judicial discretion is possible even when political principals are perfectly informed.

JUDICIAL INDEPENDENCE, DISCRETION AND SEPARATION OF POWERS

The issue of judicial independence, and thus that of discretionary power, is usually related to the question of the equilibrium of powers. Since Landes and Posner's seminal argumentation, debates about judicial independence have focused on such a question. The existence of an independent judiciary branch of government seems to be a necessity because it contributes to the check and balances required in a democracy. The greater the independence is, the better the system works. Judicial discretion also involves issues of separation of powers and equilibrium between the different parts of the state. Indeed, judicial discretion is highly contingent upon the separation of principalship between two political decision makers. A regime in which there exists only one principal allows no discretionary power to the administrative judiciary. The latitude of the judiciary depends on the preferences of the different branches of the government. The distance between the preferences of the principals determine the size of judges'discretionary power: the more separated powers are, the larger the distance between P_1 and P_2 is, the greater is judicial discretion.

However, the way powers are divided and equilibrate reciprocally differs from the traditional perspective of check and balances. The dissimilarity is important between legal regimes, according to whether they delegate the review of public litigation to regular or to specialised courts. In the first case, the system of check and balances functions by making the control of each branch by the others possible because the judiciary exists as a full-part branch of government. Administrative control is ensured by the existence of an explicitely separated branch of the state. By contrast, in the second type of systems, the administrative judiciary does not possess the whole range of attributes of a branch of government. Moreover, its discretionary power is bounded by the other branches of government. Thus, the traditional check and balances logic does not apply. Administrative control is allowed by the discretionary power of the administrative judiciary.

CONCLUSION

Judicial independence is usually defined as an outcome of the courts' search for decisional stability. Hence, it is accepted by political principals as long as the choice of a dependent agent is impossible. This definition, however, seems quite restrictive. We propose in this paper to analyze judges' power through the concept of judicial discretion. We depart from the standard *law and economics* perspective on independence in referring to models that are not usually utilized to analyze independence. Independence is a form of judicial discretion but in no case some 'absolute' power. In other words, courts remain unable to impose their preferred solutions outside the interval determined by the preferences of their principals. Their power remains strictly limited by political preferences. Our perspective is rather sketchy, and obviously some historical examples do not prove the case, but it helps to grasp a major difference between common law and civil law regimes.

REFERENCES

Anderson, G. M., Shughart, W. F., & Tollison, R. D. (1989). On the Incentives of Judges to Enforce Legislative Wealth Transfers. *Journal of Law and Economics, 32* (April): 215–228.

Backhaus, J. (1999). Administrative Law and Economics. In: G. de Geest & B. Bouckaert (Eds), *Encyclopedia of Law and Economics*. Cheltenham, E. Elgar Publishers.

Boudreaux, D. J., & Pritchard, A. C. (1994). Reassessing the Role of the Independent Judiciary in Enforcing Interest-Group Bargains. *Constitutional Political Economy, 5*(1), 1–21.

Chapus, R. (1998). *Droit du Contentieux Administratif.* Paris: Montchrestien.

Cooter, R., & Drexl, J. (1994). The Logic of Power in the Emerging European Constitution: Game Theory and the division of Powers. *International Review of Law and economics 14*, 307–326.

Cooter, R. forthcoming. *The Strategic Constitution*, Princeton (NJ), Princeton University Press.

Ferejohn, J., & Weingast, B. R. (1992). A positive Theory of Statutory Interpretation. *International Review of Law and Economics, 12*, 263–279.

Gely, R., & Spiller, P. (1990). A Rational Choice Theory of Supreme Court Statutory Decisions with Applications to the *State Farm* and *Grove City* Cases. *Journal of Law, Economics and Organisation, 6*(52), 263–300.

Harnay, S., & Vigouroux, I. (2000). Pouvoir Discrétionnaire et Choix Stratégiques du Juge Administratif: Une Analyse Economique du Gouvernement des Juges. *Politique et Management Public, 18*(2), 1–24.

Harnay, S. (1999). *Economie Positive de la Justice Administrative*, Ph.D. Université Paris 1 Panthion, Sorbonne, Paris.

Holstrom, B. (1982). Moral Hazard in Teams. *Bell Journal of Economics, 13*, 324–340.

Josselin, J.-M., & Marciano, A. (1995). Constitutionalism and Common Knowledge: Assessment and Application to the Design of a Future European Constitution. *Public choice, 85*, 177–185.

Josselin, J.-M., & Marciano, A. (1997). The Paradox of Leviathan. How to Develop and Contain the Future European State? *European Journal of Law and Economics, 4*(1), 5–21.

Josselin, J.-M., & Marciano, A. (1999). Administrative Law and Economics. In: J. Backhaus (Ed.), *Elgar Companion to Law and Economics* (pp. 115–120). Cheltenham, E. Elgar Publishers.

Josselin, J.-M., & Marciano, A. (2000). Displacing your Principal. Two Historical Case Studies of Some Interest for the Constitutional Future of Europe. *European Journal of Law and Economics, 10*(3), 217–233.

Landes, W., & Posner, R. A. (1975). The Independent Judiciary in an Interest-Group Perspective. *Journal of Law and Economics, 18*, 875–901.

Lochak, D. (1994). *La Justice Administrative*. Paris: Montchrestien.

Ma, C. T., Moore, J., & Turnbull, S. (1988). Stopping Agents from 'Cheating'. *Journal of Economic Theory, 46*, 355–372.

Marks, B. (1988). A Model of Judicial Influence on Congressional Policy Making: *Grove city* v. *Bell. Working Paper*. Hoover Institution, Stanford University.

Mercuro, N., & Medema, S. G. (1997). *Economics and the Law. From Posner to Post-Modernism*.Princeton (NJ): Princeton University Press.

Montesquieu (1989). *L'Esprit des Lois*. Paris: Garnier-Flammarion.

Ramseyer, J. M. (1994). The Puzzling (In)dependence of Courts: A Comparative Approach. *Journal of Legal Studies, 23*(2), 721–746.

Ramseyer, J. M., & Rasmusen, E. B. (1997). Judicial Independence in a Civil Law Regime: Evidence from Japan. *Journal of Law, Economics and Organization, 13*(2), 259–286.

Rose-Ackerman, S. (1994). The Economic Analysis of Public Law. *European Journal of Law and Economics*, 1(1), 53–70.

Salzberger, E., & Fenn, P. (1999). Judicial Independence: Some Evidence from the English Court of Appeal. *Journal of Law and Economics, XLII* (Oct.), 831–847.

Salzberger, E. (1993). A Positive Analysis of the Doctrine of Separation of Powers, or: Why Do We Have an Independent Judiciary? *International Review of Law and Economics, 13*, 349–379.

Sappington, D. E. M. (1991). Incentives in a Principal-Agent Relationship. *Journal of Economic Perspectives, 5*(2), 45–66.

Shepsle, K. A., & Weingast, B. R. (1981). Structure-Induced Equilibrium and Legislative Device. *Public Choice, 37*, 504–519.

Tollison, R. D. (1988). Public choice and the Legislation. *Virginia Law Review, 74*, 339–374.

Van den Bergh, R. (1996). The Growth of Law and Economics in Europe. *European Economic Review, 40*, 969–977.

Varian, H. (1990). Monitoring Agents with Other Agents. *Journal of Institutional and Theoretical Economics, 146*, 153–174.

Varian, H. (1992). *Microeconomic Analysis*. Norton.

DO ARTISTS BENEFIT FROM RESALE ROYALTIES? AN ECONOMIC ANALYSIS OF A NEW EU DIRECTIVE

Roland Kirstein and Dieter Schmidtchen

ABSTRACT

According to a new European Union directive, artists, whose works are resold, are entitled to a share of the sales price. The principal aim of this initiative is to let the artists participate in the economic success of their work. Our analysis shows that the new directive is most likely to place the artists in a worse economic position. The analysis of the relation between the artist and his dealer as an incentive compatible contract leads to further objections against the new EU directive. However, the paper also illustrates under which conditions a resale royalty is, at least, an incentive compatible contract.

1. INTRODUCTION

Economic theory may be able to provide answers to simple questions lawmakers should ask. The title of this paper is an example of such a simple question: will the effects of a new EU directive meet the expectations of

Law and Economics in Civil Law Countries, Volume 6, pages 231–248.

ISBN: 0-7623-0712-9

law-makers, or will the outcome be just the opposite? Without a behavioral theory, it is hardly possible to predict the impact of a new law on the behavior of the concerned actors. Economic analysis does not promise to be simple, nor does it promise to give simple answers. However, it provides at least some answers to lawyers' questions.

The European Council has recently adopted[1] the European Commission's "Amended Proposal for a European Parliament and Council Directive on the resale right for the benefit of the author of an original work of art".[2] As soon as the European Parliament agrees to the Councils position, the new EU directive would require the member states of the European Union to establish resale rights. This "droit de suite" provides a right for artists to collect a royalty based on the resale price of their work.[3] The European Commission's initiative was driven by three motives:

(a) to ensure "that creators of graphic and plastic works of art share in the economic success of their original works of arts" (Recital 2).
(b) "to redress the balance between the economic situation of creators of graphic and plastic works of art and that of other creators who benefit from successive exploitation of their work." (Recital 2).
(c) a better functioning of the internal market in the Union. According to the Commission, "disparities with regard to the existence and application of the artist's resale right by the Member States have a direct negative impact on the proper functioning of the internal market in works of art" (Recital 7). The application or non-application of such a right is considered to be a factor that contributes to distortions of competition as well as displacements of sales within the Community (Recital 6).

The Commission expects about 250,000 artist to benefit from the introduction of a resale royalty in the EU.[4] Currently, Belgium, Denmark, France and Germany enforce resale rights regularly. Droit de suite also exists in Greece, Italy, Luxembourg, Portugal and Spain, but there is no enforcement on a regular basis.[5] Britain, the country with the most important art market in Europe, does not have such a legislation, as it is the case in Ireland, Austria, and the Netherlands; these EU member states opposed until recently the proposal.[6] In March, the Council has agreed upon introducing the new directive, supported by the votes of 13 member states, whereas Austria and Belgium did abstain, see FAZ (2000). Since then, some modifications of the Commission's initiative have been made in order to achieve consent. In the United States, only California has adopted a droit de suite.[7]

In this paper, we take a closer look on the first of the Commission's above mentioned motives. Our analysis is based on the idea that a dealer has three different economic functions which provide the sources of gains from trade between the artist and the dealer.[8]

(a) the dealer may have better access to capital markets, i.e. pay a smaller interest rate, than the artist and therefore serves as an intermediary for cheap credits;
(b) the dealer may (perhaps as well as the artist) spend effort on the enhancement of consumer valuation in the resale market for the work of the artist;
(c) if the artist is risk-averse, the dealer may provide insurance.

The impact of the introduction of a droit de suite on the dealer's economic functions is analyzed separately in the subsequent sections. Section 2 focuses on the function of the dealer as a credit intermediary, and therefore excludes risk-aversion and effort considerations. It is assumed that the dealer's discount factor is higher than the artist's, reflecting the lower interest rate the dealer pays to obtain credit. We show that the artist's lifetime income is always decreased when resale royalties are introduced.

A similar result was derived by Karp and Perloff (1993). Their model neglects the discounting of future payoffs, whereas in our model discounting plays an important role. Furthermore, the Karp and Perloff (1993) model places the artist in a surprisingly strong market position: he sets the initial market price and the resale royalty, whereas the dealer only chooses promotional effort and the resale price. Our analysis goes beyond this in taking into account that artists may have a weaker position in the initial market.

In Section 2, the analysis is limited to the distribution of a given cooperation rent, an aspect that was particularly stressed in the EU initiative. This neglects the incentive effects a droit de suite may have. Section 3 takes into account that a droit de suite may affect the two parties' effort to promote the value of the artist's work. Promotional effort may increase the cooperation rent that can be distributed between the two parties. First, we follow Karp and Perloff (1993) and assume that the future valuation of the artist's work depends only on promotional effort of the dealer. We show that the optimal resale royalty is zero. An argument in favor of a resale royalty ("share-cropping") contract can only be derived if customers' valuation in the resale market depends on the efforts of both artist and dealer. However, it would require additional reasons to justify a mandatory droit de suite, since artists and dealers are free to agree upon resale royalties by contract.

Section 4 introduces risk-aversion on the part of the artist. In such case, the introduction of a droit de suite would have two harmful effects on his situation: it forces the artist to accept a risky lottery instead of a sure income; and secondly, even if a resale royalty had a positive net effect on the artist's monetary lifetime income due to its incentive effect, his lifetime utility may be decreased. This effect, which we call the "*paradox of risk-aversion*", can occur if the income of the artist increases over time. Section 5 briefly summarizes the arguments, and discusses in which direction legal harmonization in Europe should reasonably move.

2. RESALE RIGHTS AND LIFETIME INCOME

2.1. *Initial Market and Resale Market*

Droit de suite intends to let the artist participate in the future economic success of his work. In some cases indeed, the resale price largely exceeds the price that was initially paid by the dealer. A widely held view of the art business is the image of a

> collector who, having purchased a work of art for relatively little, resells it for a great deal more, pocketing the entire profit and leaving the artist whose effort created the work and whose subsequent accomplishments may have contributed to its increase in value, with no part of such increase. It is the image of Robert Rauschenberg and Robert Scull in tense confrontation after the 1973 auction at which Scull resold for 85,000 Dollars, a work for which he had originally paid Rauschenberg less than 1,000 Pounds.[9]

However, there is a simple economic reason for the enormous differences in the prices at which dealers buy and sell art: from the dealers point of view, the works of young and unknown artists are lottery tickets. He will frequently be unable to resell the pieces later, and of those sold only a few will be worth large sums.

Consider a simple example: a typical dealer buys one hundred pieces of art, ten of which will be worth €100,000 some years later. The others will yield no considerable return. Neither the dealer, nor the artists know the future value of a certain piece of art. Assume both parties to be risk-neutral. The interaction between dealer and artist, concerning one piece of work, takes place in three steps (for simplicity, assume that the piece is resold only once):

(1) the dealer buys a piece of art from the artist (initial market);
(2) nature reveals the artist's true type (i.e. the valuation of the collectors);
(3) the dealer sells the piece to a collector (resale market).

The initial market price is governed by three factors: the dealer's maximum willingness to pay, the artist's minimum willingness to accept, and the market conditions. Let us first derive the dealer's maximum willingness to accept. We assume the dealer to be aware of the fact that only 10% of all purchases will turn out to be valuable in the final market. Hence, when considering his situation in the initial market, he expects an average resale price of €10,000 in the resale market for each of the pieces he buys. Assume furthermore that the dealer discounts future gains by 20%. This discount factor of 0.8 reflects the interest rate and the time until the resale is realized.[10] Thus, the dealer's present value of each piece in this portfolio is €8000, which is the maximum amount the dealer would be willing to pay.[11]

The artist will accept a price in the initial market if it exceeds the present value of the expected return the artist earns if he stores the work until he sells it on his own.[12] Let us assume that the artist's discount factor is 0.6, thus smaller than the dealer's. This reflects the fact that the dealer may have better access to the capital market. Additionally, young artists will only very occasionally be able to provide collateral if they apply for a credit directly. The artist's minimum willingness to accept is the discounted value of the average return in the resale market, €6000.

The difference between the dealer's €8000 and the artist's €6000 is the cooperation rent that is created if the dealer and the artist conclude a contract. If the initial market is competitive, then the elasticities of demand and supply govern the distribution of this cooperation rent by the initial market price. In bilateral monopolies, it is the relative bargaining power of the parties that determines the price and thereby the distribution of the cooperation rent. Thus, the split rate could be a result of a competitive market process as well as of bilateral monopoly negotiations and is assumed to be independent of whether a droit de suite is introduced or not. This approach allows us to model the effects on prices without having to explicitly model the market structure.[13]

A split rate close to 1 could be interpreted as the market situation of a young artist who is already well established (in economic terms: whose work is heterogenized), and who has some market power in the inital market. This would be the case if dealers outbid each other to come into business with this artist. On the other hand, a split rate close to zero refers to the situation of a completely unknown young artist whose work, from the dealer's point of view, is a perfect substitute to the work of other artists. In this case, the artists outbid each other to get access to a dealer.

For the sake of simplicity, we assume that the cooperation rent is equally shared among the dealer and the artist. Therefore, the initial market price without a droit de suite is calculated as

$$0.5 \cdot €8000 + 0.5 \cdot €6000 = €7000 \qquad (1)$$

The cooperation rent of €2000 is split equally between the two parties. Each one gets €1000 of the cooperation rent. This is realized by an initial market price of €7000.

2.2. *Introduction of a Droit de Suite*

If a droit de suite is established, either by mandatory law or by contract, then the artist holds a right to a share $\rho < 1$ of the resale price. A resale royalty is a kind of excise tax on art that must be paid each time the piece is resold.[14]

It can also be seen as an attenuation of the buyer's property rights. Both points of view allow for the same prediction: the buyer's maximum willingness to pay is decreased. A rational dealer will discount the expected resale royalty and subtract its present value from the amount he is willing to pay if no droit de suite were in place. We assume that the dealer cannot shift forward the burden of this "excise tax".[15] Thus, the maximum willingness to pay drops to $(1-\rho) \cdot$ €8000.

The artist compares two options: to store the work yields €6000, which is the expected return, weighted with the artist's discount factor. If he uses this option, then the droit de suite plays no role. On the other hand, the artist may sell his work to the dealer. Let p denote the initial market price paid by the dealer if a droit de suite is in place. The artist not only receives the current return p, but also the claim on the resale royalty. However, this additional income is uncertain and only due in the future; it therefore must be discounted. The present value of this claim is €6000 $\cdot\ \rho$. Hence, an initial market price p is acceptable to him if $p +$ €6000 $\cdot\ \rho$ is greater than €6000. Stated equivalently, the artist accepts a price p if

$$p > (1-\rho) \cdot \text{€}6000 \qquad (2)$$

The right hand side of inequality (2) denotes the artist's minimum willingness to accept if a droit de suite is introduced. Calculating the market price p the same way as in equality (1) leads to

$$p = 0.5 \cdot (1-\rho) \cdot \text{€}8000 + 0.5 \cdot (1-\rho) \cdot \text{€}6000 \qquad (3)$$

since the split rate is assumed to be independent of whether a droit de suite is introduced or not. Thus, p equals $(1-\rho) \cdot$ €7000. The introduction of a droit de suite, therefore, leads to an initial market price which is necessarily smaller than the one without resale royalties.[16]

The difference in market price with and without droit de suite is $\rho \cdot$ €7000. The artist's return at the time he sells his piece of art to the dealer is reduced by this amount. The net effect of a droit de suite on the present value of the artist's lifetime income is the present value of the resale royalty minus the decline in the initial market price:

$$\rho \cdot \text{€}6000 - \rho \cdot \text{€}7000 = -\rho \cdot \text{€}1000 \qquad (4)$$

Under the assumptions we have made, this net effect is always negative. It can be shown that this loss is increasing as the discount factor of the artist is decreasing. Note that our result not only proves true for the example we used, but also for any other split rate or other resale market returns.[17] The net effect would be positive if, and only if, the artist's discount factor would exceed the dealer's. However, in such a case, a cooperation rent would cease to exist: gains from trade can only occur between the artist and the dealer if the discount factor of the latter exceeds that of the former.[18] If this is the case, then the droit de suite puts the artist definitely into a worse position. Hence, the EU directive not only fails to achieve its most important goal, to let the artists participate in the economic success of their work, but leads to the opposite result.

Note that the artist's loss increases in the split rate.[19] The better his position in the initial market, the more the artist looses when a resale royalty is introduced. Hence, if a droit de suite is established, successful artists have more to lose. This theoretical result explains the observation of Parachini (1990, F3), according to which 40 established artists (among them Wilem de Kooning and Roy Lichtenstein), in 1988, opposed a U.S. Congressional initiative to introduce a resale royalty in all U.S. states. According to the report, the artists' reason for their opposition was that a droit de suite "might make it even harder for unknown artists to attract the interest of collectors". In the light of our analysis this is correct, yet appears to be somewhat hypocritical.[20]

3. INCENTIVE COMPATIBLE CONTRACTING

3.1. Dealer's Effort

The analysis of the relationship between an artist and a dealer within a simple market framework might be seriously misleading. Often the relationship has a pooling character, like team production, which can best be analyzed using the concept of relational contracts. According to this concept the artist and the dealer are playing a repeated game in good faith. Neither is trying to gain an advantage at the expense of the other side. Rather, both see themselves as members of a team acting co-operatively in order to increase the economic value of the relationship.

A dealer incurs substantial costs in buying, owning, conserving and promoting sales. He has usually tied up specific investments in the work of art, expecting a reasonable rate of return or, in economic terms, a "quasi rent". If resale royalties reduces this quasi rent, the incentives of the dealers may be affected in a way that harms the artists.

As in Karp and Perloff (1993), we first analyze the situation in which only the promotional effort of the dealer is relevant for the valuation by the customers in the resale market. Let us, for simplicity, distinguish two cases:

(a) the dealer does not spend additional effort, hence the average resale price remains €10,000;
(b) or the dealer undertakes additional effort to promote the value of the artist's work.

Assume that the additional effort costs the dealer an amount of e, and increases the average value of the artists work to, say, €15,000.[21] Thus, high effort increases the average return in the resale market by €5000. In this section, we neglect discounting of future payoffs and focus on effort only. It is the promotional effect only that explains a difference in the parties' maximum willingness to pay and minimum willingness to accept, respectively, in the initial market. To analyze the impact of promotional effort on the value of the artist's work in the resale market, we have to distinguish two concepts: social and individual rationality.

The first-best effort maximizes the common profit of the dealer and the artist, disregarding the possible conflict between the two parties. It would be first-best to spend high promotional effort if the increase in valuation in the resale market exceeds the effort costs, denoted as e. Hence, it is first-best to spend high effort if, and only if,

$$e < €5000 \tag{5}$$

The individual decision of the dealer is not necessarily based on this comparison. The dealer spends high effort if his individual share of the return exceeds his effort costs. Recall that, if a droit de suite is established, the dealer only receives a share $(1-\rho)$ of the return in the resale market. Therefore, he is motivated to spend high effort if, and only if,

$$e < (1-\rho) \cdot €5000 \tag{6}$$

A comparison of the inequalities (5) and (6) leads to the following results:

(a) if $e >$ €5000, then it is efficient not to spend high effort, and the dealer makes the efficient choice;
(b) if $e < (1-\rho) \cdot$ €5000, then it is efficient to spend high effort, and the dealer makes the efficient choice;
(c) if e is in between (i.e. $(1-\rho) \cdot$ €5000 $< e <$ €5000), then it would be efficient to choose high effort, but the dealer is not motivated to do so and chooses low effort instead.

The interval in which the dealer behaves inefficiently vanishes if $\rho = 0$. Thus, from an efficiency point of view, the optimal mandatory resale royalty would be $\rho = 0$. This is not only in accordance with the result in Karp and Perloff (1993, 165),[22] but also with the standard result of contract theory, given that both the artist and the dealer are risk-neutral. In such a situation, a "sell the shop" contract would be optimal: the dealer pays a fixed amount to the artist and becomes residual claimant. In contrast to this, a mandatory droit de suite would force the parties into a "share cropping" contract, which induces the dealer to choose a suboptimal low effort.[23]

A "sell the shop" contract allocates the entire risk to the dealer. If he were assumed to be risk-averse, whereas the artist is risk-neutral, then such a reallocation of risk would be inefficient. In such a case, a resale royalty could be an efficient contract. This, however, does not seem to be the world the EU Commission had in mind when making its proposal.

3.2. *Artist's Effort*

Let us turn to the second scenario: the expected return on the resale market depends on the effort of the artist rather than of the dealer. An artist has several ways to increase the value of a piece he has already sold to a dealer, such as producing additional pieces of high quality, investing in his skills, seeking further inspiration, and making contacts with potential buyers and intermediaries.[24]

In principle, the artist's effort may have a substitutional or a complementary effect on the expected return for his earlier work. Here, we consider the complementary effect: future work of high quality is assumed to increase the valuation of the life's work of the artist.[25] If the artist spends high effort, he bears costs $f > 0$, whereas in the case of low effort his costs are 0. Let us again assume that this increase amounts to €5000. Thus, it is first-best to spend high effort if, and only if, $f >$ €5000. From the artist's point of view, it is individually rational to spend high effort if his share of the increased return (namely $\rho \cdot$ €5000) exceeds the effort costs f. Just as in the case above, we have three cases to distinguish:

(a) if $f >$ €5000, then the artist abstains from high effort, which is efficient to do so;

(b) if $f <$ €5000 $\cdot\ \rho$, then the artist chooses high effort, which is efficient to do so;

(c) if $\rho \cdot$ €5000 $< f <$ €5000, then high effort would be efficient, but from the artist's point of view it is better to choose the inefficient low effort.

The interval in which the artist may behave inefficiently vanishes if $\rho = 1$, which implies that the artist not only receives a share of the resale price, but the whole return. In such a setting, a dealer is not necessary, and the entire risk should be borne by the artist. It would be optimal if the artist simply stores his pieces and waits until they have gained their resale value.

If, however, the artist were assumed to be risk-averse, then it would be inefficient to let him bear the entire risk.[26] In this case, a contract should balance the artist's desire for insurance against the motivational effect of the residual claim. However, such a contract would not lead to the first-best solution, which is not attainable due to the risk-aversion of the artist. A resale royalty may at most be second-best: the artist sells the main part of the residual claim in turn for an up-front payment to the dealer, yet the prospect of receiving a share of the uncertain resale returns keeps the artist motivated to spend at least some effort on the enhancement of these returns.

3.3. Both parties' efforts

Things are more complicated when the expected resale market return depends on the efforts of both the artist and the dealer. First of all, the contract should deal with the fact that now both parties may have an incentive to spend less than the optimal effort (double-sided moral hazard). Secondly, the parties' efforts may influence each other. In particular, they may have a complementary or a substitutional effect. We consider the complementary effect here: future work of high quality does not only tend to increase the value of the life's work of the artist, but also increases the marginal effect of the dealers effort (and vice versa).[27]

To keep matters simple, we limit the choices of the parties to high and low effort. Let us denote the high effort of the dealer as $e = 1$ and of the artist as $f = 1$, whereas $e = f = 0$ represents both parties' low effort. The expected return on the artist's work is denoted as $q = q(e+f)$. Hence, three levels of q must be distinguished: $q(2)$, if both parties contribute; $q(1)$ if only one party spends effort; $q(0)$, if neither party contributes.

The marginal effect of either party's effort on the expected return is positive, thus $q(2) > q(1) > q(0)$. Furthermore the two party's efforts are assumed to be strategic complements, hence the marginal effect of one actors contribution is higher if the other has made a contribution as well: $q(2)-q(1) > q(1)-q(0)$.

The parties may bear different costs for high effort: let us denote the artist's cost as c and the dealer's as k. If both spend effort, the (expected) social net surplus of the two parties is $q(2)-c-k$, which we assume to be positive and greater than $q(0)$: it would be efficient if both were spending effort. However,

Table 1. The Effort Game.

artist \ dealer	$e = 1$	$e = 0$
$f = 1$	$(1-\rho)q(2)-k$ $\rho q(2)-c$	$(1-\rho)q(1)$ $\rho q(1)-c$
$f = 0$	$(1-\rho)q(1)-k$ $\rho q(1)$	$(1-\rho)q(0)$ $\rho q(0)$

this is not necessarily the outcome if the parties maximize their own (expected) payoff. Table 1 shows the interactive decision situation as a game in strategic form. Recall that the artist's share of the expected return is denoted as ρ, hence the dealer's share is $(1-\rho)$.

The efficient outcome $(e = 1, f = 1)$ is a Nash equilibrium[28] if, and only if, the following relations hold simultaneously:

(a) $\rho \cdot q(2)-c > \rho \cdot q(1)$; this condition guarantees that $f = 1$ is the best reply for the artist if the dealer chooses $e = 1$, and

(b) $(1-\rho) \cdot q(2)-k > (1-\rho) \cdot q(1)$, which implies that $e = 1$ is the best reply to $f = 1$.

Both conditions say nothing more than the individual costs of choosing high effort should be smaller than the individual gain, given the other side chooses high effort as well. The two conditions can be equivalently expressed as

$$c < \rho \cdot [q(2)-q(1)] < q(2)-q(1)-k \tag{7}$$

If the parties agree upon a value of ρ that satisfies condition (7), then this contract turns the efficient outcome into a Nash Equilibrium.[29] Note that the interval in (7) is non-empty if, and only if, $q(2)-q(1) > c + k$. If this condition is violated, then there is no value of ρ that turns $(e = 1, f = 1)$ into a Nash-equilibrium.

A numerical example might help to understand the meaning of condition (7): let $q(2) =$ €100,000, $q(1) =$ €10,000 and $q(0) =$ €0. This satisfies the strategic complement property, since 100,000−10,000 > 10,000−0. Let furthermore be $c =$ €9000 and $k =$ €45,000, which satisfies the efficiency condition (100,000−45,000−9000 > 0). Table 2 shows the decision situation in this example (the figures are in €1000).

Using these parameters, condition (7) translates to $9000/90{,}000 < \rho < 45{,}000/90{,}000$ or $0.1 < \rho < 0.5$: In this example, a very low value of ρ implements efficient behavior as a Nash equilibrium.[30] This is due to the cost structure:

Table 2. Example Effort Game.

artist \ dealer	e = 1	e = 0
f = 1	$100(1-\rho)-45$ $100\rho-9$	$10(1-\rho)$ $10\rho-9$
f = 0	$10(1-\rho)-45$ 10ρ	0 0

the dealer's costs were assumed to be nine times as high as the artist's costs. The low share for the artist is not only efficient, but also reflects fairness considerations: the party that has to bear the higher costs should get the greater share of the output.

4. RISK-AVERSE ARTISTS

Until now it was assumed that the actors are risk-neutral. It has been shown in the previous sections that, leaving aside incentive effects, the introduction of a droit de suite tends to harm the artists. If, on the other hand, both sides' efforts to promote the resale value of the work are relevant, a resale royalty can be the incentive compatible contract, as it was shown in Section 3.3, and may lead to a higher monetary income for the artist.

The assumption of risk-neutrality will be maintained in this section with respect to the dealer because he is able to spread his risk over a portfolio of different assets. The individual artist, however, relies on only one source of income, especially if he is completely devoted to his work. Therefore it seems reasonable to assume that artists are risk-averse.[31]

Risk aversion is modeled by a concave utility function. The marginal utility of income is positive (more money brings more utility), but the rate at which an additional unit of income increases the utility is diminishing. There are two reasons why this kind of utility function makes it more likely that a droit de suite is harmful for the artist. First of all, resale royalties oblige the artist to a lottery that can adversely affect his utility if he is risk averse. It could be beneficial to receive a higher (and secure) initial fixed income rather than a lower one which is combined with a risky payment in the future.[32] If the artist had the right to waive the resale right (and the dealer would agree), the artist could buy himself out of the lottery. However, a waiver is not permitted under the EU directive.

Additionally, if the artist is unable to obtain credit against his claim, the droit de suite shifts income from his youth to his older age. The artist is forced to accept a lower income now, in exchange for some uncertain future gain, shifting income to a perhaps more prosperous stage of his life.[33] This transfer of a part of the artist's current income to the future may be harmful even if the present value of the lifetime income stream is increased.[34]

A numerical example should make clear this "*paradox of risk-aversion*". Assume that a young artist has an annual income of €16.900. The introduction of resale royalties leads to a decrease of, say, €2.500. His new annual income is then €14.400. Making use of a concave utility function like $U(x) = x^{0.5}$, where x is the income and U the utility, the artist gets 130 utility units before, and 120 utility units after the introduction of the droit de suite: thus, the droit de suite leads to a current loss of ten utility units.

Assume now that, in his later life, the artist has an annual income of €90 000 and the resale royalty brings him €3.025 as additional income.[35] This is equivalent to 300 utility units without the droit de suite, and 305 utility units after the introduction of it. The introduction brings an additional utility of 5 units. These figures are displayed in Table 3, where the label "no dds" stands for the situation without a droit de suite, whereas "with dds" denotes the situation if a resale royalty is introduced.

Adding up the income as well as the utility in the two years under consideration, the artist earns €106.900 without droit de suite, and €107.425 if a droit de suite is introduced; hence, the resale royalties increase his monetary income by €525. However, his lifetime utility is decreased: without droit de suite, overall utility adds up to 430 utility units, whereas with resale royalties it is only 425 utility units. The utility loss at a younger age due to the introduction of a droit de suite exceeds the utility gain from the resale royalty.

The economic reason for this is straightforward: Having an additional € in a situation where the income is low can bring much more utility than having this additional € in a situation where the income is already high. According to our example, this even holds true when discounting of future income and utility as well as the riskiness of the resale royalty is neglected. If future income were subject to discounting, this effect would be even greater.

Table 3. Lifetime Income and Utility.

	in €		in utility units	
	no dds	with dds	no dds	with dds
young age	16900	14400	130	120
old age	90000	93025	300	305
sum	**106900**	**107425**	**430**	**425**

5. CONCLUSION

The aim of this paper was to analyze whether the introduction of a mandatory droit de suite will make artists better off. The answer is, to say the least, unclear. Leaving the effort issue aside and focusing only on the distribution of a given expected return on the resale market, the droit de suite clearly places the artists in a worse position. Taking the incentive effect into account, three cases must be distinguished:

(a) a resale royalty would be counterproductive if only the dealer's effort is required to promote the value of the artist's work. However, the droit de suite might be at least second-best if the dealer were assumed to be risk-averse, whereas the artist is risk-neutral.
(b) If, on the other hand, only the artist's effort is relevant to promoting the value of his work, then he should be the residual claimant. The artist should circumvent the dealer and sell his work on his own behalf.
(c) If both the artist's and the dealer's efforts may increase the expected return in the resale market, then a share cropping contract can implement efficient behavior.

However, even if a resale royalty forms part of a contract on the initial market, an increase in the artists' lifetime income does not necessarily mean that their position is improved. If they are risk-averse, they are likely to lose. First of all, a droit de suite increases the volatility of their lifetime income. Additionally, the income shift from younger to older age induced by resale royalties can decrease the utility derived from the artist's lifetime income even if the monetary value of his income is higher than without a droit de suite.

Even if a resale royalty were efficient, this would not yet justify a mandatory droit de suite. The artist and the dealer would have an incentive to do this voluntarily. Such a contract may yet be difficult to specify or to enforce.[36] Prohibitively high transaction costs are a standard rationale for mandatory legislation;[37] in this case the law can sensibly be seen as a standard contract. If droit de suite is inefficient, but distributes the smaller "cake" in a way that is more favorable for the artists, this might provide another reason for mandatory legislation.

However, there may arise practical difficulties in enforcing the proposed legislation.[38] Dealers may try to circumvent the droit de suite by selling works of art in a jurisdiction where no resale royalties apply. This would prevent the dealer's maximum willingness to pay from decreasing, but nevertheless Europe would lose a share of the art market.[39] Furthermore, one should carefully determine whether Europe is the optimal legal area for the issue in question.

If not, then harmonization itself is not a reasonable goal. Even if one agrees that Europe is the optimal legal area, then the additional question arises towards which direction harmonization should take place.[40] Taking into account the inefficiency of a droit de suite, harmonization should rather be directed towards the abolition of the droit de suite in the countries where it exists than towards the introduction of it in the other countries.

NOTES

We are grateful to Brandon Ahearn, Gerrit de Geest, Lewis Kornhauser, Ejan Mackaay, and other participants of the conference on "L'économie du droit dans les pays de droit civil" in Nancy, June 2000.

1. See FAZ (2000).
2. OJ (1998).
3. Perloff (1998, 645). Taken literally, this principle would give the artist a claim on a share of the resale price even if it is lower than the initial price. Karp and Perloff (1993, 167f.) discuss resale royalties based on the difference between the resale and the initial price ("capital gains"), however without deriving a systematic effect of the two regimes on the artist's income. See also Bolch, Damon and Hinshaw (1988, 75).
4. EU Commission (1999).
5. See O'Hagan (1998, 86), and FAZ (1999).
6. FAZ (1999).
7. See Karp and Perloff (1993, 163), who also mention Algeria, the former Czechoslovakia, Chile, Poland, Sweden, Tunisia, and Uruguay to provide such guarantees – however, in most countries the artists do not actually receive resale proceeds.
8. In Kirstein and Schmidtchen (2000), an additional function is analyzed: an expert dealer creates value by his ability to tell good from less talented artists.
9. Weil (1983), c.f. O'Hagan (1998, 100, Fn. 18).
10. If the annual interest rate is denoted as i and the resale takes place t years after the initial purchase, then the discount factor for the future returns is $1/(1+i)^t$. Obviously, the discount factor is higher if the interest rate is lower.
11. If the dealer had operating costs, these would further decrease his maximum willingness to pay, but the effect of the droit de suite would qualitatively be the same.
12. O'Hagan (1998, 90) remarks that the artist "always has the possibility of holding on to his/her work for investment purposes, if there is reason to believe that the work will appreciate". Only for simplicity we assume the artist produces at zero marginal costs.
13. Karp and Perloff (1993, 165) also analyze the case of an artist-owned gallery. In terms of our model, this kind of vertical integration would be reflected by a split rate of 1 (the artist internalizes the whole cooperation rent) and equal discount factors. Obviously, the dealer-artist cannot be made better off by introducing a droit de suite.
14. The EU Commission rejects the view that resale royalties are "just a further tax", since the proceeds go to the artist, not the state, see EU Commission (1999). However, the economic effect on the resale market is just the same as if a tax were imposed.

15. This assumption seems to be rather reasonable when the supply on the resale market is inelastic, which is the case in our model: the amount traded on the initial market is the constant supply on the resale market.

16. See Perloff (1998, 645), Karp and Perloff (1993), Hansman and Santilli (1996, 69).

17. See Kirstein and Schmidtchen (2000).

18. For the moment, we have left aside other economic reasons for cooperation rents, such as insurance, screening, or promotional effort. Insurance and promotion are analyzed in the subsequent sections.

19. This is proven in Kirstein and Schmidtchen (2000).

20. The bill has not passed Congress, see Karp and Perloff (1993, 163). Landsburg (1989) argues in the opposite direction: a droit de suite may shift income from less known to successful artists. However, Solow (1990) rejects this argument, see Karp and Perloff (1993, 174f.), endnote 6.

21. In principle, this increase can have two reasons: the resale value of the artists work is increased, or the probability that an artists turns out to be successful is increased (or both).

22. Even though these authors do not perform a rigorous derivation of optimal contracts, they come to the result that resale royalties reduce the dealer's incentives to spend promotional effort.

23 This holds in general if the dealer's choice set is continuous; if he chooses his effort from a discrete set, such as high or low, share cropping could be optimal as well. However, "sell the shop" would still be optimal in this case and nothing is gained by a mandatory resale royalty.

24. The impact of the artist's activities on the value of a piece of art sold is not taken into consideration in Karp and Perloff (1993).

25. The substitutional effect would be reflected by the idea of Coase (1972): the later output of a monopolist may be seen as a substitute for his earlier works which tends to decrease the value of each piece of work. See Karp and Perloff (1993, 169) and Schmidtchen, Koboldt and Kirstein (1998, 789).

26. We take a closer look on risk-aversion and droit de suite in the next section.

27. The resulting interactive decision-making situation is called a "supermodular game", see Fudenberg and Tirole (1992). In case of a substitutional effect, the marginal effect of one party's effort on the expected return is diminishing in the effort chosen by the other party.

28. A strategy combination is a Nash equilibrium if no player has an incentive to deviate from it.

29. It is possible that ($e = 0$, $f = 0$) as well is a Nash equilibrium; a case which is not of interest for our analysis here.

30. In fact, four equilibrium constellations are possible, depending on the value of ρ (and neglecting ties):

(1) $0 < \rho < 0.1$: The strategy $f = 0$ is dominant and $e = 0$ is the best reply.
(2) $0.1 < \rho < 0.5$: Both $e = f = 1$ and $e = f = 0$ are Nash equilibria.
(3) $0.5 < \rho < 0.9$: $f = 0$ is dominant and $e = 0$ is the best reply.
(4) $0.9 < \rho < 1$: The stategies $e = 1$ and $f = 0$ are dominant.

Note that $0.1 < \rho < 0.5$ implements efficient behavior as one out of two Nash equilibria.

31. A decision-maker is risk-averse if he prefers not to take part in a "fair" lottery. A lottery is called fair if the ticket price equals the expected gain. Consider a lottery

that pays €100 with probability 0.1 and nothing otherwise. Its expected value hence is €10. If the lottery is fair, then a risk-neutral decision-maker would be indifferent whether to participate or not. A risk-averse decision maker, on the other hand, would strictly prefer to keep the ticket prize. He would take part if he had to pay less than the expected gain. If the risk-averse is indifferent between the lottery and a ticket price of, say, €7, then the difference of €3 is the "risk premium" this decision-maker wants to earn before trading in the ticket prize for the prospect on an uncertain return.

32. See Karp and Perloff (1993, 171).

33. O'Hagan (1998, 89).

34. This argument was presented in Schmidtchen, Koboldt and Kirstein (1998).

35. According to Filer (1986), young artists earn less, but show a steeper lifetime income profile than the average workers of the same age.

36. A very simple way – which is completely free of enforcement costs – for an artist to guarantee participation in the increasing value of his work would be to withhold a few pieces.

37. Karp and Perloff (1993), Hansman and Santilli (1996), and Schmidtchen, Koboldt and Kirstein (1998, 790) also discuss reasons like paternalism or asymmetric information. However, these reasons appear to be less convincing, as long as perfect rationality is assumed. For a general discussion of inalienability, see e.g. Rose-Ackerman (1985).

38. See O'Hagan (1998, 88f.).

39. In EU Commission (1999) it is argued that the introduction of a droit de suite would not lead to the loss of "thousands" of jobs.

40. The EU commision complains that the works of painters like David Hockney enjoy much weaker protection than those of the Spice Girls, see FAZ (1999) and EU Commission (1999). Therefore, harmonization is claimed to be necessary not only among the member states of the EU, but also between different groups of artists.

REFERENCES

Bolch, B. W., Damon, W. W., & Hinshaw, C. E. (1988). Visual Artist's Rights Act of 1987: A Case of Misguided Legislation. In: *Cato Journal*, *8*(1), 71–78.

Coase, R. (1972). Durability and Monopoly. In: *The Journal of Law and Economics*, *15*, 143–149.

EU Commission (1999). Proposed Directive on Artist's Resale Right – Clarification; document dated Dec. 14th, 1999, downloaded on June 23rd, 2000 at *http://europa.eu.int/comm/internal_market/en/intprop/99–68.htm*

FAZ (1999). Zwist um Folgerecht für Künstler. Finnische EU-Ratspräsidentschaft drängt Briten zu neuen Vorschlägen. In: *Frankfurter Allgemeine Zeitung*, *255*, 2.11.1999, 18.

FAZ (2000). Zementiert. Neue Richtlinie zum Folgerecht. In: *Frankfurter Allgemeine Zeitung*, *66*, 18.3.2000, 51.

Filer, R. K. (1986). The 'Starving Artist' – Myth or Reality? Earnings of Artists in the United States. In: *Journal of Political Economy*, 94, 56–75.

Fudenberg, D., & Tirole, J. (1992). *Game Theory*. MIT Press, Cambridge, London, 2nd part.

Karp, L. S., & Perloff, J. M. (1993). Legal Requirements that Artists Receive Resale Royalties. In: *International Review of Law and Economics*, *13*, 163–177.

Kirstein, R., & Schmidtchen, D. (2000). Do Resale Royalties Make Artists Better Off? An Economic Analysis of a New EU Directive; Center for the Study of Law and Economics, Discussion Paper 2000–07, Saarbrücken.

Landsburg, S. (1989). *Price Theory and Applications*. The Dryden Press 1989.

O'Hagan, J. W. (1998). *The State and the Arts. An Analysis of Key Economic Policy Issues in Europe and the United States*. Cheltenham: Edward Elgar.

Hansmann, H., & Santilli, M. (1996). Author's and Artist's Moral Rights and the Droit de Suite: A Comparative Legal and Economic Analysis; Paper presented at the 5th Symposium of Law and Economics, Travemünde, 27.-30.3.96.

OJ (1998). Official Journal of the European Union 125/8, 23. 4. 1998.

Parachini, A. (1990). Artist's Rights Bill Awaiting Bush's Signature. In: *Los Angeles Times*, Nov. 6th, F3 (cit. Karp/Perloff (1990, 174)).

Perloff, J. M. (1998). Droit de Suite. In: P. Newman (Ed.), *The New Palgrave Dictionary of Economics and the Law* (pp. 645–647). London/Basingstoke/New York: MacMillan.

Rose-Ackerman, S. (1985). Inalienability and the Theory of Property Rights. In: *Columbia Law Review*, *85*, 931ff.

Schmidtchen, D., Koboldt, C., & Kirstein, R. (1998). Rechtsvereinheitlichung beim "droit de suite"? Ökonomische Analyse des Richtlinienentwurfs der Europäischen Kommission. In: B. Großfeld, R. Sack, T. M. J. Möllers, J. Drexl & A. Heinemann (Eds), *Festschrift für Wolfgang Fikentscher*. Mohr Siebeck, Tübingen.

Solow, J. L. (1992). *An Economic Analysis of the Droit de Suite*. University of Iowa Working Paper.